Never the Last Road

A Partisan's Life

Never the Last Road

A Partisan's Life

MIRA SHELUB
FRED ROSENBAUM

LEHRHAUS JUDAICA
Berkeley, California

Jewish
Family and
Children's
Services
OF SAN FRANCISCO, THE PENINSULA,
MARIN AND SONOMA COUNTIES

JFCS
San Francisco, California

Never the Last Road—A Partisan's Life

Lehrhaus Judaica
2736 Bancroft Way
Berkeley, CA 94704
Phone: 510-845-6420
E-mail: FR747@aol.com
Website: www.lehrhaus.org

In partnership with:
Jewish Family and Children's Services Holocaust Center
2245 Post Street
San Francisco, CA 94115

Copyeditor: Dorothy Shipps
Proofreader: Katie Cook

Cover and interior design: Sara Glaser

Typeset in ITC Legacy Serif and ITC Legacy Sans

Printed in the United States

To the memory of my beloved husband,
Norman Shelub

Table of Contents

FOREWORD

Mitch Braff

ON MARCH 16, 2000, near San Francisco in the wooded backyard of a man born in Lithuania over eighty years earlier, I had a conversation that changed the direction of my life. I learned of the existence of Jewish partisans. In the forests and mountains of East-Central and Southern Europe, thousands of Jews had fought back against the Nazis and their collaborators, joining and sometimes even forming armed resistance groups.

Like most others, I had had no inkling of Jewish resistance during the Holocaust beyond the Warsaw Ghetto uprising of 1943—when nearly all the Jewish heroes were killed or captured. The predominant image I had gleaned from my secular and Jewish schooling was that of Jews who "went like sheep to the slaughter." The fact that approximately thirty thousand Jews fought back, in both Jewish and non-Jewish paramilitary groups, profoundly altered my understanding of the Holocaust and my identity as a Jew. The newly gained knowledge infused me with pride in my people.

I knew that this largely hidden history could do the same for others, and I began planning to share the stories and lessons of the Jewish partisans with as large an audience as possible. I wanted to ensure that future generations would not, as I had, miss such a vital piece of history. Within six months, I founded the Jewish Partisan Educational Foundation (JPEF) to preserve and teach this priceless legacy. The idea was to interview fifty surviving partisans, create printable guides and short films, and distribute all of this freely on the web. As I began searching out former partisans to interview, I found them in cities all over the world. I did not realize that one, who would become a valued friend, mentor, and inspiration to me, was close at home in San Francisco. This was Mira Shelub.

Beginning with our initial interview in 2003, my knowledge about the partisans grew significantly. Mira was the first person I met who had interacted with Tuvia and Zus Bielski, the famous brothers who led the Bielski Brigade of twelve hundred Jews.

She shared with me the political and religious conflicts among the Jews in her hometown of Zhetel, and their fraught relationship to the local Poles and Belarusians, often ingrained with anti-Semitism. This hostility would later recur in the forest where partisan groups such as the Polish Armia Krajowa, or Home Army, that were anti-Nazi, nonetheless attacked Jews. Mira's vivid recollections also made clear the difficult position of Jewish partisans living and fighting alongside former Red Army soldiers, who often held anti-Jewish stereotypes of their own.

She spoke movingly about the vulnerability of women in partisan units, a delicate subject many surviving partisans decline to discuss. Early in her forest days, Mira convinced some of her fellow partisans to rescue her parents and brother from a German forced labor camp and bring them to the safety of another partisan group. Given the generally low status of women in partisan units, it is especially noteworthy that she was successful in convincing them. Knowing Mira, however, it is not surprising. Her tenacity, energy, and charm would be difficult to resist—character traits that leap out to the reader perfectly from these pages.

Mira met her life partner in the partisans and, importantly, their story does not end with liberation. We are gifted with descriptions of her enduring bond with her husband, Norman Shelub, their postwar lives in the DP camps, their eventual immigration to America, and the life they made in San Francisco.

Beginning in prewar Poland, Mira's love of learning runs like a thread throughout her long life. Her Yiddish schools, both in Zhetel and later the prestigious Real-Gymnasium in Vilna, were her pride and joy. As a young woman, she had several suitors, but none shared her intellectual interests as did Norman. They made sure their children had every educational advantage, and all three received advanced degrees and became accomplished professionals. In middle age, Mira enrolled in San Francisco State University to complete her own long-delayed education. Above all, her mind and soul have been nourished from childhood by the Yiddish language and its rich literature.

In the forest, Mira, Norman, and their band of partisans spent countless nights in the freezing woods, not knowing if they would survive. Their group resisted by ambushing Germans, attacking their bases, and derailing their trains. Today, Mira continues to resist by sharing her remarkable experiences with audiences throughout the Bay Area, and has made a particularly deep impact on young people. Her astounding memory and natural eloquence, her decency and courage, have given them a personal link to someone who endured one of the world's greatest catastrophes and has come to terms with it, with all her grace, humor, and humanity intact.

Now, in this book, her story comes alive in more depth and detail than ever before. *Never the Last Road* is the pinnacle of her mission to deepen our understanding of the Shoah.

PROLOGUE

Nazi-Occupied Dvorets in White Russia

Early Fall, 1942

"Escape with us to the forest," he beckoned.

The plea came from the handsome Shael Shakhnovich, a few years older than me. With a comrade named Chaim, he had slipped into the forced labor camp where I was imprisoned with my family. Shael whispered that hundreds of my neighbors had survived the mass murders that summer and many were fighting back from the woods. He was one of them.

Their camp, ten miles away, was in need of medical help and they had infiltrated this enemy stronghold looking for doctors. None were willing to flee with them, but Shael seemed happy to return to his camp with me instead.

I could tell there was more than rescue on his mind. Despite the way I must have looked under such miserable conditions, the tall, dark-haired guy was attracted to me. I felt flattered and was drawn to him, too. He did not fit my image of someone living rough in the woods: his finely chiseled face was clean-shaven and his clothes fit him well. He did not carry a rifle slung across his shoulder or wear a pistol on his belt.

But I was anxious about what I'd be getting myself into if I left my parents, brother and sister behind in the camp, linking my prospects with two men I'd never seen before. Though I had just turned twenty, I had not yet had a boyfriend. I wasn't religious, but I had been bookish in my teens. The only crush I'd had in high school had not even included touching. If freedom meant that I would be dependent on a man, I wanted him to be a soul mate and value higher learning as I did. What if that was not Shael? Would I be committing myself to him?

Armed resistance seemed just as much of a risk. Since the Nazi invasion more than a year earlier I'd seen only German tyranny and Jewish helplessness. The proud Jewish leaders of our town had been identified and quickly murdered, my father barely escaping that fate. The rest of us were forced into a cramped ghetto, subsisting on measly amounts of food and medicine. In June 1942, twelve hundred Jews, including my dear grandmother, were shot to death. In August, thousands more were rounded up and executed.

In the midst of that slaughter, my family had hidden and then fled. Now we were again caught in the Nazi net, this time as inmates of a work camp. Our treatment was better than in the ghetto but I knew we could be marked for death at any time.

Yet should I take this leap into the unknown with two strangers? Vault over a fence and trek through the dark woods to a ragtag band of Jews? What would be expected of a woman who had never held a gun? And the cold weather was nearly upon us. I had grown up near the forest and loved going into the countryside during my summer vacations, but being a year-round fugitive, or a fighter, would be something entirely different.

I took the chance. My parents approved, and we all agreed that Sara, my seventeen-year-old sister, would join Shael, Chaim, and me. But it was heartbreaking to leave behind our Mameh, Tateh, and our fifteen-year-old brother, Maeshe.

I now see this choice as my passage to adulthood. I began anew, going from victim to master of my own fate. Fighting back for the next two years shaped my character and the rest of my life. Never since, have I stood by passively in a crisis.

I also owe a lot to my upbringing before the war: the warmth and love that sustained me and the schools and community that nurtured me. That world that has vanished, but it remains etched in my mind.

ONE

Skating on Thin Ice

I was born and raised in eastern Poland in a typical shtetl, one of many hundreds of heavily Jewish, rural small towns across Eastern Europe that flourished for more than half a millennium. Ours was called Zdzieciol in Polish, and in Yiddish Zhetel, coincidentally rhyming with the word shtetl. Even more Jewish than most, only a quarter of Zhetel's forty-five hundred inhabitants was gentile when I was growing up there before the war.

Like almost every other shtetl, the livelihood of this small community depended on the weekly open-air market. Ours was held on Tuesdays and hundreds of farmers from the surrounding countryside arrived in the big town square on horse-drawn wagons, bringing for sale their fresh produce, dairy, eggs, poultry, and meat. With the proceeds they bought goods from the dozens of stores run by mostly Jewish craftsmen and merchants, or availed themselves of the services provided by Jewish professionals, from pharmacists to photographers. I'll never forget the exciting bustle of that day when town and country, Jew and Christian, met to engage in trade. I looked forward to it all week.

My parents owned one of the small stores on the town square, but they struggled to raise me and my younger sister and brother, Sara and Maeshe. My grandmother lived with us, too. We were not impoverished, like a large segment of Polish Jewry in the 1920s and 30s, but we were hardly secure. We lived week to week and money was always scarce.

Like most other families in Polish shtetls, we lacked almost all of the trappings of modern life that I take for granted today. We had electricity, but no refrigeration, indoor plumbing, or telephone. Our little one-story, planked house was heated only by a wood-burning, clay oven built into the tiled chimney. It stood floor-to-ceiling in the middle of the house, and to warm ourselves during the harsh winters, we'd stand with our backs to it. But even in mild weather it was never allowed to grow cold because my mother and grandmother also cooked our food there. When the wood burned down to coals, they would give off an even heat, good for cooking a pot of stew or even roasting potatoes.

We washed ourselves in the morning by splashing handfuls of water on our sleepy faces. There was no bathtub or shower; we used cold water fetched from a well and stored in a big pot. Perhaps once a week, I'd heat some water and, with a cloth, wash my whole body. A small child could stand in a washbasin for such a "bath," a larger person would have to lean over it. Lacking indoor plumbing also meant that we used an outhouse, supplemented by an indoor chamber pot in the coldest winter weather.

The house for our family of six was tiny with a little kitchen and only two small bedrooms. One was for my sister and me (we slept in the same bed), and our grandmother. The other had a bed

The market square in Zhetel where my parents owned a store.
(From *A Memorial to the Jewish Community of Zetel*)

From right to left, my grandmother Bubbe Henye, my parents,
my brother Maeshe and me. My sister Sara is in the foreground

Heyfgas, the street where my family lived in Zhetel.
(From *A Memorial to the Jewish Community of Zetel*)

A celebration in Zhetel's market square on the Jewish holiday of
Lag B'Omer in 1921. (From *A Memorial to the Jewish Community of Zetel*)

for my parents and a crib for my little brother.

Most of the houses were made of wood and the town was frequently engulfed in flames. My house burned down in one conflagration, my school in another. Fire had plagued Zhetel since the nineteenth century, and the *fear* of fire was so great that even a false alarm could result in serious injuries when people trampled one another in order to flee.

Yet for all the economic insecurity, daily discomforts, and even dreadful blazes, I was happy during my youth, and for the rest of my life I've been grateful for the sense of belonging I absorbed in Zhetel. I felt cared for by my family and community and proud to be part of the Jewish people. I came to value learning and literature, kindness and compassion.

Our town had every manner of Jewish organization, prayer houses and schools of course, but also an elaborate network of mutual aid societies to assist travelers, visit the sick, shelter orphans, make interest-free loans, and help the poor with everything from weddings to funerals. Zhetel's Jews looked out for one another.

We were proud of the Talmudic luminaries we had produced, above all the Chofetz Chaim, whose nineteenth century teachings on *mitzvot*, or good deeds, were revered by learned Jews throughout Eastern Europe. Our *sofrim*, or scribes, were renowned as far away as America for their expertly handwritten parchment Torah scrolls and holy inscriptions inside the mezuzahs on the doorposts of Jewish homes.

As a young woman I would witness the death of Jewish Zhetel, but as a girl I experienced its warmth and vitality.

Yet I don't want to romanticize or over-simplify the shtetl. Especially in the years when I was growing up, the Jews in small towns like ours, along with the big cities like Warsaw and Lodz, had sharply conflicting ideas and attitudes. There were Orthodox and Hasidim, socialists and communists, assimilationists and converts, Bundists and Folkists, and Zionists of every political stripe. These groups often bitterly fought with one another.

The relationship between Jews and non-Jews was even worse. More than three million souls, we Jews comprised about a tenth of Poland's prewar population—the highest percentage in any country in the world except Palestine—but anti-Semitism ran deep, and we were never fully accepted. In the new Poland that had come into existence after World War I, there were other large minorities and Jews had to deal with their hostility as well. To the east was Stalin's totalitarian USSR, and on our western border, beginning in 1933, Hitler's demonic Germany. So, amidst the joy I felt as a youth, I was also aware of danger looming.

WE WERE CITIZENS of the newly created Polish Republic, but our province, Novogrudok (named for its capital city, about twenty miles from Zhetel), was in the northeast, part of a wide swath of territory covering the eastern third Poland, known as the *kresy*, or borderlands. Anyone could feel the ethnic tension in the air. There were a lot of Poles, and plenty of Jews, but the large majority in our province was Belarusian, or White Russian.

Perhaps they were a bit less hostile than the Poles. They too were an unwanted minority and they deeply resented the thousands of Polish "settlers" whom Warsaw had brought to our region to shift the demographic balance. A few Belarusian writers even compared their lack of an independent state to Jewish homelessness over the centuries. Yet they were largely poor, rural, and uneducated. So whether they belonged to the Russian Orthodox or Catholic churches, the Belarusians, like many Poles, blamed the Jews for killing Jesus, and a lot else.

In a province south of us, Volyn, the Ukrainians had the numerical advantage. About a hundred miles north was the famed city of Vilna and its environs, with many Lithuanians. It too was part of Poland in those years. The *Volksdeutsche*, or ethnic Germans, were numerous in the western part of the country.

The new Soviet Union had coveted the *kresy* (it had belonged to Russia before World War I), but the Red Army unexpectedly lost a border war against Poland, which absorbed the area in 1921, the year before I was born. In 1939, it would revert to the Soviet Union, and only when the USSR collapsed in 1991 would these regions join newly independent countries, reflecting their ethnic makeup. Today Vilna is the capital of Lithuania and Volyn belongs to Ukraine. My town of Zhetel and the province of Novogrudok, where I grew up, is now in the western part of the country of Belarus.

But even as part of Poland in the 1920s and 30s, the influence of the Belarusians in my region was very noticeable. Their language, written in the Cyrillic alphabet, is much more like Russian than Polish. Because the *kresy* had been in the Czarist Empire for a century and a quarter before it became part of the new Poland, my parents and grandparents were far more comfortable speaking Russian, or even its sister tongue Belarusian, than they were with Polish. Needless to say, Yiddish was their first language, and mine as well.

The medley of languages no doubt rankled the Polish leaders sitting in Warsaw as they dealt with so many minority groups, about a third of the population. Following many generations of violent struggle and tragic failures, Polish independence had finally been attained and nationalism was flexing its muscles. As a condition of coming into existence, Poland had been required by the League of Nations to guarantee the "total and complete protection of life and freedom" of all people within its borders. But the promise was never kept and the Polish government later renounced the treaty.

The Poles viewed the Jewish minority as the greatest threat of all. Unlike the other sub-groups, we were neither concentrated in one region nor rooted in the land as peasants. Instead, we were spread throughout the country and largely worked in commerce. Beyond that, Polish identity was bound up with the Catholic Church and Jews were the only significant minority that wasn't even Christian. The situation would be at its worst in the late 1930s, but from its beginning the Polish Republic took punitive measures against us. As early as 1919, for example, all stores were required to close on Sundays, delivering a painful blow to strug-gling Jewish retailers, nearly all of whom, like my parents, shut their doors on Saturdays as well. In the years to follow, Polish Jews would have to contend with economic boycotts, discrimina-tion at the universities, and occasionally even pogroms.

Still, as a girl in a Jewish school, in an overwhelmingly Jewish town, I was rarely affected by anti-Semitism. One time *chuligans* (which entered both Polish and Yiddish from the English word hooligan) put anti-Semitic placards on the walls of the Catholic Church, and the priest had them taken down. In his sermon the next Sunday, he warned his parishioners not to be influenced by such bigotry.

But whether Zhetel's Jews were luckier than most, I really can't say. Decades after the war one of my older cousins still resented the spiteful boycotts. He remembered that when a non-Jew exited a Jewish-owned store, often a *chuligan* would slap his back, leaving a note that said, "I am a Christian betrayer."

I spent most of my free time with my Jewish friends in a loosely organized club of girls and boys we jokingly called the *Eiserne Guardia*, the Iron Guard, and met little hostility from the non-Jewish kids or their parents. In a way, Zhetel was a cocoon, especially for children, giving us a sense of safety from the hatred that was all around us.

YET I FELT the growing concern of my parents and teachers. How were we Polish Jews—almost a fifth of the Jewish population in the entire world—going to respond to the prejudice and poverty around us? How could we shape a better future for our families?

One answer was emigration. Some of my relatives had already

An outing of the *Eiserne Guardia*. I am the second from the right

immigrated to America, including two uncles and an aunt on my father's side of the family. My father's remaining sibling, my Aunt Nechamke, probably would have immigrated, too, but her husband was a master tailor in town, known as *Der Gott* due to the miracles he could perform with a needle and thread, so they were actually well off and remained in Zhetel.

Many less fortunate Jews did want to leave Poland but, by the time I was growing up, most of them were unable to emigrate. Almost all of those seeking entry into the United States were turned away after 1924, when the American Congress drastically curtailed the number of entry visas from Eastern Europe. Others went to Palestine, hoping to build a Jewish state, but that option, too, was hindered when the British, who controlled the Holy Land, sharply reduced the number of immigration certificates in the late 1930s. In May 1939, the notorious White Paper choked off *aliyah* almost entirely.

For those like my family, who stayed in Poland, the responses to the Jewish dilemma were wide-ranging. The majority was Orthodox, including many Hasidim, although the mystical sects were not especially strong in our region. While these traditional Jews were active in Polish politics, and vigorously defended their rights, their main preoccupation was religious observance and Talmud study.

At the opposite end of the spectrum was a far smaller group that can be called assimilationists. They thought that they could shed their Jewish skins and "Polonize" themselves completely. Some actually converted to Catholicism, but most simply declared themselves "Poles of the Mosaic faith" and changed their names. They not only spoke Polish exclusively, but also looked down their noses at Yiddish as "jargon." The assimilationists were more prevalent in the big cities in western Poland than the shtetls in the *kresy*, but we knew of them.

There were also Zionists among us who put all their energy into preparing for Jewish statehood even as it became harder and harder to make *aliyah*. I vividly recall their day school, Tarbut, and their lively youth groups and political organizations, which often clashed with one another along political lines. Whether they were right wing or left wing, most Zionists insisted on speaking Modern Hebrew on the streets of our shtetl. If you answered in a different language, even Yiddish, you'd get the sharp reproach, *Rak Ivrit*, "Only Hebrew!"

My family was in a different camp altogether, neither Orthodox, nor Zionist, and certainly not assilimilationist. Nor did we seek to immigrate to America or anyplace else. We firmly believed that we belonged in Poland. There was even a term for this: *do-igkeyt* in Yiddish, literally "here-ness." But while we wanted to stay, we insisted upon *cultural autonomy* within Poland—based on the Yiddish language.

Given everything that has happened since, the thinking of us Yiddishists will no doubt seem strange to Jews today. It can only be fully understood by someone who lived in interwar Poland. Yiddish, derived from medieval German but written with Hebrew characters and containing a good number of Hebrew words, was the language spoken by East European Jews for many centuries—truly our *Mameh Loshen*, our mother tongue. We were well versed in its fiction, poetry, and drama, all especially rich during the late nineteenth and early twentieth centuries. Yes, we knew enough Polish, Russian, and Belarusian to communicate with our gentile neighbors, and we knew some Hebrew from the synagogue and the holy books. But for us, Yiddish had pride of place among all the languages; its very cadence seemed to evoke the suffering, hope, peculiarities, and humor of East European Jewry. The Yiddish lullabies my mother sang to me are among my earliest memories. Yiddish stories, songs, and poetry have shaped the way I think; they are at the core of my soul.

When I was growing up, there were millions of Yiddish-speakers in Poland. We Yiddishists wanted to ensure Jewish continuity by maintaining that language and culture on Polish soil.

History proved us completely wrong, I know. We should have realized that Poland, even if it was a republic created after the "war to end all wars," was in no mood to grant cultural autonomy to the minority groups within its borders, least of all to the Jews whom the state and Church viewed as a cancer in the Polish body. In any case, the Poles would not be masters in their own house after September 1939. And neither we nor anyone else could have imagined that the overwhelming majority of Yiddish speakers—in Poland and throughout East-Central Europe—would be murdered.

We were also overly idealistic when it came to politics. Although my father never joined it, our family was sympathetic toward a Jewish political party known as the Bund. It had been founded in Vilna at the turn of the century as the General Jewish Labor Bund (meaning federation or union) and it drew upon the writings of Karl Marx. But its democratic notion of socialism had little in common with that of Lenin or Stalin. In advocating the eight-hour day, and equality for women, who comprised about a third of its members, the Bund was much closer in outlook to the socialist parties of Western Europe. Eastern Europe proved to be treacherous terrain for this position. Bundist leaders were deemed an enemy not only by the nationalist right, but also by the communists who claimed that they were the only true Marxists.

Anyone else on the left was labeled a dangerous revisionist.

Despite its modest size, Zhetel had a few lumber mills of fifty or more workers and a strident labor movement by the turn of the century. It was actually considered a revolutionary town. The local Bund was founded in 1903, and it remained a force until the outbreak of World War II, even attaining representation on the *Kehilla*, the Jewish community council. Especially active were the Zhetel chapters of the national youth groups: SKIF, the Socialist Children's Union; and *Zukunft*, or Future, for the teens. I was too busy with my schoolwork to belong, but many of my close friends were members.

Unfortunately, relations with the Bund's most likely non-Jewish ally, the Polish Socialist Party, were not good. They saw virtually all of us Polish Jews as "tribalists," i.e., too concerned with specifically Jewish interests. We thought they turned a blind eye to the anti-Semitism of their main constituency, the working class. But we Yiddishists—whether formally affiliated with the Bund, the Folkists or, like us, unaffiliated—were derided by the Zionists since we rejected Jewish nationalism and by the Orthodox because we were so firmly secular. Nevertheless, we comprised over 10 percent of Polish Jews, and much more in some industrial cities and towns, particularly as the economy worsened in the 1930s. Our deeply held and passionately expressed positions made our presence loom even larger.

My father, Chaim Michael Raznov, declined to be a member of the Bund, probably because his socialism was tempered by being a storeowner. But I sometimes think about the reasons he approved of it and surrounded himself with its followers when instead he could have joined the smaller Folkist party, which emphasized Yiddish as a living language and was not socialist.

He was born in the mid-1890s in a nearby village called Alexandrovich. Raised in a religious home, he attended *Cheder*, the traditional school for boys where sacred Jewish texts comprised almost the entire curriculum, and I think he went to a Yeshiva for advanced study too. Many years later we were all impressed with his ability to recite by heart lengthy Biblical and even Talmudic passages.

But even as a sheltered Jewish youth, he was dealt a horrible blow. When Chaim Michoel was twelve, his father died and, as the oldest of five children, he became the man of the house. Keeping his family out of poverty was a cruel struggle, and I wouldn't be surprised if that's when the Bundist message about social justice first helped him make sense of the world.

Then, shortly before World War I, he was conscripted into the Czar's army. This would have been a crisis for any young Jewish man. The ranks of Russian recruits were rife with anti-Semites, the living conditions were atrocious, and the hitch could last twenty years. But it was especially dire for my father who was helping to support his mother, two sisters, and two brothers.

There are all sorts of ways Jews dodged the Russian draft. Some starved themselves before the physical examination; others went without sleep for days on end; still others took on a false identity or went into hiding, but then often had to pay huge sums to blackmailers (often other Jews) not to denounce them to the authorities.

I don't know if my father tried any of these ploys, but in the end he was inducted. And he almost lost his life during basic training. One night he fell asleep on guard duty, an offense that normally resulted in execution by firing squad. But, as he recounted to us many times, he felt a tapping on his shoulder and suddenly woke up. Whoever, or whatever, had alerted him was nowhere in sight. As it turned out, the warning had arrived just in time because a Russian officer walked by only moments later.

The incident, however miraculous, did not bring my father closer to God; he was never to re-embrace the traditional faith of his childhood. But it did convince him that he needed to get out of the army. For that he willingly paid a high price. Making it look like an accident, he shot himself in the palm of his right hand. He was quickly discharged and sent home, but from then on he could never move his ring finger and pinkie together. That and a noticeable scar were lifelong physical reminders of his brief service in the Russian army and his painful exit from it. Even so, he may have spared himself a lot worse: debilitating injury or death in the terrible battles.

WORLD WAR I took a heavy toll on civilians as well. My father witnessed widespread looting and violence by retreating Cossacks, a cavalry corps of mostly Asian Russians, which fled the front in disarray and sometimes resorted to savagery. Our region was also occupied by the German army for three years. It required Jews along with the rest of the population to perform forced labor. When the Kaiser's forces finally retreated, crime, famine, disease, and anarchy gripped the area.

In Russia, the Bund had played an active role in the Revolution of 1917, and no doubt my father, around twenty years old when the Czar fell from power, was inspired by those days that "shook the world." Certainly, when peace finally came, and the old imperial order lay in ruins, he hoped not only for a better life for himself and his family, but also for a better society. His vision was that of a progressive Poland where the rights of minorities and workers would be guaranteed.

Around war's end he courted and wed my mother, a Zhetler a bit older than him, named Chana Rashke Rabinovich. Her mother, my Bubbe Henye, who lived with us, had someone else in mind for her daughter, a rich young man she knew with deep roots in Zhetel, not a poor village boy like my father. But my mother married Chaim Michoel anyway, and Bubbe Henye helped them make a living by giving them the shop my late grandfather had owned and operated. Like my grandparents before them, my mother and father sold clothing and household items from a modest store facing the market place on the town square. The economic hardship we underwent, especially in the 1930s, stirred anew my grandmother's feelings that her daughter had married beneath her station.

Unlike my father, Bubbe Henye had no sympathy for the Bund and, more important to our family's day-to-day life, she was religious. When she insisted we keep a kosher household, my parents complied. The dishes and silverware for meat and dairy were kept separate, and if even one utensil got mixed up—a meat knife used on a dairy plate, for example—she would get upset. She might run to the rabbi for advice or even bury the *treyf* (non-kosher) utensil for awhile in the hard earth near our house in order to make it kosher again, actually more of a folk custom than a requirement of Jewish law. Many secular Jews ridiculed this kind of behavior as superstition or fanaticism.

But we indulged Bubbe Henye, and although the rest of us were not God-fearing Jews, my family generally accepted Jewish observance as part of Jewish culture. Although we could barely all fit around the kitchen table, the Seder for the six of us that my father led each year was both beautiful and meaningful. So we never openly derided Bubbe Henye's Orthodoxy. Even my father got along with her, despite her opposition to my parents' marriage. Besides, we all loved Bubbe. I was especially grateful when she took me to visit my aunt and uncle in the splendid, sprawling city of Vilna, a trip she and I made together every summer.

My religious observance, or lack of it, does illustrate a young Yiddishist's attitude toward Judaism. I certainly felt no compunction to stick to the dietary laws. When I looked into the display cases of the Polish bakeries and saw the tempting *pierogi*, dumplings filled with ground beef or even pork, I usually passed them up but not due to any religious scruples. I simply couldn't afford them. And unlike Bubbe Henye, who went to *shul* every Sabbath, my friends and I attended only one day a year, Yom Kippur. Was it solemn? No, we ducked out every chance we got and played outside. Did I fast? Hardly. I got so hungry that I probably ate more on that day than at any other time of the year.

What drained all of the significance of the Day of Atonement for me was the service itself. I was naturally relegated to the women's gallery upstairs. One old lady would read the prayers and the rest of us would simply repeat them. I don't think we really paid attention because one time she said, "There's a cold draft coming in, close the door," and we all solemnly repeated, "There's a cold draft coming in, close the door." Then someone called out, "I don't remember saying that last year." She was put in her place by another woman who righteously declared, "We recite that once every four years and this is a leap year so we have to say it."

My little brother, Maeshe, five years younger than me, sat on the main floor with the men and later told me he didn't follow the services either. He says he learned more about Judaism decades later in the United States than he did in Zhetel.

Our elementary education, in a Yiddish day school, was just

the opposite, a worthwhile experience in every way. Critical thinking, not rote memorization, was prized. Founded in the early 1920s, the school was so progressive that it drew upon the educational philosophy of Enlightenment thinkers like Rousseau and Pestalozzi, as well as contemporary American educators such as John Dewey, some of whose works had been translated into Yiddish. So advanced was our primary school that it even offered a course in sociology.

The Sholem Aleichem Yiddishe Folkshule that my brother, sister, and I attended taught some Hebrew and Polish but the main language by far was Yiddish. We studied the great fiction of the folklorist Mendele Mocher Sforim, the socially conscious I.L. Peretz, and the school's namesake, humorist Sholem Aleichem. I took to Yiddish literature as a child and have treasured it my entire life.

Yiddish was the language of instruction for *every* subject: math and science, geography and history, art and music. The Warsaw-based Central Yiddish School Organization, known by its initials TSYSHO, standardized the seven-year-long curriculum and published educational materials, including full-length textbooks, in Yiddish. In geology, for example, they had to come up with new Yiddish words for scientific discoveries and technical terms.

When I started kindergarten in 1927, there were fourteen thousand children in almost a hundred TSYSHO elementary schools across Poland. There were also Yiddish secondary schools, teachers' seminaries, and adult schools. In Zhetel, the Bundist night school for workers met in the Sholem Aleichem building, which housed a substantial library.

Academics came first and the Sholem Aleichem School required much from its students. Sara, Maeshe, and I were lucky to have a helping hand from our father. He was a self-educated man, but

My parents, Chana Rashke Rabinovich and Chaim Michoel Raznov

My father, top row on the left, at a meeting of the Zhetel Tradesmen
Committee. (From *A Memorial to the Jewish Community of Zetel*)

had learned enough to assist us with our homework. He had never formally studied algebra, for example, yet just by using logic he led us through the problems step by step. Partly due to his tutoring, Sara got especially good at math and set her sights on becoming an aeronautical engineer. My goal was to go to an academic high school, known in Central and East-Central Europe as a *gimnazjum*, or gymnasium, and then to a teachers' seminary or university.

For all of its emphasis on scholarship, our school focused on "the whole child" and it aimed to produce well-rounded graduates capable in different ways of leading their community. I still remember our demanding physical education instructor, Mr. Frankel. There were also many extra-curricular activities: a twenty-instrument orchestra (in which my brother played the mandolin), a choral group, a chess club, and sports teams. I joined the dramatic society and loved acting in our class plays.

Before I was old enough for kindergarten, classes had met in rented quarters on the outskirts of town, but I started school in a new building in the heart of Zhetel. It was made of wood, not surprising for a town surrounded by ancient forests of birch, oak, linden, and spruce. Zhetlers who had immigrated to America helped to build it by sending us donations, and we considered its opening a major achievement. With about 250 students, the Sholem Aleichem School involved so many families that it became the hub of our Yiddishist community. My uncle Sroel Ber was a founder of the school and for a few years an administrator. My father was a longtime board member.

Sometimes the school was used for major cultural events such as the comic operetta *Rumanian Wedding*, performed by adults like my older cousin Moshe Mirsky. A professional actress came from the much larger city of Grodno, about seventy miles away, to play

An early photo of my grandmother Henye Rabinovich (seated) and her two children, my uncle Sroel Ber and my mother Chana Rashke

the lead. Usually the auditorium was partitioned to form temporary classrooms for the growing school, but at night the dividers were taken down to create the theater. Among many benefits, the performances generated a sorely needed stream of revenue for our school.

Commencement day was especially festive. Graduates, teachers, staff, and many parents proudly marched through Zhetel and all the way to Novayelna—over five miles—to mark the occasion. I remember that grand procession when I graduated in 1934.

Two years before, the school had celebrated its tenth anniversary with many events over several days including plays, outdoor gymnastics, and speeches. A most distinguished visitor arrived from Vilna to take part. Dr. Zemach Shabad, a Polish senator, spearheaded the nationwide program known as TOZ, aimed at improving the health and nutrition of the Jewish community, especially its children. And as co-founder and Vice-President of YIVO, the famed Institute for Jewish Research, he was the leading advocate for Yiddish in all of Poland. A statue of him stands in Vilna today. Dr. Shabad was deeply impressed with our school and, when he got back to Vilna, wrote about it at length as a model of Yiddish-language-based education for the whole country!

The school could charge only a pittance in tuition, and it received no funds from the government. Nor did it receive much from the Jewish community council, on which Yiddishists were far outnumbered by the Orthodox. But it could count on regular support from Zhetlers who, decades before, had immigrated to the United States.

At no time was that aid from abroad more needed than in February 1936 when the entire building went up in flames. It was a Friday night and the school had been closed for many hours, so thankfully no one was hurt. I was not in Zhetel when it happened, but I soon learned of the disaster from my family. Sara, two and a half years younger than me, and looking ahead to her graduation in June, and Maeshe, still in fourth grade, were devastated.

Cries of "The school is burning!" were heard through the town, but even though Zhetel was so familiar with big blazes—two hundred houses had burned in one fire only three years earlier—people didn't want to believe it. Only when they saw smoke and fire coming out of the wooden schoolhouse did they run to it. They pushed in doors and broke windows to save what they could. Miraculously they salvaged most of the library and the administrative records.

It seemed that the whole shtetl encircled the burning school, and one newspaper later wrote that the anguished crowd would have doused the flames with their tears if they could have. The volunteer fire department—my father was one of its leaders—arrived with its horse-drawn trucks and even pumped water from the nearby lakes, but it proved too late; the tinder-dry walls of the school came down. It was hard enough controlling the horses. Some were blinded by the smoke and ran off in different directions.

Yet the will to rebuild arose on the very night of the disaster. My father's close friend Avrum Barashanski, a school board member and one of the founders of the Bund in Zhetel a generation earlier, addressed the anguished crowd. He promised that a new house of learning would be constructed on the same site, and a roar of approval followed his words. So interwoven was my school in the fabric of Zhetel's life that even political opponents of the Yiddishists, many of whom had gathered with us that night, pledged their support.

We collected some money from the insurance company, but much more was required and fundraising became a big task. Large ads appealing for donations were taken out in the national Bundist paper, the *Folkszaytung;* in the big Vilna daily, *Der Tog;* and New York's Yiddish-language *Jewish Daily Forward*, which then had two hundred thousand readers in the United States. Dr. Shabad's family made a handsome contribution and thousands of children in Vilna's Yiddish schools helped out with gifts of ten groschen each, only small change but meaningful during the Depression. In days we raised a thousand zloty. It was only worth about $200 at that time, but it started us on the way to reconstruction. Meanwhile, our students met in unused classrooms in Polish schools.

The new school turned out to be even larger and better equipped than the one destroyed in the fire. Celebrities from all over northeastern Poland came to the grand opening in 1937. Dr. Shabad had passed away, but he was represented by his daughter, Regina, and her husband, Max Weinreich, the longtime director of YIVO, which he had co-founded with his late father-in-law.

Weinreich wrote a glowing report of the rededication in the *Forward*. Dozens of telegrams of support poured in especially from our American donors. A new school flag, made by the students, was unfurled and on that glorious day we thought we could overcome anything.

WE YIDDISHISTS WERE not the only ardent Jewish group in Zhetel that revolved around a day school. The Orthodox had their Talmud Torah and I believe its students were a little envious of the kind of education we received; I heard that they demanded reform of their traditional curriculum, long school day, and harsh disciplinary measures. At least one of their teachers was known to beat misbehaving kids with a leather whip. Every year the Sholem Aleichem School would receive transfer students from the Talmud Torah.

The Zionists, meanwhile, rivaled us with their school, called Tarbut, meaning culture in Hebrew. Of course, they used Modern Hebrew rather than Yiddish as the language of instruction. A Hebrew-speaking Jewish state in Palestine, they insisted, was the only way forward for the Jewish people. They even supplemented their academic curriculum with practical skills needed for immigration to the Land of Israel: courses in industrial arts, nature, and agriculture.

With Hitler's seizure of power in Germany and the rise of anti-Semitism in Poland the appeal of Zionism and the desire to make *aliyah* grew. For that reason, the Tarbut School was even more vital for its community than the Sholem Aleichem School was for ours. In 1933 and 1934, Tarbut actually arranged for the families of students to obtain immigration certificates to Palestine. *Aliyah* from Poland was not large at that time, but for Zhetlers making that choice, Tarbut paved the way. This didn't last long though; even Tarbut was unable to overcome the restrictions Britain imposed on Jewish immigration to Palestine later in the decade.

The competition between our two schools was not always healthy. Tarbut also had a drama club that invited the whole community to its productions. I can't say who was more at fault, but often our major plays and theirs were scheduled on the same night, guaranteeing that everyone had to choose. On a national level, the Zionists and Yiddishists sometimes cooperated in opposing anti-Semitism, but the ideological divide was so great that mutual contempt was more common. There was little disagreement about religion—we both opposed the Orthodox, whom we thought were backward-looking—but we were at odds politically and our differences widened with every ominous event in the late 1930s.

We young Yiddishists could usually tolerate the socialist-Zionist youth group Hashomer Hatzair, but the rightwing Betar, the creation of the Revisionist Zionists led by the militant Vladimir Jabotinsky (Menachem Begin's mentor), was another matter. I recall singing a ditty with my friends that compared the Revisionists to fascists, and likened Jabotinsky to Hitler. The Betarniks said their brown uniforms were the color of the soil of Palestine but, in order to taunt them, we could not resist the comparison with the brownshirted Nazis.

Everything in Zhetel was politically charged and our town square was a marketplace not only for goods, but also for ideas. We were linked to the outside world by a jitney going to and from the railway station in Novayelna, which sat on the main train line running north to Vilna and south to Warsaw. Whenever a newcomer came into Zhetel on that little bus from Novayelna, a representative from each of the Jewish factions was usually there to try to recruit him. As soon as the visitor stepped down from the van, he would be descended upon by an Orthodox Jew, a Bundist, and at least two kinds of Zionists. Each delegate would make a fervent pitch to win him over and would also recommend lodging where the traveler would be further implored to join one of the movements.

My father discussed world politics with us over the dinner table. Only in the last months before the war did we have a radio at home, but before that he listened to broadcasts with his Bundist friends. He regularly conveyed the news and opinion to us. Knowing that the mainstream Polish news media were often censored, he relied much more on Yiddish reports.

But my father's interests weren't limited to the plight of the Jews, dreadful as that was in the 1930s. He was also painfully aware of the oppression of other groups all over the world. One foreign crisis in particular grabbed our attention: the Spanish Civil War. Here, we were sure, was a clear struggle between democracy and fascism, and, beyond that, we knew a Zhetler who had gone to Spain to fight against Franco.

The dashing Ilusha Shapiro, just a few years older than me, was the son of a respected obstetrician in Zhetel who was a leading Bundist. Ilusha, too, studied medicine and belonged to the Bund. But he had a more fiery revolutionary temperament than the rest of us. After his arrest by the authorities in 1933, we suspected he might have been in an underground organization like the Communist Party, illegal in interwar Poland. He served a year in prison and after his release traveled to Spain where he was killed on the battlefield. We admired the whole Shapiro family and mourned with them. Ilusha's mother, Anna, a midwife, was respected for her work in bringing healthcare to the disadvantaged. His beautiful sister, Manye, became a physician and his much younger sister, Sonia, was a schoolgirl and close friend of my sister, Sara. The Shapiros were exceptional people and the loss of their son in a faraway land drove home to us the horror of the fascist movement engulfing Europe.

What newspapers did my father read every day? Well, his Polish wasn't completely fluent, but he read the *Robotnik* (the Worker), the organ of the Polish Socialist Party. Although it didn't fully condemn anti-Semitism, at least it defended the economic rights of the common man. He trusted more the Bund's *Folkszaytung*, delivered door-to-door by my neighbor and best friend, Rishe Kaplinski. Her father, Chaim, had been a founder of the Bund in Zhetel early in the century and her brother, Binyumen, or Nyome, as we called him, was one of its most charismatic and selfless leaders. It seemed Nyome, around thirty years old, had no personal life; he devoted all of his waking hours to advancing Jewish cultural autonomy and democratic socialism.

There were hundreds of thousands of Jews on the left in interwar Poland and most worked in the factories of the big cities—and protested their exploitation there—but my father saw the contradictions of capitalism from a different perspective: he worked as a merchant and later as an insurance broker. My parents' store was in a good, central location, along a row of other shops that sold leather, fabric, and lumber, but it did well only in the 1920s when I was a little girl. We sometimes called it a department store, but that was hardly the right description. It was really limited to housewares and clothing. If we specialized in anything, it was warm winter garments for the peasants and I recall some of the wool and cotton goods we carried, like stockings, underwear, and sweaters. We also sold buttons, needles, and thread, but our inventory was slight. The merchandise came from Warsaw or

Vilna and my father made buying trips to those cities every few months. By the time we paid off the suppliers, however, we were left with very little.

Even though we were secular, we could not risk offending our Orthodox customers by being open on Shabbat. The Compulsory Sunday Rest Law meant that now we had to close for two consecutive days every week. I remember one time when my father secretly met a customer at the store on a Sunday. After the purchase was made behind closed shutters, they peeked through an opening and spied a policeman lingering outside. Feeling trapped, they were afraid to leave for hours. At long last they slipped away undetected. Had they been spotted, both could have been heavily fined or even prosecuted by the authorities.

Debt was an even bigger burden for my mother and father. They often had to pay a vendor before they had the cash in their hands from past sales. Many of the peasants bought items from us on credit and were late in settling their accounts. I still remember my father's big, black ledger listing the names of the people who owed us money. So in order to pay their bills, my parents would borrow from someone, and then soon have to scramble to pay back that person by taking out another loan from someone else. The amounts were not large, maybe a total shortfall of only a few hundred dollars in today's money, but the constant stress of seeking loans to pay small debts weighed on us. Thankfully, we never went hungry, but my mother often had to put off food shopping, even for our Shabbes dinner, until the last possible moment.

By the mid-1930s, with the economy still very sluggish, my father realized that the store alone could not support our family; he had to bring in money from another source. Now in middle age, and not in good health—he suffered from chronic bronchitis—

Chaim Michoel took up a new profession: insurance broker. Given the frequent and widespread fires in our town, it was a "growth industry," as we'd say today. In fact, our own little house burned down one day in 1933 when I was eleven. I came home from school and was shocked to find a whole block of homes on our street, Heyfgas, in the shadow of the stately brick Catholic Church, blackened by the flames. We were all dismayed by the loss, but fortunately we were quickly able to rent accommodations from good friends of my parents, and the new place was bigger and more modern than the one that had been consumed by fire. My father went into the insurance business after that.

Initially, he did a brisk business, obtaining life and property policies for his local clients from major insurance companies like the Warsaw-based Polonia. There was a lot of correspondence back and forth, so in order to improve his written Polish (his fourth spoken language after Yiddish, Russian, and Belarusian), he hired Mr. Brandes, the Polish teacher at the Sholem Aleichem School, to tutor him at our home. Even as a child I was struck by his ambition to succeed in this new line of work.

But there was a major problem. In these desperate economic times, it turned out that a good number of Zhetlers purposely set their homes on fire to collect insurance money. They'd remove anything of value first—even the doorknobs, though that was a telltale sign of the fraud—and put their houses to the torch. I've since heard that Zhetel is hardly the only place where this has happened. Arson was so widespread on New York's Lower East Side a century ago that suspicious fires were often referred to as "Jewish lightning." But for a town already hit by so many blazes, this insurance scam was especially damaging. The underwriters, not thrilled with Zhetel to begin with, became even more hesitant about writing policies, which in turn caused honest property owners to pay much higher premiums or receive outright denials. It crippled my father's business, which, along with the "department store," barely sustained us through the 1930s. My aunts and uncles in America often sent us packages of used goods and we were deeply grateful for that help.

MY MOTHER, FAR less politically engaged than my father, was fully devoted to her three children. Although she worked in the store, and carried even more responsibility there once my father started his insurance business, she took time to bring our lunches to our school, as the other mothers did for their kids. On Sundays, when I'd go on nature walks in the forest with my friends in the *Eiserne Guardia*, she'd meet us with treats she'd made, like tasty latkes. Mameh was very health-conscious and served our family milk that had just been squeezed from a neighbor's cow. The milk was still warm and you could see the foam.

She had a lot of help with the housework from Bubbe Henye, especially when it came to cleaning our home from top to bottom before Shabbes, or making *cholent,* the big stew we'd leave overnight in the bakery oven and enjoy on the Sabbath day. But when a crisis arose involving one of us kids, Mameh took charge. Maeshe was often ill as a child and one time a case of whooping cough was so serious that she and Bubbe Rochel Leah, my father's mother, took him all the way to Vilna to be treated by a specialist. They came back only when father insisted upon it—the emergency had exhausted all of his meager savings. Sadly, Bubbe Rochel Leah, who lived with my Aunt Nechamke, soon died from her own medical problems. On a cold winter's day she chased after and caught a wayward cow, but also a fatal case of pneumonia.

My parents spared my brother, sister and me any domestic chores. All that was expected from us was that we excel in school. I dreamed of attending a gymnasium, a six-year high school issuing a *matura*, the only diploma that would meet the entrance requirement for any institution of higher learning. In all of Poland there was only one Jewish gymnasium accredited on that level, the Real-Gymnasium in Vilna, and its language of instruction was Yiddish. Even the several Tarbut gymnasiums throughout the country did not have the same academic standing. So the Real-Gymnasium was my first choice, but I knew it would be a long shot. Yes, the Sholem Aleichem School was perfect preparation for it, and I had good grades, but that hardly guaranteed acceptance to this prestigious institution. Even if I were accepted, how would we pay for it? My

A photo in 1909 of my grandmother Rochel Leah Raznov (right) and four of her five children: my Aunt Nechamke and (top to bottom) my father Chaim Michoel, and my uncles Yitzchak and Maeshe (who took the names Irvin and Morris after they immigrated to America)

uncle Sroel Ber, Bubbe Henye's son, had moved to Vilna and he and his wife could put me up, but could my family handle the tuition?

I thought I might have to attend a public Polish gymnasium, and if so, I felt I'd have a better chance if I applied from a Polish elementary school. So after I graduated from Sholem Aleichem, I entered a Polish grammar school in Zhetel for its seventh and final grade just to earn another elementary school certificate. I hardly felt alone there as a Jew; almost half of the student body of the non-tuition school was Jewish, including another recent graduate of Sholem Aleichem, Feigel Kaplinski, who, like me, aimed for the Real-Gymnasium, but also thought of the Polish gymnasium as her "safety school." She was a distant relative of mine, but no relation to the family of Chaim, Rishe, and Nyome Kaplinski, with whom my family and I were so close.

In the end, Feigel and I were both accepted by the Real-Gymnasium and would spend four years there, our studies ended only by the outbreak of World War II. In many ways I would be formed by the stimulating city of Vilna as much as the small town of Zhetel. But one incident brought home for me the way the Jews of the shtetl took care of their own. It happened in the winter of 1934–35, while I was attending the Polish school during my last year as a student in Zhetel.

I was skating alone on a frozen lake at the edge of the town when the ice beneath me gave way and I fell in. A Jewish boy on shore saw the accident, ran out to rescue me, and fell in too. We both flailed around in the frigid water, shouting, shivering, and terrified.

Well, a Jewish couple living near the lake risked their safety, too. They ran out of their home, came close to where we were, extended long tree limbs, and got us both out. Then they brought us to their house, dried us off in front of their stove, and fortified us with vodka. After nightfall my parents arrived—I don't know how they were notified—and took me home.

I was saved by some courageous, quick-thinking people. Later, my Polish teacher called me *topelitz*, the submerged one, and everyone in class had a good laugh about it. The story soon made its way around town.

The shtetl had many wonderful qualities, including the responsibility Jews felt for the well-being of one another. But it's also true that the shtetl could not defend itself. In just a few short years Polish Jewry, cities and shtetls alike, would be utterly destroyed even while a few of us fought back. Looking back on it now, I can see that we were all skating on thin ice.

TWO

The Capital of Yiddishland

Even while I lived in Zhetel, lively, legendary Vilna played a major role in my life. It wasn't that hard to get there. A short bus ride to Novayelna and then a two-hour train trip up north brought me to the Renaissance city, nestled in a pretty valley between two rivers. Vilna had been the capital of the vast empire known as the Grand Duchy of Lithuania in the fourteenth century, but the city had changed hands multiple times since then. In my younger years it was in Poland, and full of attractions old and new.

Only a hundred miles from Zhetel, enchanting Vilna appeared to belong to a different world. The enormous train station itself, with its stone pillars and tall peaked roof, seemed to announce that the traveler had arrived at a world-famous destination. Exiting the great hall, and walking through an ancient gate in the wall of the old city, I saw a huge assortment of churches and synagogues, hotels and apartment houses—much taller than those back home, of course, and also more solid. They were made of bricks and stone, not the combustible wood we used in Zhetel. The architecture was both grand and graceful, ranging from a Gothic cathedral built four and a half centuries earlier, to an art deco theater that had gone up in my lifetime. And if all of that weren't enough, Vilna was teeming with every manner of Jewish expression.

I went on class trips from Zhetel, sometimes lasting a week, and learned about the towering Jewish figures Vilna had produced, most notably the Vilna Gaon, or Genius, of the 1700s, possibly the greatest Talmud scholar ever. A century later in Vilna, Israel Salanter founded the *Musar* movement, focused on the ethical dimension of Judaism. The city had also been a center of the *Haskalah*, or Jewish Enlightenment, which sought to infuse Judaism with reason and link it with secular culture. Even the Gaon had been open to modern learning, and Vilna was perhaps the prime example in East-Central Europe where science, philosophy, and art could go hand in hand with a full-fledged Jewish identity.

Vilna had been the birthplace of the Bund in 1897, and four decades later it remained the most popular political party among the city's Jews. The city was home to numerous Yiddish day schools, and, after World War I, the Real-Gymnasium, the Yiddish Teachers' seminary, and the Yiddish research center known as YIVO. If there was a Yiddishland in Eastern Europe, Vilna was its capital.

But most of my childhood memories of Vilna center on my aunt and uncle and their family. Accompanied by Bubbe Henye, I'd stay with them every summer for many weeks each time. I don't know why neither my sister nor brother ever went on these marvelous vacations; I just assumed it was a privilege that came with being our family's oldest child.

My mother's only sibling, Yisroel (or Israel) Ber Rabinovich, whom we all called Sroel Ber, had moved to Vilna in the 1920s to marry my aunt. Just as my grandmother did in Zhetel, Bubbe Henye turned their house upside down to make it kosher as soon as she arrived. And just as my parents did, Aunt Mareh and Uncle Sroel Ber indulged her, even though they hardly felt bound by the Jewish dietary laws.

My aunt did stem from a well-known rabbinical family but, like many Jewish women in twentieth century Vilna, took a very nontraditional path; she became a dentist. She opened a large, well-equipped office in the city, and my uncle worked there, too, as her dental technician. They lived just inside the old city walls on a fashionable boulevard, Ulica Wielka, right across from the former city hall, a massive classical building, soon to become Vilna's main concert house. In the 1930s it was used as a cultural center for drama, music, and film productions. From Mareh's and Sroel Ber's windows in the early evenings, I'd often see finely dressed patrons arriving in fancy, four-wheeled open carriages known as droshkies.

Their well-located, second-story corner apartment, with its high ceilings, tall double-entry door, and lintels over the windows bore no similarity to my parents' plain house in Zhetel. Maybe Bubbe Henye thought that while her daughter, my mother, had married down, her son, my uncle, had married up.

During the summer, Mareh and Sroel Ber would usually leave town for awhile, bringing along their dental instruments. They would go into the outlying villages to treat peasants who, not surprisingly, were in great need of their services. I went on several of those missions of mercy and saw the poor rural folk pay her for treatment with eggs, chickens, and milk. We'd stay in the countryside for days at a time in a rented house and, while my aunt and uncle worked, I'd relax with a book in a large backyard amidst tall trees. It could not have been more idyllic.

My aunt had been married before and had two children by her first husband, a veterinarian, who died when he contracted an animal-borne illness. Their daughter, Olke, was a gymnasium student about four years older than me, and Shurke was six years my senior. I admired Aunt Mareh for her professional accomplishments, but Shurke was a role model of another kind and I loved spending time with him.

He was a highly gifted artist whose real name was Alexander Katzenbogen, later shortened to Bogen. Born in Vilna in 1916, he studied in an art academy affiliated with the local Stefan Batory University, and by the late 1930s was attracting attention for his paintings and drawings. During the war he would be an officer in Abba Kovner's heroic partisan unit and, remarkably, he remained

Alexander Bogen
in the partisans

creative even in the ghetto and the forest. The art he produced during the war, and later in Israel where he had his own gallery, vividly portrayed Jewish suffering and resistance. Even as a teenager, Shurke wanted his independence, and frequently slept nights in the waiting room of the dental office, which had a little kitchen.

My aunt and uncle also had a child of their own, a little boy named Tolenka, more than five years younger than me, who had an Estonian nanny. She and Tolenka shared a bedroom in the elegant apartment, and during my visits I slept there too.

Uncle Sroel Ber was like a second father to me. When I visited we'd walk together on the crooked, cobblestone lanes of the old city's Jewish quarter, a district of ten thousand people crammed into seven square blocks. This was another side of Vilna, and the colors and smells, and the profusion of Jewish life never ceased to fascinate me. Stone arches framed quaint street scenes, but unlike my aunt's neighborhood there was also a lot of poverty. I recall being approached by children dressed in rags begging for handouts.

Sroel Ber would point out the historic sites. The *alte kloyz,* or old prayer house, dated from the fifteenth century. Near it stood the Great Synagogue, built a century later. When Napoleon first saw it in its full grandeur in 1812, he hailed Vilna as the "Jerusalem of the North." The Great Synagogue had been badly rundown for generations, but the giant stone structure still drew five thousand worshippers for the high holidays in the 1930s. Marc Chagall captured something of its faded elegance in a painting of its interior in 1935. Sroel Ber also showed me where Theodor Herzl, the founder of modern Zionism, passionately addressed the Vilna Jewish community in 1903, only a year before his untimely death.

Of course there were more modern attractions. I often went to the movies in Vilna, mostly to see Hollywood films. In one eight-block stretch of town were seven movie theaters. You could watch everything from musical extravaganzas with Fred Astaire and Ginger Rogers to comedies with Charlie Chaplin. I still remember my aunt and uncle taking me to the musical *Rose Marie*, a love story set in the Canadian Rockies starring Nelson Eddy, Jeannette MacDonald, and Jimmy Stewart. It was shown with Polish subtitles, but by then I was studying English at the Real-Gymnasium and could follow most of the dialogue. What a contrast with little Zhetel! Its single cinema rarely drew my interest.

Yet alluring though it was, interwar Vilna, was no metropolis like Warsaw or Lodz. With only two hundred thousand people and no manufacturing base, it was a lot smaller, if much more charming, than the great Polish industrial cities to its west. It did not even have a proper streetcar system; people got around on droshkies, or horse-drawn carriages, and rode sleighs in the winter, giving it a fairyland quality. Vilna also had a great deal of open land within its borders and its green hillsides made it a feast for the eyes.

It was a Catholic city; the Poles and Lithuanians had their ethnic conflicts, but they shared the same religion. You were reminded of this daily because of the huge neo-classical Cathedral of Vilna, the imposing baroque St. John's Church, and the tall, graceful St. Anne's Church—all three barely a hundred yards from the Jewish Quarter. And clearly seen in the distance was the Hill of Three Crosses, the monument to seven Franciscan monks martyred at the end of the Middle Ages, around the time Christianity finally subdued paganism in Lithuania. During the day the white crosses stood out against the blue sky; by night they were illuminated by a band of electric lights, making these spiritual symbols eerily visible for miles around.

Polish nationalism was also in the air. Soon after the Poles formally incorporated Vilna in 1922, they changed the street names from Russian to Polish. They also played up the Polish patriots who had stemmed from Vilna and its environs. Adam Mickiewicz, Poland's greatest poet, had immortalized the mythic founding of Vilna in his epic *Pan Tadeusz,* written while he was in exile in Paris in 1834. Born near Novogrudok, about eighty miles away, he spent four years as a university student in Vilna protesting for Polish independence before being arrested and banished to central Russia. Mickiewicz is often credited with the concept of long-suffering Poland as "Christ among the nations," and there were prominent historic markers showing where he and other early Polish nationalists had lived.

The greatest Polish patriot of my time was Marshal Josef Pilsudski, the heroic leader in World War I and the architect of the victorious war against the Soviets, which won Vilna and the rest of the *kresy* for Poland. Born in a Lithuanian village, he attended a gymnasium in Vilna and then dedicated his life to Polish independence. The Czarist authorities exiled him to Siberia for five years. But after his return, and his later victories on the battlefield, he became a symbol of Polish nationhood and was elected president of the republic in 1926. He served with distinction—even the oppressed Jewish minority much preferred him to any other Polish leader—until his death in May 1935.

I was visiting my aunt and uncle during a school vacation when, through their window, I viewed his somber funeral procession through Vilna. I watched thousands of people slowly making their way up an incline and through the archway known as the

Gate of Dawn, only about a hundred steps from Sroel Ber and Mareh's apartment. Since the eighteenth century this entryway in the original city wall had served as the foundation for a Catholic prayer room above, home to one of the most famous paintings of the Virgin Mary in the world. The link between Polish nationalism and Catholicism could not have been clearer.

Like many other departed Polish heroes, Pilsudski's body was interred in the hallowed crypt of the Wawel Castle in Krakow. But his heart, encased in a silver urn, was laid to rest at the foot of his mother's grave in Vilna. The flower-strewn tomb is a place of pilgrimage for Poles to this day.

There was no doubt that Poles as well as Lithuanians had a strong claim to Vilna. But the Jews, numbering about sixty-five thousand before the war, constituted a third of the population and maintained over two hundred religious, cultural, and social welfare organizations. And we had our own age-old connection to Vilna.

YIDDISH COULD BE heard and seen everywhere. I wasn't surprised to learn later that in the census of 1931, 85 percent of Vilna's Jews declared Yiddish as their native language. You could function in that city with no other language and many did so. We even rendered the new Polish street names into Yiddish. Usually, these were just translations. So Ulica Wielka, meaning "broad street" in Polish, was *breyte gas* to us. Intersecting it was Ulica Szklanna, or "glazier street;" we called it *glezer gas*. Sometimes, we changed the name altogether. An alley in the Jewish Quarter was named Sw. Mikolaja (Saint Nicholas), but we dubbed it *gitke toybe's zaulek*, "Gitke Toba's alley" for the widow of a Jew who had owned property there.

The well-known historian of East European Jewry Lucy Dawidowicz, born and raised in New York, spent a year in Vilna as a young *aspirant*, a research fellow at YIVO, while I was at the Real-Gymnasium. Here is how she described the "realm of Yiddish" she encountered:

> We had Yiddish newspapers to inform us about what was happening in the world. Shop signs were in Yiddish. People at work conducted their business in Yiddish; you could get a receipt in Yiddish for your transactions. At the Jewish banks you could write a check in Yiddish. Trade unions and craft guilds managed their affairs in Yiddish. Doctors talked to their patients in Yiddish. Political parties competed with one another in Yiddish and posted Yiddish placards in the streets. Young poets wrote their verses in Yiddish and composers set Yiddish songs to music. Nature-study hikes had Yiddish-speaking guides and Maccabi boxing matches had Yiddish-speaking referees. Even the Jewish underworld, the pickpockets and horse thieves, plied their trades in Yiddish.

The predominance of Yiddish supported her belief, as it did mine, that Jewish survival in the modern world was guaranteed. Yiddish literature was the cultural life-blood of Vilna's Jews, many of whom, including young people like Dawidowicz and me, were quite secular. Jewish Vilna produced artistic prodigies such as the violinist Jascha Heifetz and the painter Chaim Soutine, but even art and music were overshadowed by the Yiddish word.

An excellent dramatic troupe often visited us from Warsaw, but in truth the homegrown Yiddish stage in Vilna was not especially distinguished. There were a few powerful productions of Shakespeare in Yiddish, like the *Tempest* in 1939. *Carmen, Aida,* and other operas were presented in Yiddish as well. But most of the shows were popular light comedies with song-and-dance routines, not unlike New York's Lower East Side at the time.

Yet Yiddish prose and poetry were taken very seriously. Even before World War I, Sholem Aleichem, Mendele Mocher Sforim, and I.L. Peretz frequently came to the city for readings, and Mendele had studied in Vilna. But it was a younger generation of writers, men and women just a decade or two older than me, who led the literary renaissance in the 1930s. They formed an association called Yung-Vilne, a collection of idealistic, working class youths brought together by Zalmen Reisen, editor of the daily *Der Tog*, one of the six Yiddish newspapers in town. Although not as well known as the trio of Sholem Aleichem, Mendele and Peretz, in my opinion he was just as gifted.

Yung-Vilne was not especially ideological; there were many different genres and themes ranging from poems about the glories of nature to plays about the evils of capitalism. What all its members had in common was an unwavering commitment to Yiddish. Dozens strong, they published their own little magazine and supported one another at packed readings throughout the city. Many in the group had been mentored by the charismatic Yiddish playwright, poet, and novelist Moshe Kulbak, who had taught them at the Real-Gymnasium during the mid-1920s. He left Poland later in that decade, but his impact could still be felt.

The works of two members of Yung Vilne in particular, both poets, touched me deeply. Chaim Grade, later to win fame for his novels, wrote verse in the 1930s about the ascetic *Musar* Yeshiva in Novogrudok where he had studied. He seemed to capture for me the tension between the traditional and secular Jewish worlds. Avrum Sutzkever's voice put form ahead of content. His classical

Yiddish poetry drew upon Pushkin and Mickiewicz and showed that Yiddish could be as sublime as any language.

Some of the leading Yiddish poets were so young that there was one even my age, Hirsch Glick, whose work was published when he was only in his teens. In 1943, he would compose the partisan anthem *Zog nit keyn mol,* or "Never Say." That song would be the most inspirational of my entire life. It was further proof for me of the uncommon creativity nurtured by the Vilna of my youth.

IN THE SPRING of 1935, with my heart set on the Real-Gymnasium, a letter from Vilna was waiting for me when I came home from the Polish elementary school. I tore it open and saw that I was accepted. Better yet, I was awarded a full-tuition scholarship for the first year. I already knew that I could live in Vilna with my

Members of the Yung-Vilne literary circle in 1930. In the back row, Avrum Sutzkever is second from the left, Chaim Grade is second from the right. (From the Archives of the YIVO Institute for Jewish Research, New York)

The cover of the first issue of the journal *Yung-Vilne*, published in 1934, the year before I began my studies at the Real-Gymnasium. In the lower right is a drawing of the old Jewish quarter of Vilna; on the left side of the page are smokestacks representing twentieth century industry. (From the Archives of the YIVO Institute for Jewish Research, New York)

aunt and uncle, so my hard-pressed parents wouldn't have to pay for room and board either. I ran to my folks' store to tell them the great news and the whole family celebrated that evening. At thirteen, it was the most exhilarating moment of my life. Given my upbringing, I can't say I was much of a believer in God at that point, but that letter sure felt like answered prayers.

The Real-Gymnasium, established after World War I, was already highly regarded among East European Jews by the time I enrolled. It drew seventeen-year old Abraham Joshua Heschel for two years in the mid-1920s; he would later become one of the world's foremost interpreters of Judaism. The large, renovated three-story building on Rudnitski Street in the heart of the Jewish Quarter was quite impressive. It had been the palace of a Polish count and its grand staircases, parquet wooden floors, and stained glass windows were still intact.

Everything, even rigorous science courses like physics and chemistry, was taught in Yiddish, and that caused some anti-Semitic administrators in Warsaw to delay certification of the school until 1930. But in fact, the science program in particular was outstanding. The word "Real" (pronounced ray-al) in the school's name actually hearkened back to prestigious Prussian gymnasiums in the nineteenth century, which dropped the study of Latin and Greek in favor of the practical or *real* subjects such as the physical sciences and mathematics. The Real-Gymnasium required a modern foreign language, however, and the one I chose was English.

Not every teacher or student was a Bundist. Many, like me, were wholeheartedly Yiddishists and politically progressive, but did not embrace the Marxist thinking that underlay the Bundist movement. At the other end of the scale were faculty members to the *left* of the Bund, communists who deeply admired Stalin. In fact, a couple of leading teachers, including the influential Moshe Kulbak, immigrated to the Soviet Union in the 1920s to live in the "workers' paradise." Despite the variety of ideologies, I felt the prevailing political atmosphere at the Real-Gymnasium was close to the Bundist idea of democratic socialism. The mood was highly progressive, concerned with the Jewish plight but also the sufferings of other peoples.

Our core curriculum was similar to that taught in the Polish gymnasiums of the day, but we also studied Bible, Jewish history, and, of course, the Yiddish language and its literature. In addition, we were offered workshops in practical skills ranging from embroidery to bookbinding. Whatever the subject, the outstanding faculty was invariably devoted to us students. They were all specialists, but their broad-minded pedagogy went beyond lecturing and testing. They often taught us one-on-one, both inside and outside the classroom. Like my instructors at the Sholem Aleichem School, they encouraged cooperation among the students. We worked on many projects together and then relaxed in the school's big, grassy inner courtyard.

Many of my teachers are before my eyes today—Mr. Stolicki who taught physics and chemistry, Mrs. Gordon, our Polish history teacher, Miss Sheinuk, my English teacher whom we dubbed the "yellow picture" because of her yellowish-red curls, and especially Mr. Gershteyn, the strapping Yiddish instructor, with youthful energy despite his silver-gray hair. Mr. Lubotsky taught my favorite subject, math, and he and Gershteyn affectionately called Feigel Kaplinski and me the Zhetlekhes, the little ones from Zhetel. We were our shtetl's only representatives in a student body drawn from all over Poland.

Gershteyn also taught Yiddish music and supervised the school chorus, and there were many other extra-curricular activities, too. The drama group was one of the most popular and many of the kids performed in Yiddish versions of Shakespeare and other classics. Because I needed to get my scholarship renewed each year, my studies came first and I had little time for clubs.

There was no high school romance for me either. Well, virtually none. You might think that we freethinkers would experiment with sex at an early age. I did have erotic stirrings as a teenager, but I never acted upon those feelings, and I doubt many of my classmates, about a third of whom were girls, did either. The closest I came was to exchange dreamy, affectionate looks with a cute, dark-haired boy named Avrum Brumberg every time our paths crossed in the hallways. Our eyes met, and expressed longing, but we never touched one another. We never even spoke.

The faculty and senior class of the Real-Gymnasium four years before
I arrived. In the center of the top row is Mr. Turbovich, the head of
school, flanked by Yakov Gershteyn on the left and Mr. Lubotsky
on the right. In the second row Mr. Stolitzky is fourth from the left;
Miss Sheinuk, the "yellow picture," third from the right; and
Mrs. Zeiden, our Polish teacher, on the far right

My Yiddish and music
teacher Yakov Gershteyn

Bookish though I was, I left the confines of the Real-Gymnasium from time to time, even if it was usually for the purpose of conducting term paper research. That took me into some of the other extraordinary Jewish institutions of Vilna.

One was the renowned Strashun Library, in the *shulhoyf,* or courtyard, of the Great Synagogue and only a few blocks from the school. It held more than five thousand rare Hebrew books and manuscripts, acquired by the bibliophile and philanthropist Rabbi Mattityahu Strashun and donated to the community after his death in 1885. In the twentieth century, countless more volumes were added, many of them in Yiddish, and the collection of tens of thousands of works was opened to the public as a reference library. There was no proper catalogue, but the Strashun Library drew hundreds of readers every day and was even open on Saturday afternoons. In its reading room you really saw the diversity of Jewish Vilna: secular girls like me, reading modern Yiddish books, sat across the table from black-coated religious scholars poring over medieval Hebrew texts.

An even more vital organization was YIVO, almost a mile outside the cramped Jewish Quarter in a spacious, two-dozen-room villa set back from the street. YIVO, or the Institute of Jewish Research, held a huge Yiddish library including rare books and newspapers, a museum of permanent and changing exhibits, and an archive of folkloric materials and artifacts from the Yiddish theater—playbills and posters from all over Eastern Europe. The institute had more than a dozen employees in the late 1930s, about half of them accomplished scholars covering Yiddish philology and literature, but also history, economics, and sociology. YIVO published a raft of books and articles, not just on the Yiddish language, but also on the culture of the Yiddish-speaking masses. Sigmund Freud and Albert Einstein were on the board of its academic advisors.

On pleasant, tree-lined Wulska Street, YIVO had a comfortable, sunny reading room open to the public and I'd go there often to read a book or do research for a term paper. At every desk there was a reading lamp and, unlike the Strashun Library, everything was easily accessible. The capable, friendly staff brought me any of the institute's quarter-million items that I requested.

Vital though Yiddish scholarship was, YIVO signified something even more with its inviting landscaped setting, its modern spotless quarters, and its outreach to the general public. The institute seemed to fly in the face of the negative stereotype of Yiddish that many Jews and non-Jews held in the 1930s, and some believe even today: that it's merely an odd dialect of the medieval German ghetto, and not a proper language at all. Its peculiar characteristics, according to this view, might make it suitable for self-deprecating humor and sentimental folk-sayings, but not for anything truly significant. The Zionist Hebrew speakers often looked down on Yiddish as belonging to *Galut*, the despised Diaspora, while the Polish-speaking assimilationists ridiculed our mother tongue as evidence that we were backward and clannish.

YIVO challenged all of these assumptions by putting forth Yiddish on a high intellectual plane, and as the language for the *future* of Polish Jewry, not only its past. Even the sophisticated New Yorker Lucy Dawidowicz came away from YIVO thinking, "it had class (as) a place from which distinction and excellence would issue." I felt the same way. If Vilna was the capital of Yiddishland, YIVO was its citadel.

Given my family background and my years at the Sholem Aleichem Yiddishe Folkshule and the Real-Gymnasium, I had never doubted the legitimacy or value of Yiddish, but I could see it needed defenders. Fortunately, it had them. The driving force behind YIVO was Max Weinreich, a prodigy who had been raised in a German-speaking family in Czarist Russia, but became enthralled with Yiddish. He bristled when people sneered at Yiddish as a mere dialect and not a real language, a misconception he felt flowed from the homelessness and defenselessness of the Jewish people. So he often shot back with the quip that the only distinction between a dialect and a language is that the latter has an army and a navy.

No dry, pedantic philologist, Weinreich could be called a *socio-linguist* in that he studied the development of Yiddish in its cultural and social context. After World War I he earned a doctorate in Germany, but in 1923 he came to Vilna to teach at the Yiddish Teachers' Seminary, while he also worked as a journalist for a local Bundist newspaper and New York's *Forward*. He co-founded YIVO in 1925, at the age of only thirty-one. For its first four years, until the institute obtained its fine building, he housed the documents in his own apartment. He would direct the organization until the war, and in 1940 undertook the Herculean task of reconstituting YIVO, with most of its archives intact, in New York. There it would grow over the decades to become the world's preeminent archive of East European Jewish life.

I remembered Max Weinreich and his wife Regina from their visits to Zhetel for graduations at the Sholem Aleichem School, when they were often accompanied by her father, Dr. Zemach Shabad, a healthcare advocate, parliamentarian, and preeminent Yiddishist. In fact, it was Regina herself who had encouraged me to apply to the Real-Gymnasium, and given me hope that I'd get a scholarship. In Vilna I saw her often and admired her immensely. Although her primary job was teaching at one of the leading

Yiddish elementary schools in the city, she also taught a workshop that I took at the Real-Gymnasium—in the embroidery that decorated peasant blouses and delicate handkerchiefs. Although she wore plain dresses, and tied her long, red hair in a bun behind her neck, she was very attractive and the closest thing to a queen that Yiddishland had.

Her two sons, Uriel and Gabriel, were still in elementary school in the late 1930s, but everyone predicted great things for them. In postwar America, Uriel, a professor at Columbia, would write the classic textbook *College Yiddish* and compile the most authoritative English–Yiddish dictionary.

The younger one, Gabriel, became a noted physicist at the University of Michigan, although late in his life he took a path none of us could have imagined; he converted to Christianity and became an Episcopalian priest, claiming that he was not converting from Judaism but rather from atheism. Yet even this Weinreich says that when he prays, he does so in Yiddish to be sure that God understands him.

It might be too much to say that Regina took me under her wing, but she certainly boosted my confidence every time we met. When I expressed concern about whether or not my one-year scholarship would be renewed—several students were forced to drop out because their families couldn't pay the tuition—she told me not to worry, and I did receive the grant all four of my years at the Real-Gymnasium. I'll never know to what extent she lobbied on my behalf, but surely a word from Regina Shabad Weinreich carried a lot of weight.

ESPECIALLY AFTER THE death of President Pilsudski, who had protected the Jews somewhat, anti-Semitism worsened in Poland,

and during the half-decade before the outbreak of World War II we witnessed severe discrimination against us in the professions, and poisonous propaganda emanating from the press and the Church. In a pastoral letter read in the pulpit of almost every Catholic Church in 1936, the Polish Primate, Cardinal August Hlond, accused us Jews of being communists and usurers, and even blamed us for pornography and prostitution. He urged a boycott of all Jewish businesses, but stopped short of advocating violence. After all, he concluded, Jews might come to their senses one day and accept Jesus as the Messiah.

The government, too, approved of the anti-Jewish boycott and passed a new raft of laws against us. Kosher slaughtering, now deemed barbaric by the authorities, was outlawed and therefore had to be performed in secret at the risk of fines and even arrest. A nationalist political party known as Endecja, which exerted much pressure on the Polish government in the late 1930s, advocated the segregation of Jews in public places and even their expulsion from the country. The Nazis had come to power in Germany in 1933 and the Endeks, as they were called, imported many of Hitler's ideas into Poland.

As a student in a Jewish high school, enveloped by a large, vibrant Jewish community, I was mostly shielded from the rise in bigotry, much as I'd been in Zhetel. We read in newspapers about the upsurge in anti-Semitism, and discussed it, but my world revolved around my studies, my family, and my friends, and I felt fairly safe. If my aunt's dental practice suffered from discrimination during this time, she spared me the details.

But I did know of attacks against Jewish university students and faculty. Vilna was the home of the Stefan Batory University, a hotbed of anti-Jewish thought and action. The main buildings of the campus were right next to the Jewish Quarter and we gymnasium students, hoping to enter a university someday, couldn't ignore the intolerance and violence there.

All across Poland, the campuses were hubs of anti-Semitism. First of all, there was a quota for Jews, a *numerus clausus*, as it was known, that dropped sharply during the thirties; the Endeks actually demanded a *numerous nullus*. The relatively few Jewish students who were admitted (only 8 percent of Polish university students by 1938, down two-thirds from the prior decade) were required to sit in a segregated section along the left side of the lecture halls. This area was known as the "ghetto benches" and the enforced separation was humiliating. A good number of Jewish students and a few non-Jews silently protested by not sitting anywhere. Instead they stood in the back of the hall. Any Jew who flouted the rule and sat in the main section was likely to be forcibly ejected by a "patriotic" Polish student.

But the danger Jews faced was far greater than the shame of segregation. In 1931, a student rampage at the Stefan Batory University spilled into the Jewish Quarter, and some Jews fought back. Sixteen Jews and four Poles were injured, and a few days later one of the Poles died from his wounds. Among the Jews most seriously hurt was Max Weinreich who happened to be leaving a conference and walking on the sidewalk. A hooligan hit him in the eye with a stone and he was virtually blinded in that eye for the rest of his life. Because a Polish student died in the melee, militant nationalists claimed that *they* were the true victims, so each year on the anniversary of the riot they fomented fresh violence against Jews.

I witnessed a particularly bloody clash in early 1939. A number of us young people were encircling a badly injured Jewish university student already being treated by a Jewish doctor on Yat-kova Street in the Jewish Quarter. The doctor, probably thinking about our future, looked up at us and said in despair, "Children, see what is happening to us."

By the academic year 1938–39, I no longer lived in my aunt and uncle's house. We all felt it was becoming too crowded, and at sixteen I was ready to be on my own. With Feigel Kaplinski, I moved into a small room in a private house on Targowa Street where we had kitchen privileges. It was an easy walk to school and, having my own place, I felt like a real grown-up. But truth be told, I still missed my family back in Zhetel. My father visited me whenever he came to Vilna on a buying trip for the store. We would talk, eat some sweets together, and when he had to leave I'd cry openly.

But the next day I would once again become engrossed in my studies, not only out of my love of Yiddish but also for practical reasons. The Real-Gymnasium was preparing me for a career as a teacher, always my goal. I was advancing academically, and seriously thinking about entering the Yiddish Teachers' Seminary in Vilna after graduation, only two years away.

Even so, it was hard to put the ominous international situation out of my mind. After *Kristallnacht* in Germany in November 1938, when many hundreds of synagogues were put to the torch on a single night, I lost any illusions about the savagery of the Third Reich. And the Nazis seemed to be expanding their reach. The spring before, Hitler had annexed Austria, and, in September 1938, timid West European leaders signed the Munich Pact, allowing the *Fuehrer* to occupy the mountainous Sudetenland. That agreement rendered the Czechs, our southern neighbors, defenseless. And in March 1939, the spring semester of my fourth year at the Real-Gymnasium, the German army marched into Prague ending democratic Czechoslovakia's existence. That same month they seized the Baltic seaport of Memel from Lithuania.

As the school year was coming to a close, Hitler was threatening Poland. He demanded the return to Germany of the Free City of Danzig and the right to build a highway and railroad lines through the "Polish Corridor" so he could link East Prussia with the rest of the Reich. Poland refused, afraid of losing its access to the Baltic Sea.

As the two countries moved closer to war in mid-1939, there was a slight rapprochement between the rightwing Polish nationalists and the Jewish community. After all, we now faced the same adversary, Nazi Germany. But anti-Semitism was so ingrained that even under the threat of a common enemy, the nation's Jews were not widely trusted by the Polish majority.

While I was back in Zhetel during the summer break, my father listened to a little home radio—a station and transmitter had been opened in nearby Baranovich months before—and he anxiously discussed the Yiddish and Polish broadcasts with other men in the market place, and later in the evening with us. The military dictators in Warsaw tried to suppress the media, but none of their censorship or bluster could ease the sense of impending disaster. At times we would pick up a news report from BBC, which left no doubt that Europe was on the brink of war. I later learned that in Vilna that summer, in expectation of an attack, the population carried out fire drills.

Then, on August 23, 1939, the handwriting on the wall could not be clearer. The Molotov-Ribbentrop Non-Aggression Pact, named for the Soviet and German foreign ministers, cut the legs out from under Poland's independence. Prior to that, we all felt that Hitler would be reluctant to attack us because he'd face the kind of two-front war that had spelled Germany's downfall in World War I. An invasion of Poland, we reasoned, would pit Britain and France against Germany in the west, while drawing the Soviet Union into war against Hitler in the east. But the freshly signed non-aggression treaty between the two totalitarian superpowers suddenly gave Hitler a much freer hand in crushing us. Even if the western powers did go to war over Poland, he no longer had to worry about a second front in the east.

In fact, a secret protocol of the pact actually divided East-Central Europe, including Poland, into German and Soviet spheres of influence. In late August, there were continued "negotiations" over the territorial issues, but we all knew the very survival of our country was in jeopardy.

Early on the morning of September 1, the *Wehrmacht* invaded Poland, and Britain and France quickly announced that they stood by their Polish ally. The Second World War had begun, with the USSR remaining neutral. Like everyone else in Zhetel, I was horrified at the prospect of our nation being overrun by Hitler's forces.

We soon heard rumors of the Polish army's rapid retreat and of German brutality against Jewish civilians. Tens of thousands of Jewish refugees fled east, just ahead of the advancing German troops, and some arrived in Zhetel with stories of mass execution and other atrocities so appalling that many of us reacted with disbelief. But even those who didn't take the refugees at their word understood that a catastrophe was almost upon us. The front was still a few hundred miles away, but the distance was closing fast. People gathered in the streets and anxiously asked one another, "What do you hear? What's in the newspapers? What's on the radio?" In those opening weeks of the war, each night seemed like an eternity. I don't know if anyone got any sleep.

Then on September 17, with Germans already at the gates of Warsaw, we heard electrifying news of another kind: the Red Army had invaded Poland from the east. We were naturally overjoyed. Only a couple of days later we saw well-armed Soviet soldiers in the streets of Zhetel. The older generation, like my parents, who had grown up under the Czar, had no problem conversing with them in Russian, and some Red Army men even spoke Yiddish.

The downcast Poles and even the Belarusians would never forgive us for our reaction. To them, the warm welcome we gave the Soviet invaders was further proof that our true sympathies lay with a foreign regime, and a communist one at that. But for us it meant rescue at the last moment from the Nazi beast, which halted its assault at a secretly prearranged line of demarcation less than a hundred miles west of us. A mighty, mobilized nation of two hundred million people, who inhabited the largest landmass in the world, was now our protector.

The Red Army, we could plainly see, was highly disciplined, and well-equipped with wide tanks and high-caliber artillery. It was not the rag-tag crew that had lost the border war against Poland two decades earlier. This time, with little resistance from the already-battered Polish army, they conquered eastern Poland—in all of two weeks.

We Jews waved little red flags, literally threw flowers in the path of the Soviet "liberators," and even kissed their tanks. In turn, they seemed friendly, patting small children on the head. Despite the bad Soviet record on Judaism and Jewish nationalism, even the Zionists and Orthodox felt a kind of deliverance from disaster. Even if Soviet rule turned out to be evil, could any Jew doubt that it would be the lesser of two evils?

But nothing matched the excitement of Zhetel's leftist Jews, some of whom, upon hearing that the Soviets' forward units had reached Novogrudok, streamed onto the surrounding country roads, forming a kind of welcoming committee for the on-coming Red Army. Their joyous anticipation and high expectations were like the parents of a bride or groom at the wedding, meeting the *mechutonim*, or in-laws, for the first time.

Bundists were especially jubilant. Although the political party was shut down almost immediately, that was the fate of all the Polish parties, Jewish and non-Jewish alike. Before long many Bundist leaders would be deported by the Soviets to Siberia, but for now, greatly relieved that we wouldn't fall into the clutches of Nazism, Bundists and those of us who sympathized with them, rejoiced.

Beyond that, a new political and economic system would soon be in place, one, we fervently hoped, with more social justice than the Polish regime it had swept away. Nothing less had occurred than a "revolution from abroad," as one historian later put it. In 1939, most of Poland's natural resources were still controlled by the land-holding gentry and we looked forward to their downfall. We weren't sorry to hear that some communists were already looting the upper classes' estates. My father assumed that he'd lose his store as well as his insurance business, but they were barely providing us with a livelihood anyway, and he enthusiastically welcomed the change of regime.

But the ensuing turmoil also gave us many reasons to harbor doubt. One of the earliest Soviet decrees was to make their currency legal tender in occupied Poland, and on par with the zloty, which before the war had been worth many times a ruble. Then they disbursed hundreds of rubles to each soldier as advance wages. The Soviet men, not used to seeing so many consumer goods available, immediately bought up everything in our shops.

They were likened to a swarm of locusts by storekeepers. In our shop, entire shelves of goods were picked clean in minutes. I remember some troops buying coarse linen nightgowns for their wives or girlfriends, thinking the garments were fancy dresses. The buying spree, amidst all the disruption and shortages of wartime, was a problem we could not have foreseen. The goods they bought could not be replaced and our store soon closed. We were left with a stack of rubles, which had little value.

I fell for this currency switch myself. A Soviet soldier eyed my wristwatch and politely offered me many times what I'd paid for it. Or so I thought. I foolishly sold it to him for rubles, and ended up with little buying power at all. Ration cards and long lines would be our lot.

AMIDST THE CHAOS and confusion of those weeks, school was suspended as we all watched Stalin formally annex our region, making it part of the Byelorussian Soviet Socialist Republic.

At first, Vilna, too, was incorporated into the BSSR, but in October it was awarded to Lithuania, which, since its modern reincarnation in 1918, had coveted the historic city. Lithuania somehow retained its independence even after World War II began, although it would be a satellite of the USSR, required to allow Soviet military bases on its territory.

With the fighting in our region finally over, the Real-Gymnasium opened late for a shortened fall semester. But would it be safe for me to attend? My parents were concerned that I'd be stranded in a foreign country in this most uncertain of times. Would I be allowed to cross the border to come home? And what dangers might befall little Lithuania, perched as it was between Nazi Germany and the Soviet Union?

Months before hostilities had broken out, my parents and I had decided that if war came, I wouldn't return to Vilna. Instead, I would finish high school as close to home as possible. So I hedged my bets, just as I had done four years earlier when I attended an extra year of primary school in case I was not accepted by the Real-Gymnasium. In the spring of 1939, I was accepted by the public, tuition-free Polish gymnasium in Novogrudok, a school that housed out-of-town students in a modest, low-cost dormitory. Of course, the language of instruction there was not Yiddish, but the year I'd spent at the Polish school in Zhetel, we all thought, would serve me well in making the transition. Feigel Kaplinski also decided to transfer to the same gymnasium—this would be the fourth school we'd attend together. In late September 1939, we two seventeen-year-old girls set out for Novogrudok. She had an aunt living in that city who could put us up until we were ready to move into our dorm.

Given the widespread damage caused by the war, it was not surprising that public transportation was at a standstill. In fact, peace had not yet fully arrived because of attacks by roving bands of Polish militiamen who refused to accept defeat and their country's loss of sovereignty. So how did we cover the twenty miles to Novogrudok? We hitchhiked and were picked up by a truck full of Soviet soldiers headed our way. It sounds like we were courting trouble, but in fact they could not have been more courteous. They delivered us safe and sound to the door of Feigel's aunt.

But the benevolence of the new rulers in these early encounters would prove transitory. Although the Nazis would ultimately destroy Jewish life in Poland, our *way* of life ended with the Soviet occupation. Nothing would be as it had been before.

THREE

The Assault

I spent the next two years as a student in Novogrudok, returning to Zhetel only for summer vacations. Except for its brief
war with Finland in the winter of 1939–40, my new country
was at peace while I continued my schooling. In Western Europe
by contrast, especially after May 1940, war raged as Hitler conquered France, the Low Countries, Denmark, and Norway and
bombed Britain.

My home in the Byelorussian Soviet Socialist Republic was a
leafy hilltop settlement on a tributary of the Neman River. It was
built on a flat area atop a mountain, so you walked uphill to get
to the center of town, which hosted a lively farmer's market every
Thursday.

With over ten thousand people, Novogrudok was more than
twice the size of Zhetel. On the eve of the Soviet invasion the
roughly seven thousand Jews (including about five hundred refugees from Nazi-occupied western Poland) formed a lively, diverse

community, not much different from that of my childhood home. Here, too, there were many Bundists and the Zionist movement was especially strong. Even so, like Zhetel, most Jews were Orthodox and Novogrudok was justly proud of its centuries-long line of distinguished rabbis, cantors, and Talmud scholars.

Of course, it was nothing like the matchless metropolis of Vilna, and I sorely missed the intellectual stimulation of the Real-Gymnasium. But while not the "Capital of Yiddishland," Novogrudok had made its own contribution to my beloved mother tongue. It was the birthplace in 1863 of the pioneering Yiddish philologist Alexander Harkavy, who compiled the first Yiddish-English dictionary at the end of the nineteenth century, preceding Uriel Weinreich's by two generations. Harkavy was educated in Vilna, lived in Paris, and immigrated to New York in 1903 where he wrote for the *Forward*. But he never forgot his hometown. For the rest of his life he raised funds among New York émigrés from Novogrudok to ease the hunger and devastation of his town after the German occupation in World War I, reconstitute the many Jewish social service agencies, and later alleviate the suffering during the Depression.

Like Vilna during the interwar period, Novogrudok gloried in its Polish past. Adam Mickiewicz, Poland's national poet, was probably born on his uncle's estate in 1798, only a few miles out of town. A monument was placed there and I saw him hailed in Novogrudok as I had in Vilna. But by the time my friend Feigel Kaplinski and I arrived, the Jewish and Polish, and even Belarusian character of the town was in the process of being swept away by the Soviet occupation and annexation.

The Soviets made a special effort to win over us young people. The academic high school we attended got a lot of attention from the authorities and was completely transformed. It had been a Polish gymnasium and Feigel and I had assumed that the year we'd studied at the Polish elementary school in Zhetel would help us make a smooth transition to Polish from the Real-Gymnasium's emphasis on Yiddish. Well, we were wrong. Replacing the Polish language was among the highest priorities of the Soviet regime. By the beginning of the spring semester every course was taught in Russian. The Russian language itself was taught by teachers sent to us from deep in the USSR.

Poland conquered by Nazi Germany and the Soviet Union in 1939

In some cases in newly annexed provinces like ours, minority languages of the former Polish state were allowed. Belarusian, Ukrainian, and even Yiddish continued to be the language of instruction in a few schools. Theoretically, parents were supposed to decide the issue by voting at town-wide assemblies. But often, political pressure was brought to bear, and Russian generally carried the day.

Even when Yiddish was taught, as it still was at the Sholem Aleichem School in Zhetel, where my brother, Maeshe, attended classes, the Soviet pedagogues changed the spelling in order to sever the language from its Hebrew roots. The word *emes*, for example, meaning "truth" in Yiddish and Hebrew, was altered by replacing the letter *aleph* with an *ayin* so that it was not spelled as it was in the Bible or in Modern Hebrew. To us, such changes seemed like glaring errors, and a joke went around that the Soviets could write the word Noah with seven mistakes.

Needless to say, instruction in Hebrew (which represented both Jewish nationalism and Jewish piety) came to an abrupt halt and all the Tarbut schools were closed. I found out later about heart-wrenching scenes like the one in Pinsk, about a hundred miles south of us, where a Hebrew teacher and his class burst into tears after he announced, "Children, I am speaking to you for the last time in Hebrew."

Polish fared only slightly better. It was retained in only a tiny minority of schools throughout our region and our new rulers often forced those schools to move to inadequate facilities or adopt an inconvenient afternoon class schedule. Naturally, portraits of Polish statesmen came down from the walls, as did the crucifixes that had hung in the classrooms.

Not only did the language of instruction change, but also the whole school system was soon overhauled to match the rest of the Soviet Union, where private schools no longer existed. Now, a four-year elementary school would be followed by a seven-year secondary school in the rural areas and a ten-year secondary school, the *desetiletka,* in cities and towns.

Overnight, the curriculum changed too. Science and history would be taught from a different perspective, and the Soviet regime even objected to our mathematics lessons, which frequently mentioned the prices of commodities. New textbooks had to be shipped in from the east for every subject.

While our Soviet rulers exiled to Siberia most of the former political office-holders and civil administrators, they valued the expertise of policemen, firefighters, postmen, and teachers, and generally kept them on. But all public employees, and especially those responsible for instructing the youth, quickly needed to master Russian and the party line. Teachers were now required to take a crash course in communist ideology as well as the Russian language.

The Soviet education system was more advanced than the Polish schools had been, so I was set back two years, as was my brother in Zhetel. But I relished my studies, and the Russian language came easily to me. I'd often heard it spoken at home because my parents, like other Zhetlers of their generation, had grown up when our region was still part of the Czarist Empire. Feigel also took quickly to Russian; the languages of Eastern Europe had always been her main academic interest.

Especially at the outset of Soviet rule, we all looked forward to a better life as citizens of the USSR. Because of the rampant anti-Semitism we'd witnessed in the late 1930s, for us, as for many other Jews, the loss of Polish sovereignty, along with the country's language and school curriculum, was no great cause for despair.

I don't recall being inundated with Soviet propaganda. But veneration for Comrade Stalin—his picture was everywhere—almost replaced the Judeo-Christian God whom the communists rejected. Yet the Soviet assault on religion did not disturb us very much. Jews were now expected to work on Saturday, and could no longer observe their sacred day of rest, but except for Bubbe Henye my family had not kept the Sabbath anyway. Jews were allowed the holiday of Passover, no doubt because of its message of social justice, but it was limited to just one day, rather than eight. That, too, seemed reasonable to us.

I seriously thought about joining the Komsomol, the spirited Soviet youth group, which offered recreation, political education, and a sense of purpose that appealed to me. In the end I chose not to apply. I was not worried about indoctrination, but simply concerned it might drain precious time from my studies. In Zhetel my little brother wanted to join Komsomol's club for children, the Young Pioneers. For a while they wouldn't accept Maeshe because its leaders considered our father "bourgeois" or "capitalist" simply because we'd owned a little store. Finally, though, they relented and Maeshe became a Young Pioneer and proudly wore its uniform: the red neckerchief against a white shirt.

My father also adapted well. He soon got a new job as a bookkeeper, yet another profession this ambitious man taught himself without any formal training. He quickly rose in the ranks to become the supervisor of a number of other bookkeepers for our region's state-run bakeries. Like all of us, he was pleased to see Jews employed on almost every rung of the government bureaucracy, which had certainly not been the case in prewar Poland. He was not the only one to laugh at a gibe about the dejected Poles:

Before the war they wanted a Poland without Jews, now they still have the Jews, but no Poland.

But as the months wore on, even our family began to see that our sense of safety and well-being under the new system might have been an illusion. The Soviet Union's clamps of censorship were much tighter than Poland's had been. You could not criticize the government in the press, but neither could you express your disapproval in the classroom or on the streets. Many, fearing they'd be denounced to the authorities, were afraid to voice dissent in front of their neighbors, or even family members at home. A child might later blurt out something he or she had overheard and dire consequences could follow. During my visits home from school I remember politics openly discussed in our house, but the conversation around many other dinner tables in these times was largely about the weather.

You could pay a high price just for having been a businessman in the old regime. While the only consequence of my father's "capitalism" was Maeshe's delay in entering the Young Pioneers, other former entrepreneurs were imprisoned and/or exiled.

Father was vulnerable in another way, as a Bundist sympathizer, or "fellow traveler" to use an American term from the 1940s and 50s. In the eyes of the Soviets, Bundists were the wrong kind of leftists, too concerned with specifically Jewish interests and not fully committed to communism. They were considered deviationists like the Trotskyists who Stalin had brutally purged before the war. Now this ideological purity would be imposed on the whole *kresy*. During the twenty-one months of Soviet rule in the former eastern Poland, a million people, including Bundists as well as many others who had been tainted by their past politics or business activities, were deported to the Gulag. A disproportionate number of them were Jews and a few were our friends. These included the Kaplinski clan that lived next door to us: Chaim, who had founded the Bund in Zhetel, and his grown children Nyome, a dedicated leader, and Rishe, my closest friend. Many others were imprisoned in Novogrudok. A large financial center was converted into a jail just for political prisoners.

Of course the greater threat facing us was Nazi Germany, now lurking just over the border. But we were deluded about that as well, and not only because of the August 1939 peace treaty between Hitler and Stalin, or by the censored news reports that gave us little reason to suspect any impending hostilities. Most wrongheaded of all was our belief that the Soviet Union was infallible militarily. We thought that its huge army, wide tanks, and big bombers could repel an attack from the Germans or anyone else.

Early on, my perceptive uncle Sroel Ber voiced his doubts. He and his family, feeling that Vilna was unsafe, had come to Zhetel during the Soviet occupation. He noticed that the Soviet tanks had left deep ruts in the cobblestone streets of the town, grooves that deepened after September 1939, and that no one fixed. The ruts soon became a hazard for any vehicle. To Sroel Ber it was a glaring sign that the Soviets would neglect even the basic infrastructure, and he worried that it foretold a breakdown of services beyond the roadways. Meanwhile, we all noticed growing shortages of basic commodities like salt and sugar and feared they indicated even bigger inefficiencies in the Soviet distribution system. This was the nation that was protecting us from Hitler. Maybe it wasn't as powerful as we'd once thought.

WHEN IT FINALLY came, the suddenness and scale of the Nazi invasion was astounding. On June 22, 1941, the Germans and their allies sent almost four million troops across the borders of the USSR along an eighteen hundred-mile-long front. Operation Barbarossa would be the largest military operation in world history in terms of combatants and casualties. By late fall the *Wehrmacht* was at the gates of Moscow, and occupied half a million square miles of Soviet territory, an area nearly twice the size of Texas.

Close on the heels of the regular army was a far smaller group of German invaders with a special mission, the infamous *Einsatzgruppen*, part of the SS. Only three thousand strong, their job was to round up—and execute—Jews and other civilians. This was the first phase in Hitler's plan to annihilate European Jewry. Later, he would bring the victims to the executioners at death camps like Auschwitz, Treblinka and Belzec. But between mid-1941 and mid-1942, the executioners came to the victims. In all, about a million and a half Jews, and hundreds of thousands of gypsies and political prisoners, were murdered by these mobile killing units.

In many ways, this was the opposite of the Soviet invasion of eastern Poland in September 1939. Then, we were spared the Nazi aggression that had taken place in the western part of the country, while the Poles mourned their loss of statehood and brooded about the imposition of communism. Now, with the rapid retreat of the Red Army, we Jews were exposed to the full brunt of German barbarism, while gentiles either passively watched or actively collaborated in the slaughter. In our area, some of them were encouraged by rumors that the Germans intended to set up an independent Belarusian state after the fall of Soviet rule.

I'd recently come back to Zhetel from Novogrudok for summer break when my hometown came under German attack. The opening round was an aerial bombardment lasting a few days.

Most Zhetlers were horrified by the extensive damage and longed for it to stop. But there were some wise people who knew this air attack would be the least of our troubles. One was a teacher, the mother of my sister's closest friend, who looked up at the planes in the sky and gravely said, "Let them bomb forever, as long as they don't come in."

Yet the bombing did stop and forward units of the German army arrived in Zhetel on June 30. They parked a few of their vehicles in our backyard, and I remember some soldiers distributing candy to Jewish children. But that sort of behavior changed almost immediately. Even before the arrival of the *Einsatzgruppen*, German infantrymen shot eight Jews to death.

Most of them had been active in the Soviet administration, but one, Osher Gertsovsky, was a young friend of mine in our club, the *Eiserne Guardia*. I was appalled when they pinned him to the ground, put a pistol into his ear and shot him right before my eyes. It was the first time I'd seen the Nazi killing machine in action and one of its victims had been someone I knew well.

The carnage let up for a while once the army moved on to the next town, but as early as July 14 we were all required to sew a yellow Star of David on our outer clothing, front and back.

Nine days later the *Einsatzgruppen* arrived in Zhetel for their first sweep. With the aid of the local police, comprised of Poles and Belarusians, they had drawn up a list—numbering a hundred twenty, I soon learned—of Jewish leaders to be arrested, trucked to a forest twenty miles away, and executed. I later came to understand that their plan was to eliminate at the beginning anyone likely to organize resistance once the Jewish community was slated for destruction. There were doctors and lawyers on the list, businessmen and bureaucrats, and prominent rabbis. One of the hundred twenty was a woman, Shifra Dunyetz, a respected nurse in town.

My father's name was on that list, too. At the time, he was bed-ridden with his chronic bronchitis. So when they came to our house to arrest him, I tried to use his illness as an excuse to save him. We all knew it would be a long shot.

Several local cops barged through our front door. But as luck would have it, I knew one of them and I can recall his name to this day, Vladek Sosinski. Like me, he had been a gymnasium student before the war and although we'd attended different schools, I'd known the handsome youth and we'd had some friendly conversations. At this critical moment we barely spoke, but when he saw my distress and my father's condition, he nodded as if to convey his understanding. Finally he said, "Alright, he's sick, let him die at home." Vladek and the others then left and went to the next house on their list.

This miracle may have saved our whole family, not only father. For he soon regained enough strength to be assigned work at a lumber mill, becoming our family's only wage earner. The following spring, a far larger Nazi action, or *sh'chiteh*, literally slaughter in Yiddish, would murder twelve hundred Jewish Zhetlers, and those families without a major breadwinner were particularly at risk for selection. By then I was working too, three days a week in a milk factory, but I don't think that my part-time employment would have been enough to spare our entire family.

Killings on a much greater scale followed the first roundup, but that atrocity vividly remains in my mind. Even as they were marched through the streets toward the waiting trucks, those hundred twenty Jews were jeered by gentile onlookers. A few were even mocked by being made to sing the Zionist national anthem,

Hatikvah. Nearly all those selected were executed in the next two days. Yet somehow our besieged community raised enough money to bribe the local police to release two prominent figures: the chief rabbi and Alter Dvoretzky, a courageous young attorney who would later become a resistance leader.

Meanwhile, our plight worsened. Jews weren't allowed to use the sidewalks anymore; we were required to walk only in the street. Still absorbing the shock of the massacre, we were made to surrender to the Germans virtually anything of value including jewelry (even wedding rings were not exempted), gold, and furs. The confiscations took place in mid-summer, but it was easy to imagine how we'd freeze during the cold weather that would arrive in just a few months. Many took the risk of stowing their heavy clothing out of sight. Maeshe remembers hiding something else, the few gold pieces we had, behind some tiles in the walls of our house. But when the time came to flee Zhetel, retrieving that stash was not on our minds and I haven't the slightest idea of what happened to it.

In August, a *Judenrat*, or "Jewish Council," was formed, a group of remaining influential Jews charged with carrying out the German decrees. We would not actually be ghettoized for another half-year but both before and during our confinement the *Judenrat*, while completely at the mercy of the German military administration, acted as a puppet municipal government. Invested with power over housing, food rations, forced labor, the confiscation of valuables, and much more, it controlled our lives.

The *Judenrat* supervised a small Jewish police force, armed not with guns but with clubs. Some were compassionate toward us, their fellow Jews, while others turned corrupt and cruel. Facing German demands, they would be expected to turn over community members for deportation and death, although in shtetls like ours many in the Jewish police refused to comply, feeling that was a moral line they couldn't cross.

The role of the *Judenrat* in Nazi-occupied Europe is highly controversial. In some communities its members (a dozen in small towns like ours, but as many as twenty-four in Warsaw) have been accused of outright collaboration with the Germans. Others have viewed them more sympathetically, pointing out that the Jewish councils attempted to reduce, however slightly, a level of oppression unmatched in its ferocity. Rarely did they fully cooperate with the Nazis, even in the big cities. The head of the Warsaw *Judenrat* committed suicide rather than carry out the worst German demands, and some of his counterparts chose the same course.

Zhetel was unusual because our *Judenrat* chairman, Alter Dvoretzky, headed the resistance as well. The charismatic left-wing Zionist was only in his mid-thirties and retained his youthful demeanor. He had studied law in Berlin, among other cities, so his German was flawless. Fair-haired, and without the typical physical features many associated with East European Jews, he may have had an advantage in ingratiating himself with the occupiers. That direct interaction with the Germans may have been a reason why, unlike almost every other *Judenrat* leader, he grasped the Nazi goal from the outset: nothing less than the complete extermination of the Jewish people.

So Chairman Dvoretzky, who lived with his wife and small son as well as his parents in Zhetel, played a risky double game. During the day he consulted with the Nazis; at night he made contact with former Soviet soldiers in the forests. Some had gone into hiding after the Germans routed them, others had been taken prisoner but escaped the POW camps. These ex-Red Army men were forming the nucleus of a partisan force to attack the Germans. By the fall, Dvoretzky had also formed an underground group in Zhetel itself, twenty cells of three young men each, some of whom were armed with guns bought with *Judenrat* funds and smuggled into town. Dvoretzky too carried a loaded pistol.

He also arranged for ten members of the resistance to infiltrate the Jewish police force. This was especially important because the young, relatively healthy cops, many with prewar military training, had special privileges such as the ability to be out after curfew. Beyond that, Dvoretzky tried to affect public opinion by printing anti-Nazi circulars and distributing them to local non-Jews. Although he was a fairly recent transplant from Novogrudok, my family knew and trusted him; we felt he had the interests of our community at heart. Even so, in late 1941 his plans for fighting back were so secret that we remained unaware of the details.

Alter Dvoretzky, chairman of the Zhetel *Judenrat* and simultaneously leader of the resistance, and his family.
(From *A Memorial to the Jewish Community of Zetel*)

Eventually, the Germans tightened their grip by announcing the ghettoization of Zhetel's Jewish community. On February 22, 1942, posters went up requiring all Jews to leave their homes and move to a small, crowded, circular-shaped area encompassing the synagogue and Talmud Torah. It was fenced in by wood and barbed wire, the only gate guarded by local policemen. As it turned out, our apartment was within the boundaries of the confined area so we did not have to move. But along with other households within in the ghetto we had to take in Jewish families who were no longer allowed to live anywhere else.

Most slept cheek to jowl on our living room floor or on makeshift bunk beds. Usually we had four or five families, often strangers, under our roof. Remarkably, we adapted to the awkward, difficult conditions of sheltering about thirty people in our two-bedroom house and I recall few conflicts. My father and I left the crowded apartment for forced labor each day with a special identity card, a *Schein* in German. It allowed us through the ghetto gate, but we were accompanied to our respective factories by armed escorts. Exhausted by nightfall, we were brought back by them.

The people in our household were among the lucky ones. It was mid-winter and some could find no accommodations other than the great synagogue, no longer used for services and unheated. One woman, whose husband was among those executed back in July, lived on the *bimah*, the platform in front of the Holy Ark, with her six children. Many hundreds of Jews in town were not even Zhetlers, but rather refugees from other shtetls where things were even worse, and their arrival further aggravated the housing crisis.

At twenty, I witnessed desperation of all sorts in the ghetto. Even those who had dragged their furniture from their homes through the February snow now threw out, or burned for heat, those same tables and chairs. Making room for bunk beds and keeping warm were greater needs. As the weather got a bit milder, some buried in the earth the valuables they'd managed to hide from the Germans, even their bridal trousseaus. Others gave their treasured possessions to non-Jews, hoping they might be repaid later with potatoes or other basic foods. Some Jews packed their most essential belongings into knapsacks; they thought they might be transferred to another ghetto on short notice.

Each of us Zhetlers tried to make sense of the shocking events. Needless to say, virtually all of our town's Jewish cultural and educational activity, so vibrant before the war, came to an abrupt halt. So everyone was seeking consolation on his or her own. Some families, although not mine, became more religious. Men who had been secular Jews now donned a *tallis* and *tefillin* and prayed three times a day. Women, looking skyward, poured out their hearts to God. Other ghetto-dwellers sought solace in literature. One book that passed from hand to hand was Franz Werfel's classic *Forty Days of Musa Dagh*. The Prague Jew's novel, based on the Armenian genocide perpetrated by the Turks during World War I, had been translated into both Yiddish and Hebrew.

Some of us turned to spiritualism, a movement that had appeared in the big cities of East-Central Europe at the turn of the century, but had not taken hold in little Zhetel until our desperation made us more receptive. Now, in the depths of our misery, some of my fellow Zhetlers thought their dreams provided omens, or that voices they heard in their heads gave them a sign from another world. A number of us, mostly young people, held séances, seeking to communicate with spirits. We hoped that when the table seemed to levitate, it was a sign that our suffering would soon end. Some of us even spoke to the table, "*Tischele, tischele*, when will the war be over?" I participated myself, believing that even if the séances were only wishful thinking, at least they couldn't do any harm.

Our confinement in the ghetto affected everything, even the way children played in the streets. In their games, they acted out the drama we endured in real life. One Jewish kid would assume the role of a German and bark orders while another would play the role of a deportee and beg for his freedom. It broke my heart once to see a kitten squeeze through the barbed wire fence and hear a little girl shout after it, "*Katzele*, you can't do that, you don't have a *Schein*."

We weren't entirely isolated. Peasants were allowed inside to barter food for any leather or clothing we still had. One of those farmers wanted something else from us. He offered to smuggle the blossoming young Sara out of the ghetto and hide her on his land for the duration of the war. Not yet seventeen, she would be too vulnerable, my father and mother decided, and they turned him down. That time at least, we'd stay together as a family, but the goal of saving their children by somehow getting them out of the ghetto remained uppermost in our parents' minds.

We knew the United States had entered the war after being attacked at Pearl Harbor. But after we were ghettoized two and a half months later, we heard virtually no news of the outside world and thought of ourselves as being in a big prison or labor camp. We saw no end in sight. Then, on April 20, 1942 came word that Alter Dvoretzky, with six other members of the resistance, had fled the ghetto for the forest. This could only mean that a catastrophe was brewing, and the whole ghetto braced itself for what would come next. In fact, the Germans had learned of Zhetel's underground movement. The reprisal would be merciless.

Dvoretzky's plot, conceived more than a year before the Warsaw Ghetto Uprising, called for an armed revolt in Zhetel, even to the point of occupying the town's Gestapo headquarters. But on April 19, one of his most trusted comrades, the young Shalom Fiolun, posing as a furrier, was arrested by the Germans in the countryside as he sought to purchase weapons from the peasants. He had been set up by a former Soviet pilot, posing as a partisan, whom the Germans used as a double agent. Fiolun was tortured to death but somehow got word out that the enemy knew of the bold resistance plan. "Save yourselves," he implored his comrades. Some stories about this episode, including the one told in Zhetel's memorial book, report that Fiolun's chilling message came in the form of a note, written in his own blood, and passed to a Jewish worker in the prison where he was being held. The Germans immediately put a price of twenty-five thousand Reichsmarks on Dvoretzky's head, arrested all of the other *Judenrat* members, and began preparations for a massive assault on the ghetto.

It began early on the morning of April 30, warm, sunny, and the day before May Day, previously the occasion of many joyous celebrations among the leftists in our town. I happened to be looking out my window and saw the *Einsatzgruppen*, other German units, and their Polish and Belarusian collaborators surrounding the ghetto. They commanded us all to assemble in the market square, just inside the ghetto boundaries. The mood was one of dread, but most Jews complied. Others, though, had to be forced out of their homes at gunpoint. By now the involvement of the Jewish police was negligible. Not only had the small force in Zhetel been infiltrated by the resistance, but as in many shtetls, few Jewish cops could bring themselves to round up for extermination their Jewish friends and acquaintances. It is both tragic and despicable that many of our non-Jewish neighbors willingly served in that capacity.

By mid-day, almost three thousand people, young and old, healthy and infirm, cowered in the market square, clinging to each other family by family, while fierce dogs barked and leather-jacketed officers shouted orders. As the selection began, the six in my family locked arms. We came to the ghastly realization that we might be together for the last time.

If there was any method to the madness it seemed to be a forced separation between those who could work and those who couldn't. Local policeman came over and, grabbing Bubbe Henye, pulled her from our arms. Sara and I ran after her, but we were pushed back by the cops' rifle butts and told that if we continued to interfere, they'd seize us, too. I can still hear my grandmother's screams as she was led away: "*Ich bin a Bubbe!*" My sister and I now went back to Mameh, Tateh, and Maeshe and we all linked arms again, painfully aware that our family was now smaller.

We remained under guard as we heard shots and shrieks in the distance. They came from the Kurpiscz woods, at the southern end of town, where the killers had already dug three long ditches. The victims were lined up, shot in groups of twenty, and fell into mass graves, which Poles and Belarusians covered up with earth. Astonishingly, more than a hundred people survived this *sh'chiteh* even after they'd been selected for death. At the last moment they produced ID cards to show that they were skilled craftsmen. They were allowed to return to the ghetto and told the rest of us the gruesome details of the killings. I learned later that the number of Jews gunned down that day was twelve hundred.

The murder of Bubbe Henye devastated my family, mother

especially. She would never be the same again.

If up to April 30 the ghetto had felt like a prison, afterwards we all thought we were on death row. If the devils could slaughter over a thousand innocent people, mostly children and elderly, clearly the rest of us, the other two-thirds of Zhetel's Jewish population, were also doomed. Yes, many of us were useful to them as laborers now, but how long would that last? We heard rumors that other towns had been wiped out completely and now all we could think of was the impending annihilation of ours.

Only days before the slaughter, Dvoretzky, on the run in the forest, linked up with Soviet partisans. Although his plan for an uprising within Zhetel had gone terribly wrong, he still hoped to prevent the impending mass murder by convincing his Russian hosts to join him and his men on a raid of the ghetto. But the Soviets, wary of him from the beginning, did not share his goals. They refused to risk their lives for Jews.

Even after the *sh'chiteh,* the bitter and desperate Dvoretzky still tried to convince the Soviet partisans to save the remaining Jews by fighting the Germans not only in Zhetel, but also throughout the area. By now his bold strategy and strong will threatened the Russians so much that they ambushed and killed him and his second in command, Moshe Pozdonsky, on May 11.

The news of Dvoretzky's murder did not come to Zhetel immediately. But after April 30 we held out little hope of seeing him alive again, although another of Zhetel's underground leaders did return to the ghetto from the forest. Shalom Gerling had been one of Dvoretzky's closest comrades. But once our chief was lost, the resistance never regained traction. The ghetto continued to function, my father still worked at the lumber mill and I labored at the milk factory. Like us, nearly every Jewish Zhetler had lost a family member or close friend in the *sh'chiteh*. Our community was saddened and embittered beyond description.

Now the thought on everybody's mind was preparing for the next *sh'chiteh*. For many Zhetlers, including us, that meant finding or building hiding places. Everyone in my family helped by nailing boards or shoveling dirt during the night. Maybe we could be out of sight the next time the killers came.

My household built two hideaways. Our apartment, in a two-family house, shared a root cellar normally used for keeping food cool in the summer months. There we fashioned a hidden room, which would be concealed, we trusted, from the eyes of any raiders.

The second hiding place was outside, in a shed that was used as a chicken coop. We built a double wall there, hoping to create another safe haven. But the food rations were so sparse, and the produce we could obtain from the farmers so meager, that only the cellar hiding place was stocked with provisions. Our neighbors meanwhile prepared hideouts in gardens, attics, and garages—anywhere to make capture more difficult.

The liquidation of the ghetto began even sooner than we'd anticipated, the morning of August 6, 1942. Once again I was standing by the kitchen sink, looking out the window, when I saw the danger in the distance. This time we all moved quickly. The *Einsatzgruppen* and their local collaborators found the streets and most of the houses empty. They'd have to ferret us out one family at a time. A loudspeaker blared that all Jews had to assemble in the cemetery, but clearly that meant nothing other than an invitation to be murdered.

My whole family ran first to the hiding place in the cellar. Maeshe was suffering from a painful boil in his throat that had just burst, but thankfully he was able to follow us downstairs.

We knew too that the dank air below ground, and the crowded quarters, could only aggravate father's bronchitis. Even so, we all felt this was the safest of our choices.

We found the cellar already crowded with more than a dozen people, including a few who had moved in with us since the ghetto had been formed, but also other Jews, some of whom we barely knew. Among them were small children and babies. Sara and I were naturally afraid that as the murderers above stalked their prey, the cries of the little ones might give us away. So the two of us made a snap decision that we'd have a better chance at survival hiding in the chicken coop. Later we heard from Maeshe, who remained in the cellar with my parents, that one of the babies did wail loudly. Its mother smothered the infant to death, rather than put the whole group at risk. Such were the impossible choices made during this time.

I would later learn from him, too, that my resourceful mother, until now a rock upon whom we all leaned, became delirious in the midst of this life-and-death crisis, barely three months after her own mother had been torn away from us and executed. Now separated from her daughters, she was frantic about our fate. In a state of utter confusion, she began murmuring about preparations for her children's weddings.

Sara and I crouched in the hiding place within the double wall at the back of the chicken coop. Before long we had company. Two men entered after we were settled in. Although we couldn't get a good look at their faces in the darkness, I didn't fear them in any way. We assumed they were young Jews seeking safety just like us.

Everything depended on not making a sound. For much of the time the hunters seemed right outside the coop. At one point, we even heard a few German soldiers chasing a chicken, just a few feet from us. From further away, came the sounds of marching, shooting, and explosions, and of people being dragged out of nearby homes. We couldn't tell if one of those houses was our own. "*Raus, Raus,*" the Germans yelled. We heard, too, the whoops of locals evidently embarked on a looting spree.

That night, after the commotion of the "Jew hunt" had quieted down a bit, I was startled to hear my father's voice calling out our names, "Mirele, Sorele," and knocking on the outside wall of our hiding place. Filled with anxiety about us, he'd rightly guessed that we'd taken refuge in the shed.

But we didn't answer him. I made a hand sign to Sara and the two guys to keep quiet. All sorts of dark thoughts passed through my tormented mind. Maybe someone was impersonating him. Maybe he'd already been captured by the Germans and they were holding a gun to his head to make him flush us out. But even if such scenarios were unlikely, there were more basic reasons to keep silent. Without his knowledge, the enemy could have observed his walk to the chicken coop and any conversation between us might be overheard and reveal our refuge. So all of my self-preservation instincts told me to be still. But to this day it hurts me that I couldn't relieve his dread that Sara and I had been dragged away. We remained safe but he became further distraught.

Then we had another visitor. Yoshke, a Jewish policeman originally from Vilna, stood outside our wall. He had shown a romantic attraction to Sara in the ghetto so his voice was familiar to us. I had no idea where he'd been hiding, but somehow he knew of our haven and in low tones urged Sara to come out of the chicken coop and flee Zhetel with him. She was a lot more restless in the shed than I was, and seemed desperate to leave, but I insisted that despite his persistent plea, she remain silent again. I felt certain the ghetto was being liquidated and it was too early to come out of hiding the first night. My sister later said I probably saved her life with that that judgment.

While the roundup continued, we sat in that chicken coop through the night and the next day, without any food or water, and without knowing what had happened to our parents or Maeshe. With no toilet facilities we had to relieve ourselves inside the shed; in this life-threatening situation we could not allow modesty to be an issue. But at least the stench did not give us away. After all, we were hiding in a poultry pen.

One of the strangest moments came during the second day when a drunken German soldier found Sara's mandolin in the house, brought it outside, and tried to play it. The sounds he made were awful, and even in those horrible circumstances we might have laughed if it weren't so dangerous to let out a peep.

BY SUNDOWN ON the second day I knew we had to leave the coop. Although the *sh'chiteh* was coming to an end, we were still in great peril. But the simple fact is that we could not have survived much longer without food or water. The worst part of it was our parched lips. I was afraid that the intense thirst and dehydration could incapacitate us if not drive us mad.

Sara and I, and the two guys hiding with us, stepped out of the shed. We were enfeebled of course, dazed, and unsure about where to go next. So we just ran away from our house. I made quite a clatter by stepping on wires and other items in the yard but luckily that drew none of the soldiers. As soon as we could, we voraciously drank water scooped up from nearby puddles on the ground.

We all made it through a gap in the ghetto fence but were quickly stopped by local policemen. They easily could have turned us over to the Nazis and our lives would have ended then and there. Instead, they separated Sara and me from our two fellow fugitives, and I have no idea what happened to them. But the cops told us to go to another ghetto, Dvorets, even smaller than Zhetel's, which the Germans had not yet liquidated. They'd converted it into a work camp to build an airstrip for the *Luftwaffe*. In fact, four hundred skilled Jewish Zhetlers had been sent to Dvorets for construction work a year earlier, in July 1941, near the beginning of the German occupation. The policemen even pointed the way for us, southeast in the direction of Baranovich, a hike of about eight miles. We completed the journey that night.

BEFORE THE WAR, Dvorets was a shtetl of fewer than a thousand Jews and, like the rest of our region, under Soviet occupation for almost two years. Now, in the grip of the Nazis, it was a cramped ghetto near a construction site.

Jews had been moved in from neighboring towns, swelling the population. In addition to the four hundred Zhetlers, three hundred were brought from the town of Lubcha, east of Novogrudok, and later hundreds of other Jews were transferred from Ivye, forty miles to the north. The ghetto became terribly overcrowded and it was not unusual for an average-sized apartment to house twenty people.

In mid-1941, the work consisted of breaking and hauling rocks from a quarry for the construction of a railway bridge. The pitiless Germans even made Jews pull up tombstones from the Jewish cemetery for use on the work site. By the spring of 1942, three months before we arrived, attention had shifted to building the landing strip. It was under the command of the engineering unit *Organisation Todt,* which in the course of the war would exploit 1.4 million forced laborers. After its founder, the engineer Fritz Todt, died in a mysterious plane crash in early 1942, most of his duties were taken over by Albert Speer, a more ambivalent Nazi (and later the only defendant at the Nuremberg Trials to show any remorse). He nevertheless imposed harsh conditions on his work force, little more than slave laborers.

Still, Dvorets was not as strictly controlled as Zhetel had been. As in my hometown, local police escorted us ghetto-dwellers to and from our workplaces, but along the way they often allowed us to be approached by peasants with whom we could barter clothes or other items for food. That was much needed because our daily rations were merely one bowl of soup and a slice of bread.

Sara and I were in Dvorets only a day or two when our parents and Maeshe showed up! That family reunion was one of the most joyous moments of my life. When we'd set out from Zhetel, we didn't know if they were alive, and they didn't know we had escaped. In fact, my father had looked for us a second time in the chicken coop, after we'd left. He found the door open, and thought we'd likely been captured.

But on the journey to Dvorets, they and we had received the exhilarating news of one another's survival. My brother remembers that on their trek (longer than ours because they'd stopped to rest in a small forest along the way) their group had sent some scouts ahead to Dvorets who came back and reported that Sara and I were there. Soon after we had entered the work camp, other newly arrived Zhetlers told us they'd seen our parents and Maeshe on the way. So we were all in a state of high anticipation before the reunion.

But we weren't truly relieved until we saw each other face-to-face. When I finally threw my arms around my mother I saw that she was still in a state of confusion. I hoped that reuniting with her daughters, even in this dismal place, would soon bring her back to her senses.

Fortunately, my father had some influence in Dvorets. He became the spokesman of the many Zhetlers there, and, more important, one of his friends was the man in charge of picking people for the construction crews. He was usually able to keep my family off the lists. Neither my parents nor I ever had to work, and Sara and Maeshe were recruited for hard labor only infrequently. We weren't prime candidates anyway. Maeshe, a small fellow at fifteen, was too young; my mother and father, well into middle age, were too old; and Sara and I hardly filled the bill as menial laborers. But many others, even less suited than we, were regularly pressed into this backbreaking work, so I was immensely grateful to have been spared.

We and other newcomers lived with a Dvorets family in the ghetto and, perhaps understandably, the local Jews did not show a lot of warmth to the many strangers they were now required to house. On our part, we tried to conserve our strength, subsist on the meager rations, and plan our next move.

Within a few weeks I got a chance to get away. A chatty, strong-willed man four years older than me named Melech Zuckerkopf wanted me to go into the forest with him and join a partisan unit. From an Orthodox family in western Poland, Melech was among the hundreds of thousands of Jews who had fled into the Soviet zone when the Germans invaded in 1939. For two years he had lived in the shtetl of Molczad (Meitshet in Yiddish) in our region. In Dvorets he was the representative of that town's contingent.

Before a big *sh'chiteh*, he had warned his townsmen to flee to Dvorets. Few heeded him and, like Zhetel and hundreds of other shtetls, Molczad was annihilated in the summer of 1942.

I respected Melech but sensed that he was looking for more than a companion on his escape to the forest. He desired an intimate relationship with me, and I didn't feel the same way about him. He wasn't as interested in literature and learning as I was, and I quickly concluded we had too little in common. I declined his invitation, but our paths would cross again soon.

Another opportunity to leave Dvorets soon emerged and that one I took. At the beginning of the fall, about six weeks after we'd arrived, two Jewish partisans from the nearby Lipiczanska Puscha, or forest, sneaked into the ghetto. Shael Shakhnovich and Chaim Slomke, Zhetlers whom Sara recognized from home, although I didn't, were not carrying weapons and didn't fit my image of fighters in the forest. But they said that while three thousand Zhetlers had been murdered in the second bloody *sh'chiteh* of August 6-8, many, like us, had escaped—over six hundred, I later learned—and quite a few of them, along with Jews from other shtetls and Red Army men, were organizing armed resistance groups in the woods. Shakhnovich and Slomke had made the dangerous fifteen-mile trip into the enemy territory of Dvorets to look for a couple of doctors sorely needed in their partisan camp. But they couldn't find any willing to leave—ghetto doctors were treated better than the rest of us—and the two partisans left with Sara and me instead.

The good-looking Shakhnovich took a romantic interest in me and I was attracted to him as well. Still, I had my doubts. Shael was a tailor and, like Zuckerkopf, did not have the intellectual curiosity I sought in a man. But I made the fateful decision to go with him and Slomke. They had not asked my younger sister, but the impetuous Sara refused to be left behind. She later remembered telling them, "If you don't take me, you'll have to shoot me."

My parents and Maeshe would remain in Dvorets but they were not opposed to Sara and me accepting Shakhnovich and Slomke's offer to leave, especially as their two daughters would remain together. They knew the camp could be surrounded by the Germans and liquidated at any time. They also understood that we were much better suited for life in the partisans than they were. And once established in the forest, we might well be in a position to send for them. After an emotional farewell with our family—such tearful leave takings were occurring throughout our region at this time—Sara and I walked with Shael and Chaim from the ghetto into the woods. I held no gun in my hands, but I felt I was taking the first step in fighting back. Right away Sara and I removed the yellow stars from our clothing.

FOUR

Life in the Forest

In the light of the early morning sun, we four weary trekkers beheld a sight I scarcely could have imagined while in the grip of the Nazis—a camp of Jewish partisans organized to fight back against the Germans and their collaborators.

I now know how fortunate Sara and I were to have gone directly from Nazi oppression to the partisans in one night. During the late summer of 1942, as the shtetls in our region were liquidated, thousands of Jews fled in small groups but they often wandered in the forest without clear direction. Unarmed, they begged peasants for food or ate wild mushrooms, slept on beds of damp leaves, and were terrified about their future in the freezing winter that would be upon them in just a few months. If they were lucky, they would meet partisans in the woods before being attacked by local fascist bands. And even if they succeeded in reaching the partisans, many were turned away because they lacked guns.

But our journey, in the light of a full moon, took us straight to the heart of the resistance, on the north bank of the Shchara River. It was the Zhetler Battalion headed by Hershel Kaplinski. In his early thirties, he wore a belt of hand grenades around his waist and a Mauser pistol on his hip. He was not related to my close friend Rishe Kaplinski and I didn't know him well, but our mothers had been good friends back home. His parents, like mine, had run a store on the market square. Unlike the Kaplinskis with whom I'd grown up, Hershel was not a Bundist, but rather a staunch leftwing Zionist. In fact, in the late 1920s and early 30s, he had been the General Secretary of the local Hashomer Hatzair youth group, which advocated the building of socialist kibbutzim in Palestine as the best hope for the Jewish people. Later, Kaplinski served in the Polish army. His military training and organizational skills, his determination and courage earned him great respect as our leader.

While Soviet partisans had been functioning in the forest since late 1941, and some Jewish fugitives joined them, Kaplinski's all-Jewish group coalesced much later, following the final destruction of Zhetel and nearby towns. Kaplinski himself had lost his

Hershel Kaplinski before the war. (From *A Memorial to the Jewish Community of Zetel*)

entire family in the massacres and set up camp only twelve miles from his hometown.

By the time we arrived, there were about a hundred twenty people in the Zhetler Battalion. Kaplinski had organized it into three platoons, one of which he commanded. He was in close contact with the leader of the Soviet partisans in the area, Nikolai Vakhonin, known as Kolya, with whom he coordinated missions and pooled resources.

The Kaplinski fighters protected a family camp, or *mayak*, a few miles away, which we all called Tel Aviv. After Sara and I pleaded with him, Shakhnovich arranged for two partisans to go back to the Dvorets work camp and bring my parents and Maeshe to the forest, exactly as he and Slomke had recently done for us. My father actually needed coaxing; utterly debilitated by his bronchitis at this point, he was reluctant to leave.

With dozens of others, including children and the elderly, my parents and young brother would live in the *mayak*. Their shelters in the family camp were something like half-buried log cabins, which the partisans in this region and throughout the *kresy* built quickly with the wood from the forest's endless supply of tree trunks. Known by the Russian word *ziemlanka,* each unit was long and narrow and about three and a half feet below ground and four feet above. In one *ziemlanka* a dozen or more people could sleep, close to one another for warmth, with no thought given to gender. Most *ziemlankas* had wood-burning stoves vented by a pipe made of stacked tin cans. The pitched roof was covered with tree branches, both for insulation and camouflage. In the fighters' camp we had to be more mobile, so we stayed in tents or slept under the trees. When the weather got colder, we commandeered peasants' houses.

We obtained food by sending fighters to nearby farms. When the provisions weren't willingly surrendered, we would take them by force. If the peasants weren't home, we would often leave "receipts" detailing our haul and identifying ourselves as partisans. We wanted them to know they had helped a vital cause and weren't the victims of common thieves. We even brought livestock back to the camp, horses, cattle, and sheep, although we generally left pigs behind out of respect to the minority of traditional Jews among us.

Sometimes members of the family camp would go unarmed to nearby villages and beg for food, perhaps from farmers they'd known in better times. Maeshe recalls nighttime hikes with father from the *mayak* to the village of Chaim Michoel's early childhood, Alexandrovich, where his family was still remembered. There they obtained much-needed provisions.

No less vital for survival were weapons. Our fighters seized these too, as well as ammunition, on raids in the countryside or into the towns. Arms the Soviets had left behind in their retreat, local policemen's guns, peasants' hunting rifles, and even captured German ordnance all became part of our growing arsenal.

I could see that Kaplinski was an able leader and that, given the horrors that had just occurred, Sara and I had landed in the best place possible. Because of the Lipiczanska forest's dense growths, swampy terrain, and poor roads, it would be very difficult for the Germans to come after us. That gave us time, we thought, to build up our strength to take the fight to them. And the woods were not all that strange to me. My upbringing in Zhetel had not only given me some knowledge of the timberland, but also instilled a love of nature. Above all, I felt a sense of purpose in being given a chance to fight back after sixteen months of unchecked Nazi brutality.

Yet uplifted as I was, I also saw the dark side of partisan life.

Jews and Russians in the Lenin Brigade, operating near us in the Lipiczanska forest and including many Zhetlers. In the bottom row, Rochmiel Lichter is at the far left and Shleimele Shifmanovich is second from the left. At the very top is Neach Rosenfeld. In the row below him, Aaron Gertsovsky is at the far left. (From *A Memorial to the Jewish Community of Zetel*)

The Zhetler Battalion was semi-autonomous at best and in many ways an appendage of the much larger, better armed Soviet Orlanski *otriad* (Russian for partisan detachment), sometimes named *Borba* or struggle. It had in its ranks numerous anti-Semites, including its leader, Kolya. While there were some Jews in the Orlanski *otriad,* the attitude of many of the Russians was that the *Zhydy* (the derogatory term they used for us), and certainly those in our exclusively Jewish battalion, were by nature weak, cowardly, and selfish. We felt as if we had to constantly prove ourselves to the non-Jews, but no matter what we accomplished on our missions, we usually couldn't change their ingrained prejudices.

Kolya sometimes fabricated charges against Jews in his group and ours, such as the claim that carelessness on the part of two Jewish partisans had led to a vehicle being blown up. The false accusation resulted in their expulsion. The conflict between Russian and Jew could be even more serious than that. It was soon after I arrived in Kaplinski's Battalion when I learned that back in May Russian partisans had killed the leader of Zhetel's Jewish resistance, Alter Dvoretzky.

SOON AFTER BRINGING us to Kaplinski's outpost, Shael Shakhnovich mysteriously vanished from the camp. In fact, he had left to search the region for another Soviet *otriad* that would take us under its wing, one more tolerant of Jews than Kolya's. Almost everything depended on the attitude of the Russian commander and there were some who would not tolerate anti-Semitism. But Shakhnovich had said nothing to me about his intention to leave. I was as surprised as everyone else by his sudden disappearance.

Because he and I had been so close, the Soviet leaders of the Orlanski *otriad* believed I knew Shael's whereabouts and proceeded to interrogate me. I was put in a wood-framed room and grilled by the detachment's top intelligence officer, Voroshilov. He pressed relentlessly: "Where is Shakhnovich?" But I had nothing to tell him. That was the truth, but I had to repeat it again and again. He never used physical force, but the encounter was terrifying nonetheless. If Voroshilov concluded that Shakhnovich had deserted and that I had somehow aided and abetted him, I would have been severely punished.

I soon found out that a few Jews in our battalion had overheard my grueling interrogation. Maybe Voroshilov knew they were outside the room and wanted to intimidate them. In any case, the way I handled his harsh questioning convinced my comrades that I could stand up to pressure and they told Kaplinski and his top lieutenants. Before long I was entrusted with one of the most important tasks in the partisan camp—guard duty. I carried a loaded gun but ammunition was so precious I'd been given no practice using it.

We guards patrolled the camp's perimeter at night in pairs and I was matched with a young man from Novogrudok named Nuchem Shelubski, whom everyone called Nonye. Little did I know that this was a turning point in my life.

ABOUT TWO YEARS older than me, and quite a bit taller, he was handsome, with dark, curly locks of hair. He stood erect and confident, seemed to know his way around the forest, and was clearly comfortable holding a rifle. He was also educated and intelligent, kind and gentle. I immediately felt we had the right chemistry.

But this had to be one of the strangest "first dates" in history. When we met in the woods guarding a camp of Jews fighting the Nazis, we were both covered with foul-smelling black tar. This was the home remedy we used to control a contagious skin disease that tormented many of us in the forest. It broke out as a rash—often between the fingers, but it could show up anywhere on the body—and itched terribly, a source of misery day and night. Ideally, we ought to have mixed the tar with lanolin and sulfonated shale oil, but in our circumstances all we could do was slather on our skin some of the tar we used to lubricate the wheels of the camp wagons.

I'll always think of this affliction by its Yiddish name, *kretz*, but it was similar to the ailment we call scabies in English. It resulted from mites, prevalent in the forest, which burrowed under our skin. The egg-laying insects should have been washed off in the first place, but obviously sanitary conditions were not good. We bathed in the creeks and ponds, and occasionally cleansed ourselves with buckets of water, but it wasn't enough protection against the stubborn mites and the rash they spread. Of course, when you scratched the blisters they'd often get infected, making things worse.

Yet irritated as we were by the *kretz*, Nonye and I tried to put it out of our minds as we patrolled the perimeter of the camp through the night. We quickly realized that we had a lot more than mites in common. We'd both been gymnasium students—he had graduated from the academic high school in the town of Baranovich—and his younger brother, Simcha, had gone to the one in their hometown of Novogrudok when I had been there during the Soviet occupation. Although I hadn't known Simcha well, we were in the same grade and I clearly remembered my former classmate. Nonye and I also shared a connection to Vilna where I'd studied at the Real-Gymnasium. There he had attended the famed Stefan Batory University for a year and spoke about the benches set aside for Jews along the left side of each lecture hall. He had his sights set on a career in chemical engineering, but of course the war completely disrupted his education.

While we shared a deep desire for higher learning, our backgrounds were not entirely similar. He came from a religious family and for his primary education went to *cheder* where he studied the classical Jewish texts. As a youth he broke with Orthodoxy, gravitating to socialist Zionism. He was a proud *Shomrak*, as the members of the Hashomer Hatzair youth group were called, and like our leader, Hershel Kaplinski, had received some paramilitary training in its ranks, an education that would prove invaluable in the partisans.

Naturally, my Yiddishist attitudes clashed with Nonye's Zion-

Nonye's parents, Yitzchak and Elke Shelubski

ism, but as we made our rounds night after night, we spoke more about our recent experiences than our ideological differences. He was emotionally shattered by what had happened to him and his family since the German invasion. Calmly and deliberately he told me the story.

Just as we in Zhetel had been horrified by the murder of about one hundred twenty leading Jews only a month after the occupation of our shtetl had begun, so Novogrudok suffered a similar sweep. The Germans bombed the town several times in late June and entered it on July 4, 1941. Three weeks later, using the pretext of the medieval blood libel, they claimed that a fifteen-year-old Polish girl had been killed by Jews to use her blood for ritual purposes. About a hundred Jews, many of them community leaders, were taken out of their houses to the German military headquarters where they were subjected to sadistic cruelties. They were made to carry heavy pails of water from a well in the courtyard up to the third floor, while German soldiers brutalized them. Those who fell down were killed immediately. Among those who survived, fifty-two were forced to line up in the market square. They were executed by a firing squad.

Nonye was supposed to be one of the victims. He was only twenty-one, but was likely selected because of his part-time work as a tax collector while a student in Baranovich during the Soviet regime. Probably local Poles or Belarusians had given the Germans his name for their list of Jews to be seized.

The SS demanded that the roundup be carried out by the newly comprised *Judenrat*, which felt it had no choice but to comply. But when Jewish officials burst into the Shelubski home and demanded that he come with them, Nonye's father announced that *he* was Nuchem Shelubski and they left with the older man instead. It would never be known if the Jews who carried out this vile decree actually fell for the trick, or if they knew the Shelubski family but went along with the ruse thinking that the Germans would not be able to verify their captive. In the end, all that mattered was that the father went in place of the son.

Nonye sat in another room of the house, stunned as he overheard the drama unfolding around him. Later that day, Yitzchak Shelubski was one of those shot to death in the market square.

Nonye couldn't have known the outcome of his father going in his stead, but survivor's guilt over this shocking episode would haunt him for the rest of his life. And the atrocity led to his flight from Novogrudok into the woods in the fall of 1941, many months before the ghetto was formed.

Nonye's father, Yitzchak, had been a surveyor and worked in a big lumberyard, and often showed his son the wooded terrain around their hometown. He also instructed him on how to use the tools and machinery needed in the woods. So the forest, even with the onset of cold weather, and even before the organization of partisan groups, was less intimidating to this former *Shomrak* than to many others. Beyond that, Yitzchak had been away from home a lot working in the forest, sometimes for many weeks at a time, and Nonye, as the eldest son, took on a great deal of responsibility. This upbringing added to the self-confidence he felt in later years.

He wandered into the Lipiczanska Puscha alone, but soon joined a group of Soviet soldiers who had fled into the woods after being routed by the Germans. From time to time, he sneaked back to Novogrudok to make contact with his mother and brother. It was on one of those visits home when a far worse massacre occurred.

On December 5, 1941, still before the formation of the ghetto, over five thousand Jews were forced into the front yard of the main courthouse, while about a thousand children and old people were confined in a nearby Catholic convent. They would be the first to be killed. Among the Jews huddling together outside the courthouse were Nonye, Simcha, and their mother. Finally, in the middle of the freezing night, the door swung open and the waiting throng entered.

The captives were now out of the cold, only to encounter the dreaded selection. Only a small minority, those with work certificates of the highest priority, would be spared for the time being and sent home. The rest remained under guard for another day. Then, fifty at a time, they were packed into trucks and driven two miles to a *Wehrmacht* base near the village of Skridlevo. In a clearing, in the bitter cold, they were made to undress in front of German machine-gunners who mowed them down. Their bodies fell into long, narrow pits that had been dug by locals the day before.

Of the more than five thousand Novogrudok Jews rounded up, almost all were killed in that *sh'chiteh*, about two thirds of the entire community. Nonye's mother and brother were among the victims and for a while he, too, stood on the line of the doomed in that courthouse. The situation was so grave that he went into a stupor and temporarily lost his will to survive. But at the last minute a spirited, strong-willed young woman saved his life. By coincidence, I knew her. Sulia Wolozhinski (later Sulia Rubin) had been a classmate of mine in the gymnasium in Novogrudok. Both of her parents were dentists and the Wolozhinski family had been directed to the line of those few allowed to live, at least for a while. Sulia saw Nonye, a family friend, on the other line and, shouting, "He's a great bootblack," pulled him towards her. The SS did not object.

But if *his* life was saved for the time being, his mother and brother remained among those condemned to die.

Nonye and the other fortunate ones were taken out of the building. Later he would learn more from one of the very few who remained and yet survived that gruesome day. He heard that an SS officer went over to Simcha to pull him out of the line! Probably the Nazi had sized up the good-looking, muscular youth as a potential worker. There was a verbal interchange between oppressor and victim that could have included anything from coaxing Simcha with special privileges, to ridiculing him with sadistic taunts.

Whatever was said, Simcha stubbornly refused to abandon his mother and held her tightly. The officer did not persist; other Jews suitable for labor could be easily recruited. Simcha and his mother were taken to the killing fields a short time later.

Nonye did not stay among the remnant of Novogrudok Jewry, which in a few days was ghettoized, partly in the courthouse and the buildings surrounding it, and partly in the suburb of Peresika. Once again, he escaped and went back to the forest. Even in deepest despair, his mind was set on surviving and fighting back.

But he had to face the facts that his father had gone to his death in place of him, and his beloved brother would not leave their mother even to save his own life. For decades afterwards, Nonye would recount the story of his strapping "little" brother clinging to his mother in their last moments. Within four months, all the members of his intimate, caring family had been killed and he had been with each of them on the day they were slaughtered. As close as we would become, I could never fully grasp the desolation Nonye felt, the weight of his burden.

By the summer of 1942 Nonye learned of the Kaplinski partisan group, still in embryo, and felt that his struggle against the Nazi beast should be waged as part of a Jewish force led by a fellow *Shomrak*. So he left his Soviet comrades and took the risk of slipping back into Novogrudok again, this time to convince other young Jews to join him, first on a perilous journey to the Lipiczanska Puscha, and then as fighters under Hershel Kaplinski.

On August 9, he entered the ghetto by hopping over the fence, poorly guarded by paramilitary Ukrainian auxiliaries whom the Germans sometimes stationed in Belarusian towns. He arrived only days after a second great *sh'chiteh*, in which the *Einsatzgruppen* and Estonian fascists they'd recruited killed an additional two thousand Jews, including some from the surrounding villages. Novogrudok was actually their next stop after they'd decimated the Jews of Zhetel while Sara and I were hiding in the chicken coop. After the second massacre in Novogrudok only about a thousand Jews remained, mostly craftsmen whom the Germans felt they could exploit.

Nonye quickly teamed up with a Zhetler named Aaron Gertsovsky (unrelated to my friend Osher Gertsovsky, who had been shot by the Germans at the beginning of the occupation). He was one of hundreds from my hometown who had earlier been sent to Novogrudok for forced labor. Given the recent *sh'chiteh*, a sense of desperation naturally gripped those Jews still alive, and in short order Nonye and Aaron were able to recruit thirteen young men to escape the ghetto and fight back from the forest. One of them was another Zhetler, Eliyahu Kowienski, a man of such extraordinary physical strength that he was said to be able to bend an iron bar with his bare hands.

The Novogrudok *Judenrat* was still functioning and one of its officials was an uncle of Nonye's, named Isakovich, who fully sympathized with his nephew's cause. (As in Zhetel, key members of this *Judenrat* aided the underground and earlier in the summer the head of Novogrudok Jewish Council had been executed for his contacts with the partisans.) On the daily list of workers he had to produce, Isakovich replaced the escapees with others so they wouldn't immediately be missed. At midnight on August 20, the group distracted the Ukrainian guards with vodka and young girls, dug a hole under the ghetto fence, and fled.

By morning they had already covered more than ten miles. Given the mission of the *Einsatzgruppen* in the summer of 1942, this was one of the most dangerous times to be traveling in the area, so during the daylight hours they often split into groups of three or four and moved slowly, if at all. A lone escapee joined them along the way so their number rose to fourteen. Their only weapons consisted of a single pistol and several knives.

On the second night they encountered four or five men with light machine guns coming toward them. It could have been the end of their journey and their lives, but at the last minute they heard one of them call out to his comrades in Russian, "Don't shoot! These are Jews who escaped from the ghetto." The two groups met and actually embraced one another. The former Soviet soldiers shared some food with the Jews and told them they were headed east, to rejoin their units. They also confirmed the existence of Jewish partisan units in the Lipiczanska Puscha and gave the fugitives directions.

That encounter went extremely well but it further convinced Nonye and Aaron of the vulnerability of their band while it remained so poorly armed. So as they cautiously moved west, some of the men passed the homes of peasants they'd befriended or traded with before the war and, one way or another, got guns from them—a couple of rifles and a few more pistols. By now about half the force was carrying weapons. And they saw that arms were needed not only for protection from hostile forces, but also to commandeer food if farmers were unwilling to part with it.

Most of the men in the group had just lost close relatives and when a few began reciting the Mourner's *Kaddish*, all of the others joined in. But revenge more than religion was in their hearts. Perhaps the most emotional part of the ten-day journey was the arrival of two scouts sent by Kaplinski just as the fourteen men got within a few miles of the camp. One of them was Shael Shakhnovich. He brought food for the Novogrudok group as well as weapons. Nonye and his men were elated.

Kaplinski too was overjoyed with the reinforcements. He had had only twenty-five fighters at that point; the number of his guerrillas now grew to thirty-nine. But Nonye's group, which arrived around August 30, was just the beginning. The unit swelled in the next few weeks to one hundred fifty as young Jews like us, who had survived the slaughter in towns throughout our region, made their way to the forest sanctuary. They could join the fighters as Sara and I did, or, like my parents and Maeshe, be protected in the *mayak*.

NONYE TOLD ME too of the missions he'd undertaken in the month and a half he'd been in the camp before my arrival. Kaplinski's strategy was an aggressive one: he wanted to bring Jews out of the ghetto to the safety of the forest, but no less of a goal was to disrupt the Nazi war effort and, in the process, kill as many Germans and their collaborators as he could.

This often meant attacking the railways, such as the north-south Lida-Baranovich line or the east-west Minsk-Baranovich line to disrupt the *Wehrmacht's* vital supply route to its troops, now fighting deep in the Soviet Union. The Germans tried to guard these railroads with sentries and even set up little watch-towers along the tracks. Among a group of four partisans, Nonye went on horseback to such an observation post one night, opened fire, and killed the several Germans manning it. With explosives they'd brought—fairly primitive mines at this early stage—they blew up the watchtower and the nearby train tracks. But first they searched for weapons and Nonye found a machine gun that he took back to camp.

When the four returned, their comrades were thrilled to hear of the successful raid. But perhaps most impressive was Nonye's ability to take apart the German machine gun and then reassemble it. Others in the camp had tried and failed to master its workings. Nonye's knowledge of mechanics and his manual dexterity caught the attention of Kaplinski and the whole partisan leadership. They also received reports of his ability to remain calm under fire.

He was sent on many more missions: blowing up bridges, cutting telephone lines, and mining more railroads. One of the most ambitious attacks was an assault on an enemy-occupied village, Ruda Yavorska. It was launched by the Zhetler Battalion joined by other Jewish units as well as better-trained and better-equipped Russian partisans. Not only machine guns, but also two mortars and an armored vehicle were brought to bear against the Nazis.

The operation was a major success. More than fifty Germans and their Ukrainian allies were killed, many weapons and sixty thousand rounds of ammunition were captured, ten Germans were taken prisoner, and all of this was accomplished with the death of only two partisans. Years later Aaron Gertsovsky, who stood shoulder to shoulder with Nonye during the battle, recalled that he was almost too brave. "With fire coming at us from the village," Gertsovsky related, "I had to tell him to keep his head down."

Once we became close, I learned of such missions when Nonye and his comrades returned to our base. It was rare for women, even in the fighter's camp, to participate in combat or even food-foraging missions. Beyond guard duty, most of us did the cooking and laundry, nursing and secretarial work, and maintained the base. We also supplied the *mayak* with food, clothes, and medicine, so I remained in contact with my parents and Maeshe.

But Sara did participate in one operation, "usually a man's job," as she later put it. Kaplinski was initially reluctant to let her go out in the field. But her persistence wore him down and he relented: she would be the only female among a party of twelve sent to dynamite a rail line.

They carefully selected their spot, midway between two German watchtowers and close to the forest to make for the easiest escape possible. Each partisan carried a gun—she wasn't sure how to use hers—and a dynamite stick, to be set off near the train tracks by lighting a long fuse. But when the time came it was raining hard. Her matches got wet and she couldn't get a flame going. All of the men had somehow managed to light their fuses, and they ran back across soggy brush toward the cover of the forest. But she stubbornly remained at the rail line trying in vain to light her fuse too. It was a moment of great danger because the charges set by the men were about to go off. The commander ordered her to run. She still stayed near the tracks and he sent someone to forcibly bring her to safety. But that proved unnecessary. At the last instant she managed to set her fuse alight and then got away on her own. As soon as she reached the others in the woods the blasts went off and the group counted them. All of the dynamite sticks exploded, including Sara's. Much later she looked back on her courageous act with pride but also some self-deprecating humor: "After all, how would the war have ended without that?"

SARA WAS ONE of the very few females to prove herself on the battlefield but that did not spare her from the unwanted sexual advances of numerous men in the camp. This behavior was typical in the Russian and Jewish partisan network throughout East-Central Europe. Many of the young male fighters felt entitled to sleep with any unattached woman they chose.

Often a single woman would give in and take one man as a lover—usually physically strong, well-armed, or high up in the partisan chain of command—in order to protect herself from all the others. He might also bring her gifts such as a fur coat confiscated on a mission or a stash of food that was in short supply. But his main asset was being a defender against sexual assault by others. This led to quite a few unusual pairings. Refined, even upper-class Jewish women partnered with crude, uneducated men, matches that would have been almost inconceivable before the war. The Hebrew term *Tavo*, meaning, "Come here," was the word for these newly found male shields. There were no wedding ceremonies, but the pair lived together in the same tent, house, or *ziemlanka* and was considered a couple by the rest of the camp.

I found out much later that many of these seemingly unsuitable liaisons survived for decades after the war. Perhaps this could be explained by the intense partisan experience that bound the "forest wife" to her *Tavo* as nothing else could. And many who were thrown together in the woods had recently lost their entire families, making the new relationship, imperfect though it may have been, a kind of emotional replacement for a lost world. In another Belarusian forest, Sulia Wolozhinski, for example, the well-educated daughter of two respected Novogrudok professionals, created a union with the manual laborer Boris Rubierzewski (later Rubin). At first she was put off by his coarse manner; later she was impressed with his courage as a fighter and scout. They remained together for half a century.

Sara and I wanted to avoid pairing up with a stranger out of necessity and we both succeeded. In her case, she was harassed by none other than the interrogator Voroshilov, but was able to fend him off, and others as well. Very soon, I had Nonye as my protector but he was far more than that. We fell in love and he would be the only romantic partner I'd ever have.

Even amidst the danger and deprivation of the Lipiczanska Puscha, we partisans made time for pleasure. Aaron Gertsovsky played the violin and had brought his instrument into the forest. When the men came back from a mission there was always a little food and whiskey to go around, and Nonye would invariably say, "Aaron

I want to be happy now, play your violin." Soon enough, we'd hear the *Waltz of the Blue Danube* or a Polish *mazurka*. It brought back a little taste of the world we'd known before the war.

Yet in the Lipiczanska Puscha in late 1942, not everyone wanted Nonye and me to be together. Surprisingly, Shael Shakhnovich returned to the camp not long after he'd disappeared. While in another part of the forest, he had been unable to communicate with Kaplinski and Voroshilov, who gladly took him back now. He was furious when he saw that Nonye and I were a couple; I actually thought Shael wanted to kill him. Sexual jealousy was all too common in the midst of our struggle for survival and I didn't want any of us to become a victim of it.

Thankfully, the two men were able to talk it through and whatever Nonye said to Shakhnovich (it remained a secret even from me) calmed him down. He not only accepted the fact that I'd chosen Nonye, but before long the two renewed their friendship. I still remember the fine pair of pants the tailor Shakhnovich made for my man. This time, comradeship prevailed over raw emotion.

SEVERAL MILES FROM us in the Lipiczanska Puscha was another Jewish partisan camp, also with many Zhetlers, and we in the Kaplinski group cooperated closely with them. Counting about one hundred fifty fighters, this battalion was headed by a most improbable leader, a short, slim medical doctor, Yechezkel Atlas.

Around thirty years old, he had been born near Lodz, but because of the low quota of Jews allowed into Polish medical schools, he studied in Paris and at the University of Bologna where he received his degree just before the outbreak of the war. He returned home, but soon left again, this time under duress. With his parents and sister, he was among the hundreds of thousands of

Jews from western Poland who fled east into the Soviet zone after the outbreak of the war in September 1939. He and his family settled near the town of Slonim, about thirty miles south of Zhetel, in a shtetl called Kozlovshchina where he began to practice medicine.

After the German invasion in June 1941, Kozlovshchina was ghettoized and Atlas still worked as a physician until May of the following year when it was liquidated. Nearly the whole population was murdered, including Atlas' family. Yet because he was a doctor, he was left alive and sent to the village of Wielka Wola, on the Shchara River near the Lipiczanska Puscha, to treat peasants. Completely broken in spirit, he worked there for two months. Meanwhile, he learned of the existence of small, and as yet poorly organized resistance groups in the woods. He soon made contact with these forest bands and tried to heal their wounds and diseases.

He remained based for two more months in Wielka Wola until another shtetl, Dereczyn, about twenty miles south, was annihilated on July 24. Ninety percent of the town's three thousand Jews were murdered in that *sh'chiteh* but among the survivors about eleven quickly found their way to Dr. Atlas. As they told him the horrendous story of the slaughter, similar to that in his home village of Kozlovshchina, his feelings of revenge became white-hot. To him the *sh'chiteh* in Dereczyn was proof that the Germans intended to kill every last Jew they could find.

A plan began to crystallize in his mind. He would leave his medical practice, go into the forest, and organize a partisan group to fight back. In mid-summer he carried out this daring strategy and many Jews followed him into the woods. These were refugees from Kozlovshchina and other ravaged shtetls who became fighters or found shelter in the small family camp he protected. While most of the Zhetlers who escaped after the massacre of August 6–8 went to Kaplinski's group, several joined Atlas, including the strong-man Eliyahu Kowienski who served as his second in command. Meanwhile, Atlas strengthened his ties with the nearby Soviet bands, which had coalesced under Red Army captain Boris Bulat. Atlas convinced Bulat to unite in an attack on German-occupied Dereczyn, one of the boldest partisan operations in the course of the war. Bulat agreed—usually the Russian leaders in the forest were not nearly as cooperative—and the assault took place on August 24. The tiny Kaplinski unit was barely organized at this point (even Nonye's group of fourteen would not arrive for another week), but it took part as well, and the joint Russian-Jewish partisan force of about three hundred won a resounding victory. They drove the Germans out of their garrison, took complete control of the town, and executed forty-four Lithuanian policemen who had collaborated in the murder of Dereczyn's Jews. In fact, the stunning reprisal was carried out at the same pits where the *sh'chiteh* had taken place a month earlier.

Beyond that, Atlas' and Bulat's fighters returned to their forest camp with a valuable trove of captured weapons and ammunition. Later the Atlas group blew up bridges and sabotaged railway lines, but nothing gained them glory throughout our region as did the attack on Dereczyn, even if they had to pull back after a few weeks. With hindsight, I can see that Alter Dvoretzky's plan in the spring for a partisan attack on Zhetel, only slightly larger than Dereczyn, was not as far-fetched as it may have seemed. And Dvoretzky had wanted to strike *before* the second massacre so it might have been an act of rescue as well as revenge.

By the time Sara and I arrived at Kaplinski's group in October, his and Atlas' partisan bands were in close cooperation, sharing weapons, food, and intelligence. I saw the doctor once in our camp and, small though he was, he made quite an impression on Sara and me with his clear blue eyes, high Russian boots, and revolver on his hip.

In no area in East-Central Europe were the partisans more effective than in Belorussia. But a change was coming with November's cold weather. The Germans, hurt by the disruption of their transportation lines to the Russian front, humiliated by their defeat in Dereczyn, and concerned about our growing supply of arms and explosives, decided to wage an all-out offensive against us. It was the feared *oblava*, the Russian term that partisans used for a major enemy raid. The Germans deployed *Luftwaffe* reconnaissance planes and surrounded the forest with heavy cannons and tens of thousands of troops fresh from the Russian front. Belarusian police and Baltic units allied with the Nazis prepared to enter the Lipiczanska Puscha to track down and attack our fighters.

AS NEWS OF the impending *oblava* filtered into our camp, Kaplinski, Kolya and the other leaders felt it would be too dangerous for Sara and me and the other women to remain at the fighters' base during the combat. We very much wanted to stay, but were forced to leave.

So we were spared the big battle, which turned out to be a painful defeat for the Jewish partisans in the Lipiczanska Puscha. The much larger, better-armed, and more organized enemy forces killed about fifty of our best fighters and wounded many others. Worst of all, they decimated our leadership. On December 5, Dr. Atlas was shot and killed while leading his platoon into combat. His last words to his comrades were, "Pay no attention to me. Go on fighting." Atlas died in the arms of Eliyahu Kowienski who took command of the company.

We were even more devastated to learn of the death of our leader, Hershel Kaplinski, in the same battle. The blow was especially severe because we heard reports that after he had been wounded and taken refuge in a barn, he was slain by non-Jewish partisans who wanted his machine gun.

Within barely half a year the three great resistance leaders in our region had all been killed: Dvoretzky in the early spring, and now Atlas and Kaplinski. Decades later, I learned that historians questioned the choices of these men, thinking they took the fight to the enemy too soon because they were overly swayed by feelings of revenge. But we partisans rather remembered what they'd accomplished despite their early deaths. They brought Jews out of the ghetto to the forest and I'll forever be grateful to Kaplinski for his support of the family camp that sheltered my parents and brother. Many of their ambushes, acts of sabotage, and larger attacks—even on an enemy-occupied village in Atlas' case—were highly successful, dealing a blow to the Germans and their local allies. In the end, they even caused the *Wehrmacht* to divert forces from the Russian front. And, damaging though it was to us partisans, the *oblava* in the fall of 1942 would not put an end to the armed Jewish resistance in the Lipiczanska Puscha. Atlas' and Kaplinski's groups were depleted but they continued to function.

Even before the *oblava* Nonye's courage and leadership skills had come to the attention of the top Soviet partisans in the area. In the reorganized detachment he was given a promotion: commander of a *zvod,* or platoon, of more than a dozen men who, Aaron Gertsovsky recalled, welcomed his appointment. In the winter of 1942–43, he would be the leader of missions.

In February 1943, he conducted a major operation, an ambush that lured many German soldiers and their Belarusian collaborators from a garrison they'd built in the forest—and killed them. Nonye selected his ten best Jewish fighters and they met with peasants in a village about two miles from the German military post. They told the peasants to bring food to the village school for a banquet. The partisans knew through their spies that some of the peasants would go directly to the Germans and tell them where the Jews would be. And indeed, the *Wehrmacht* commander sent out about one hundred fifty men on sleighs toward the village to kill the ten Jews. Nonye found out later that the Germans told the Belarusians with them to look under the lapels on the Jews' coats; that's where they hid their gold, they said.

While the large force was driving toward the school, the partisans were lying in ambush with automatic weapons on two hills on either side of the road. Scores of enemy soldiers were shot dead. It was unusual for so many enemy combatants to be killed in one battle with the partisans and the Germans were so demoralized that they dismantled their post and moved out of the woods for good.

But with the deaths of Atlas and Kaplinski, the Soviet partisan leader Kolya became more powerful than ever. His anti-Semitism would make it harder and harder for Nonye and many of the other Jews to remain in the orbit of the Orlanski *otriad*.

Meanwhile, Sara and I, without weapons, tried to survive in the forest during one of the coldest winters of the century. Our first hiding place was a huge tangle of roots from a big tree that had come down at an angle. In that unlikely refuge we concealed ourselves for three days while the *oblava* still raged. We were so near the fighting that German shells intended for the partisans flew over our heads.

After the battle ended, Kolya would not readmit us into the

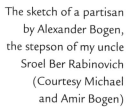

The sketch of a partisan by Alexander Bogen, the stepson of my uncle Sroel Ber Rabinovich (Courtesy Michael and Amir Bogen)

Orlanski *otriad*. For much of the next few months—and many of the details of this harsh, treacherous period have faded from my memory—we wandered in the freezing Lipiczanska Puscha, sometimes staying in friendly peasants' houses, sometimes loosely attaching ourselves to small partisan groups, themselves on the move. There was great risk even walking from place to place—footprints in the snow could give you away—but sometimes we were escorted to our family's *mayak* by friendly Russian partisans; by no means did they all share Kolya's prejudices.

Somehow the *oblava* that had ravaged our fighters' base had missed the little family camp, and our parents and Maeshe continued to be sheltered there; it remained a well-concealed hiding place throughout the entire winter. But Maeshe was quite ill. His feet were frostbitten and then got infected. Lacking medication, our mother—she and my father were also sick that winter—nursed him back to health by constantly cleaning the affected area. Sara and I, still seeking to join a fighters group, visited them frequently, bringing food whenever we could and on one occasion a thermometer.

THE ARRIVAL OF spring brought some relief. The Germans rarely entered the forest now; it must have felt to them like there was a sniper behind every tree. But one morning in May, on our way to see our parents and Maeshe in the *mayak*, Sara and I heard gunfire from that direction. By the time we arrived it was clear what had happened. The local police had learned about the family camp and raided it, shooting anyone in their sights. Before they rode off, about half a dozen Jews were murdered. My mother was among them.

When the attack had begun, my parents and Maeshe were beginning the day in their semi-underground *ziemlanka*. Their instinctive response to the commotion was to get out and seek safety elsewhere. My father hid behind the *ziemlanka*. Maeshe was naked as he ran for cover into a nearby tree grove. My mother ran, too, but the wrong way, into a clearing where she met her death.

Sara and I had arrived to find the camp in disarray and could not find our mother. We were sure she was hiding somewhere, alone and frightened, and while father and Maeshe were still traumatized, we set out looking for her. We walked around the *mayak* and only hours later did some of the camp residents show us what they'd tried to hide from our eyes.

They took us to her body, still covered in blood, laid out among the corpses. In tears, we buried her in the woods. But there could be no headstone, not even a marker for her grave. At least her husband and all three of her children were there to put her to rest and mourn together.

To this day it hurts me deeply that I cannot visit her burial place. She had sacrificed a lot for each one of us—in the shtetl, the ghetto, and the forest. Maeshe in particular was overcome with grief. Mother had saved his life only months before and now she lost hers. We were all mired in gloom that spring, and of course we knew that the police could launch another raid against us at any time.

About a month after we lost mother, we were startled to see Nonye walking into the *mayak*. He had come to the family camp to take me with him to another forest. Our separation over the past five months had deeply pained him, he said. He didn't want to be apart from me again.

He had left the Orlanski *otriad*, he told us, because Kolya's anti-Semitism had grown intolerable. The final straw was the death sentence given to two Jewish partisans accused of stealing a few things from peasants while on a mission. One was able to flee the camp, but the other was executed and buried in the swamps.

Nonye was one of the leaders of twenty-five Jewish partisans who would depart the Orlanski *otriad* at this time; they would later be known as the Forest Boys. They wanted to carry on the fight about sixty miles northeast of Lipiczanska, from a base in the larger, jungle-like Naliboki Puscha, one hundred sixty square miles filled with swamps and marshes, and crisscrossed with dirt roads. There they would be part of an *otriad* known as Ordzhoni-kidze, and be in collaboration with three brothers from a village near Novogrudok. These were the legendary Bielskis who maintained a family camp that would eventually number over twelve hundred Jews, the largest Jewish-run refuge in all of war-torn Europe.

Nonye was one of four spokesmen of the Forest Boys who had already met with the charismatic leader of the camp, the tall, powerfully built Tuvye Bielski, whom everyone called Tevye. He could easily see that the experienced Lipiczanska fighters would be a great asset and was eager to have them.

It was a heart-wrenching decision to leave the Lipiczanska Puscha with Nonye because I felt so close to my family, and so needed by them in the immediate aftermath of mother's death. But I chose the man I loved. Hopefully, it would be similar to Sara's and my escape from Dvorets to Kaplinski's partisans the autumn before, when Maeshe and my parents were able to follow us and find safety in the *mayak*.

My father fully agreed with my decision to go with Nonye. And as it turned out, he, Sara, and Maeshe would eventually reach the Bielskis, too. There they would be protected in Tevye's huge family camp. But I would not see them again until after the liberation. From May 1943 on, I would be bound to one person, Nonye Shelubski.

FIVE

From War to Peace

Nonye and I, among a group of twenty-two, walked from the *mayak* to the safety of the Bielskis in the Naliboki Forest, a distance of about sixty miles. We went slowly, usually at night, sometimes sheltered by friendly peasants, sometimes sleeping in the pine groves that dotted the countryside. Three other young Jews who had heard of the miraculous "forest republic" joined us along the way and by the time we reached the safety of the Bielskis our group numbered twenty-five. One of them was Melech Zuckerkopf whom I'd last seen in the Dvorets labor camp on the eve of his flight into the forest. He and everyone else could see that Nonye and I were a couple. I even carried the magazine of bullets for my man's light machine gun.

In the midst of the forest, Tevye, the oldest Bielski brother, somehow found us. He told us we were on the right path to the camp, but that we needed to report to the Soviet General Vasily Chernyshev (codenamed "Platon"), the supreme partisan commander of western Belorussia, an area of about six thousand square miles. Without his authorization, we'd just be considered Jews wandering in the woods with no standing in the partisan movement. Four of our men, including Nonye, were led by Tevye to Platon's headquarters, and the Soviet leader "legalized" us although he needed to be bribed with a gold watch to close the deal. He did not share the anti-Semitic attitudes of Kolya, but was still somewhat wary of partisan groups organized along ethnic or religious lines like the Bielskis'.

We still had to finish the journey to the Bielski camp. The month-long expedition, during which we sometimes spotted German troops in the distance, was one of the most frightening experiences we ever had. It was also one of the most grueling. The ground was swampy after the spring rains and for long stretches every step was a great effort as we pulled one foot and then the other out of the dense bogs. Having to hold our guns and belongings above our shoulders, while moving through murky water almost waist-deep, made it more difficult still. It wasn't long before we were exhausted.

Nonye was our leader. But at one point, near the end of our trek, something in him snapped. Up to his chest in muck, he didn't think he could go on. As strong and confident as he normally was, Nonye now took out his pistol to finish himself off, end it all with one bullet to the head. Maybe it was the severe physical pain he suffered carrying heavy equipment aloft for hours, and made worse by hunger, scabies, and fatigue. Or maybe it was the way the water and mud seemed to pull us all backwards into the pain of the past just as we were trying to move forward. I comforted him the best I could and bolstered his spirits. I simply refused to let him do it. "You promised me an *Itzikel* (a little Yitzchak)," I

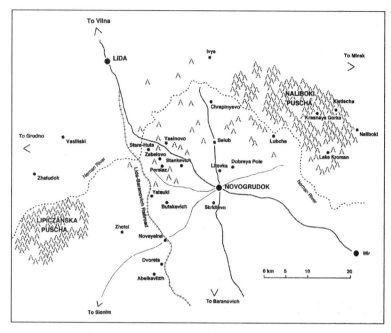

Our theater of operations in White Russia, 1942–1944.
(Courtesy Jeffrey Cuyubamba/Peter Duffy)

reminded him, "and we're going to get out of this." To this day, I've faced crises the same way; I just put one foot in front of the other and go on.

That black cloud soon passed. We all reached the Naliboki Puscha safely.

TEVYE HAD BROUGHT six hundred Jewish refugees, protected by about two hundred fighters, from the Stara-Huta woods near the Bielskis' hometown of Stankevich, to the shores of Lake Kroman in the remote southern part of the Naliboki Puscha. There, with his brothers Asael and Zus, (there was another brother, Aron, who was fourteen) he set up a community, with woodworking and tailoring workshops, that was fed by nearby farms and villages. The Bielskis' policy, based more on rescue than revenge, was to turn no Jew away. Tevye even took in the elderly and children, the ill and disabled. The camp gradually grew. Nonye's friend from Novogrudok, Shlomo Kantorovich, soon went to the *mayak* in the Lipiczanska forest to bring my father, Sara, and Macshe to the Bielski family camp where all three would remain until the liberation.

By the time we entered the large forest and arrived at the Bielski camp, General Platon already had the plan of splitting it in two. He wanted many of the fighters to leave the Bielskis, serve under Soviet commanders, and defend the western entrance to the forest along the Neman River. He thought the Bielskis put too high a priority on protecting and providing for the family camp, and that their fighters could be better deployed by disrupting German troop movements. Tevye felt he had no choice but to comply since he was dependent on the Soviets, not least in reining in rogue partisan groups that roamed the forest attacking and disarming Jews. He was allowed to keep about a hundred fighters in the civilian camp, but the other hundred formed a separate detachment. It became known as Ordzhonikidze, in honor of a Red Army commander, Grigory Ordzhonikidze, a close friend of Stalin and fellow Georgian who had mysteriously died in 1937.

The fighters in this new *otriad* were permitted to bring their wives or girlfriends. Our group from the Lipiczanska Puscha was among the very first to join it; you could say we formed it. Ordzhonikidze soon grew to almost a hundred and eighty, of whom about thirty were women. Most of the group were Jews from Zhetel and Novogrudok but there were also some Soviet soldiers who had retreated from battle or escaped from POW camps. The leadership, under the command of Red Army Captain Lyshenko, was overwhelmingly Soviet but the key position of head of reconnaissance went to Zus Bielski, a Red Army veteran. In 1943, he commanded his own mounted, sixteen-man platoon in the Naliboki forest and played a crucial role in setting Ordzhonikidze's agenda, carrying out its missions, and even running its spy network in the countryside. An avid Zionist, Zus would immigrate to Palestine as early as 1945 and later fight in Israel's War of Independence.

Thirty-one years old when I met him, Zus had lost his parents, wife, and baby in the same German *sh'chiteh* in Novogrudok in December 1941 that took the lives of Nonye's mother and brother. Six feet tall and broad-shouldered, and six years younger than Tevye, he was the most volatile of the Bielski brothers and many who knew him have recalled his heavy drinking, womanizing, and acts of violence. While still in the family camp he had a heated argument—involving both gold and a woman—with a partisan named Kaplan whom Zus shot to death.

But I remember Zus Bielski differently. Yes, he did swagger around with a pistol on his belt at a 45-degree angle, intimidating everyone. But he was also a courageous fighter valued for his expert knowledge of the wooded area along the Neman River. And he was well known and respected by the local population. Before the war the Bielski family had operated a farm and flourmill and they had done business with peasants for miles around.

Nonye and I had our own connection with Zus. Nonye knew his second wife, Sonia Boldo, because she was a neighbor who came from an admired family in Novogrudok. As fighters he and Zus worked together during the year they were both in Ordzhonikidze.

There were two special platoons in our *otriad*; one for Zus' reconnaissance activities and another, headed by a Russian named Yaki-movich, devoted to punishing informers, "capturing a tongue," as it was known. But most of the fighters were organized into two companies. Each of these had two platoons, and each platoon had two sections. Nonye, only twenty-three, quickly became *Kommandier Roti*, the head of a company of about fifty fighters, most of them older than him. He conferred with Zus; took orders from Sergei Vasilyev, commander of the Kirov Brigade of which Ordzhonikidze was one of four detachments; and sometimes even reported to General Platon. We closely coordinated our attacks with other *otriads* in the Kirov Brigade, particularly that of Viktor Panchenko of the October Detachment.

Like Kaplinski's battalion in the Lipiczanska Puscha, our goal in Ordzhonikidze was to disrupt the German war effort by blowing up railways, roads, and bridges, and destroying telephone lines and post offices. Sometimes we attacked or burned down enemy outposts and police stations. We also conducted "economic missions" to obtain provisions from the peasants. Sometimes fighters from our detachment would take extra food we'd obtained, especially "luxury" items like salt, vodka, eggs, and fat to the Bielski family camp. Occasionally, we engaged in propaganda work, meeting with locals to spread the word of the Nazis' evil deeds and make the case for the Soviets as being more humane.

Many of the fighters were already armed when they joined the detachment, but other weapons and ammunition came from local peasants, or from captured or killed enemy soldiers. Virtually every fighter in Ordzhonikidze had his own gun.

Nonye and Zus shared intelligence with the Bielski family camp, and our fighting *otriad*, poised at the entry to the forest, gave some protection to the many hundreds of non-combatants in Tevye's group. But contact between our two groups was otherwise limited. I was out of touch with my father, Sara, and Maeshe during the whole year we were in the Naliboki Puscha.

AT THE FOREST'S western edge we were in striking range of the key north-south Lida-Baranovich railroad and the highway that went northwest from Novogrudok to Lida. At first, our mines were quite primitive, four sticks of dynamite in a cigar box detonated by a grenade with a long fuse. As one of our fighters later told the journalist Peter Duffy, "We planted them on railroad tracks and... on roads. I remember we dug a hole in a road, a gravel road, and we put the mines in the hole and used branches from the pine trees to (camouflage) them." Later, when Ordzhonikidze collaborated more closely with other detachments in the Kirov Brigade, our explosives became much more potent.

Because we were part of the Soviet partisan structure, detailed reports of Ordzhonikidze's combat missions were sent to the high command. These accounts have survived and they document more than three dozen attacks that we carried out from the spring of 1943 until the liberation in July of the following year.

As a company commander, Nonye led many of those missions, often at the head of a platoon-sized unit of about fifteen men. I knew when he was gone from the camp, but for everyone's safety the details of missions were kept secret and I usually heard about them only when Nonye returned. One of the earliest operations was a foray to get food and supplies from a storage depot only half a mile from a German post. On the way back to camp they encountered the local police, opened fire, and killed two of them.

By March 1944, his missions were much more ambitious. With intelligence provided by the staff of the Kirov Brigade, Nonye led two platoons in mining the Lida-Novogrudok highway. The powerful bombs destroyed three enemy vehicles and damaged two others. No fewer than eighteen German soldiers were killed and two wounded.

Nonye led an even larger assault on the Lida-Baranovich railway line near the Yatsuki station, only about seven miles from his native Novogrudok. Heading a group of twenty-six this time, he derailed two German locomotives and sixteen railcars. They were carrying twenty motorcycles, ammunition, and food, all intended for *Wehrmacht* troops in the east. It took the enemy more than twenty-four hours to repair the tracks and remove the damaged trains.

Not every mission was successful. In January 1944, Nonye and his men went out to ambush a German convoy on the Lida-Novogrudok highway. They lay in wait for a long time until they saw a fleet of twenty trucks approaching, protected by a tank. Concluding such a large force could overpower them, Nonye ordered his crew back to camp without engaging the enemy. He was never reckless with his men's lives.

The actions of Ordzhonikidze required good camouflage, but sometimes concealing explosives had lethal repercussions for us. During one mission to blow up a train, a bomb was hidden on a hill and covered with earth, but when one of our fighters gave the mound its last few pats, he set off an explosion that killed him and two others. I found out when I saw the three bodies brought back to camp slung over horses. I'll never forget the sorrow and anguish we all felt as we encircled our fallen comrades. I was among those most shaken. I knew all three, including Leizer Leibovich, only eighteen years old, who had grown up in Zhetel. And I learned that Nonye was standing near the hidden bomb, and that he just happened to move away at the moment of the explosion. Otherwise, he too would have been among the casualties.

Like the other women in the Ordzhonikidze *otriad*, I did not go on any missions; I stayed in the camp when Nonye was in the field. When he left, I became frantic with worry. These emotions were among the most intense in my entire life. And then, usually a day later, I'd see him riding back on his white horse. I'd run out to embrace and kiss him, and in those moments of reunion the whole world belonged to me.

THE GERMANS WERE not our only enemies in the forest. The Armia Krajowa (AK, or Home Army) was an underground group of Polish nationalists, especially strong in the Novogrudok area, where they operated eight of their own partisan units. Often known as White Poles, at first they collaborated with the Soviet partisans in order to stop the German invaders. But when the Soviets tried to incorporate them into a movement devoted to communism and Stalin, it wasn't surprising that hostility arose between the two groups. The Polish Government-in-Exile in London, to which the Home Army was loyal, wanted to undermine Soviet power in the region and eventually the AK fought battles against the Russians. The White Poles formed an alliance with the Germans, who provided them with weapons, medical care, and military intelligence.

Although I was not aware of it at the time, researchers have uncovered several cases in which Jewish civilians roaming the Naliboki forest were attacked and killed by the White Poles. The eminent historian Nechama Tec quotes the head of the AK, General Tadeusz Bor-Komorowski, justifying assaults against "wild bands of all sorts of refugees living by robbery... a terrible plague to people who were visited nearly every night by bandits who gradually deprived them of their last belongings... I issued orders to the regional Home Army commanders to undertake the defense of the population against the violence of the disturbing elements." Another leader of the AK was more explicit: "Jewish bands in the forest (are) robbing and looting the peasants."

In late 1943, Soviet headquarters ordered the destruction of an entire battalion of White Poles in the Naliboki Puscha, the Kosciuszko unit, many of whose members belonged to a Polish fascist group known as the National Armed Forces. The Ordzhonikidze Detachment was not involved in that attack, but Tevye Bielski sent fifty of his fighters from the forest camp to help the Russians rout the Polish partisans. Ordzhonikidze did join Soviet groups in another battle against the White Poles a few months later in March 1944. We killed forty-seven of them and wounded twenty more.

Another pro-German group in the Naliboki forest was the Cossacks. Many thousands of them had fled north to the Novogrudok region in the winter of 1943-44 after the Red Army occupied their homeland in the Caucasus mountain range, between the Caspian and Black Seas, and began to collectivize their farms. The Germans allowed the Cossacks to set up their own military regiments of a thousand men each, and they too attacked Russian and Jewish partisans. In May 1944, Zus Bielski led an ambush that killed eight Cossacks.

There was also a cavalry corps of about one hundred fifty pro-German Belarusians led by the young Nazi collaborator Boris Ragula. Before the German invasion, his family of Belarusian nationalists had been imprisoned and tortured by the Soviets and now he was ready to take revenge. He and his men donned German uniforms with the Belarusian national colors on the collar.

So, by early 1944 the forest was crowded with different fighting groups including the local police, known as Black Crows because of the color their uniforms. At first, they did the bidding of the Germans but when it became clear that Hitler would lose the war, many of them defected to the Soviet partisans. In one of his attempts at political maneuvering, Zus wrote to the Novogrudok police chief, Volodiya Picta, that the Black Crows' past crimes against us would be forgiven if they would form an alliance with Ordzhonikidze. The police chief even met in person with Zus, but the hoped-for alliance never materialized.

Of course, not every local non-Jew collaborated with the Germans or turned a blind eye to our suffering. There were righteous gentiles who sheltered Jewish refugees, and one whom we relied upon was Konstantin Kozlowsky, known as Koscik. With his three grown sons, he had a *hutor,* an isolated farmstead, not far from Novogrudok, an ideal refuge for runaway Jews and Soviet partisans. Koscik, a Belarusian who spoke fluent Yiddish because he had lived with a Jewish shoemaker in his youth, felt affection for Jews, admired their culture, and deplored the Germans' murderous deeds. He hid hundreds of Jews on his property in the course of the war, providing them food, clothing, and even vodka from his homebrew distillery. Koscik directed refugees to our *otriad* and to the Bielski family camp. Once he even entered the Novogrudok ghetto and persuaded some young men to escape with him.

But in the spring of 1944 the local police found out about his activities and raided his home. He was away at the time, so they tore apart the house and beat one of his sons unconscious. Koscik himself had to flee to the forest to survive. He survived the war but we lost a valuable ally.

ORDZHONIKIDZE COULD BE much more mobile than the Bielski family camp and we moved frequently. I'd carry Nonye's bullets, usually in an ammunition belt, from place to place. At strategic spots along the Neman River, we'd pitch tents but sometimes we simply slept under the trees. As in the Kaplinski battalion the year before, when the weather got colder we took over peasants' large houses –dozens of people could sleep in one. Sometimes, like other partisan groups, we built the semi-underground bunkers, or *ziemlankas*. Indoors we removed our boots, but slept in our clothes in case we had to flee immediately.

And just as in the Lipiczanska Puscha, our food supply in Ordzhonikidze was adequate because we were living on the land. We could obtain fruit, vegetables, bread, milk, and livestock from the peasants, by force if necessary. Unlike the family camp, where the top echelon sometimes had its own kitchen and better food than the others, I had no special provisions, or any other privileges as the forest wife of a company commander. But overall, I felt healthy. Although some of my comrades suffered from frostbite, our *otriad* was spared the two outbreaks of typhoid fever that hit the Bielski family camp.

But of course our group needed medical and dental care from time to time. Fortunately, we had the services of some first-rate doctors. Our primary physician was Zvi Isler from Novogrudok, an experienced dermatologist in his early forties, who, with his wife, Riva, a nurse, served the family camp as well. With medicine scarce, Isler worked under the most challenging conditions, but he managed to save many lives. Sometimes he used the sulfur from inside bullets to fight infections; he'd mix it with fat to create a cream for skin diseases. Other times patients were injected with boiled milk to induce a fever that would stimulate the body's immune system.

There was an outstanding surgeon, too, who visited us from

time to time, Dr. Miesnik, who partisans had smuggled out of the Lida ghetto. In the forest he was required to perform operations without proper medical instruments or even anesthesia. He sometimes used just a knife to remove bullets from a fighter's body. Our visiting dentist pulled out teeth with a pair of pliers and no painkillers. She told us to strengthen our gums by boiling chestnuts and drinking the chestnut juice.

I don't remember any pregnancies in the Ordzhonikidze Detachment, but there were quite a few in the family camp. It had a gynecologist named Dr. Hirsh who delivered several babies, but performed many more abortions because it was so difficult to ensure the survival of an infant.

As I had seen in Kaplinski's battalion, a single woman was vulnerable to the sexual advances of the men, and often had to choose one to protect her from all the others. But this was less the case in Ordzhonikidze than in other *otriads*. We were formed much later than most other partisan units, and many who joined us were already couples.

The union of a couple in the forest was not performed by a rabbi. But sometimes it was solemnized by an informal ceremony created by the partners themselves. I heard of one couple in the family camp that pledged themselves to one another on a clear night—the moon is our rabbi, they said, and the stars are our guests.

We celebrated May Day and the anniversary of the October Revolution while I was in the Ordzhonikidze *otriad*, but I can't recall observing any Jewish holidays. We didn't even know what day Passover was. I was only fifty miles from Zhetel where I'd grown up, but it seemed like another planet. Later I learned that Zus even led a mission on Yom Kippur. Thirty of his fighters got up early, had a hearty breakfast, and went out to ambush a German convoy on the main highway.

IN THE SPRING of 1944, as the war turned against the Germans and their collaborators, a number of retreating enemy soldiers fell into our hands. They were now prisoners of the partisans. How would we treat them? Virtually everyone in our *otriad* had lost a loved one and many, like Nonye, had suffered the loss of their entire family. We'd been ghettoized and then forced to live and fight in the forest through two brutal winters. All of it simply because we were Jews. We didn't have a great deal of pity for those who did this to us.

In the Bielski family camp, captured German soldiers were sometimes beaten by mobs of furious people and then shot to death. When one plead to be spared, remembers an eyewitness interviewed by Patrick Duffy, his partisan captor wasn't moved at all. "He thought back on the way Jews had begged for their lives before being dragged to the execution ditches."

In Ordzhonikidze, we carried out our own acts of revenge. One of my friends in the *otriad*, Chiena Ratner, who had been my class-mate in the Novogrudok gymnasium and knew Nonye's family well, remembers when a Ukrainian collaborator was brought into the camp. A Jewish fighter, a Zhetler she recalls, grew so enraged that he severed the man's head with an axe.

I did not witness that killing, but I saw an act of vengeance just as severe. A Jewish partisan tied a German soldier to the ground and beat him with a club until he was dead. After each blow, he shouted, "This is for my father," or "This is for my brother."

Many of the partisans, including Nonye, did not have it in them to participate in such payback. But neither did they try to stop it.

THE RED ARMY liberated us in mid-July 1944, and my partisan life came to an end. At first, when we heard guns in the distance, we thought it was the Germans, but grew elated when we saw the red flags with their hammer and sickle. The Soviet commander called us together and announced that the area was firmly in the hands of his troops, and we were free to go. The Russians also told us about D-Day the month before—it was the first we'd heard of it. Hitler's forces were collapsing on all fronts.

Many of my comrades were not jubilant, however. Given all they'd been through, and all they'd lost, the news actually left them "numb." Both Sara and Maeshe also used that word when they described their reaction to liberation in the Bielski family camp around the same time. But I felt excited and thrilled. The days of anxiety about Nonye on missions were now a thing of the past. World War II continued, yet *our* war was over.

But we didn't simply disband. We stayed a little longer to savor the moment—and for a special purpose. Nonye and I and a few other couples got together that night, had some vodka, and wished one another a long and happy future. Each couple also promised that it would stay together for life. Nonye and I, and most of the other pairs, remained true to those vows. That night in the forest there was no rabbi and no formal wedding. But I cannot imagine any marriage ceremony that could have meant more.

We also looked back over the past two years and took stock of what we'd accomplished in the Ordzhonikidze Detachment and the Orlanski *otriad* before that. We had withstood the German army. And the damage we inflicted on them was considerable. While the Bielski family camp saved the lives of twelve hundred Jews, the largest rescue operation anywhere in Nazi-occupied territory, we in the combatant group, about one hundred fifty by the liberation, derailed German trains, mined vital railway lines and highways, and hindered the enemy's efforts to supply its troops on the eastern front. Overall, we killed hundreds of German soldiers and their collaborators and we suffered only a handful of deaths ourselves, a far lower percentage even than other partisan groups because our commanders, like Nonye, were so careful with the lives of our fighters.

Of course we could have achieved even more with better supplies of arms, ammunition, and explosives. But we felt we did our part in the victory over Hitler and reversed some anti-Jewish stereotypes in the process. Our actions flew in the face of the myth that Jews went like sheep to the slaughter. In fact, I found out later we might have inspired others. News of the Bielski family camp was covered in the underground Jewish press in the Warsaw ghetto prior to its uprising.

When Ordzhonikidze split up, some of the fighters went with Zus to Lida to put out fires set by retreating Germans. About a third of our group was conscripted into the Red Army and fought as regular soldiers. Tragically, many of them did not live to see VE Day on May 8, 1945; they were killed on the battlefield in very high numbers.

Nonye and I followed a different path. We spent the last nine months of the war about fifty miles southwest of the Naliboki Puscha, in the town of Baranovich where he had gone to the gymnasium and worked part time as a tax collector after the USSR occupied eastern Poland in 1939. From mid-1944 until the end of the war, we both served there in the Soviet civil service.

But first we left the forest for Nonye's hometown of Novogrudok where our hearts sank when we saw the devastation the war had left in its wake. Even the most basic foodstuffs were in short supply. The large, attractive home that had belonged to Nonye's family had been chopped up into three small units and lost all its charm in the process. One room was actually full of chickens and their filth. In another room lived Zus Bielski's in-laws, the parents of Sonia Boldo, and Nonye was grateful to see that they had survived. But we had come for a much more pressing reason. My father was very ill and Sara and Maeshe were caring for him in that house. The three had hiked there after the Bielski family camp dispersed. We'd sent them word of Nonye's home in Novogrudok; they found it, and moved in.

It was the first time I'd seen my family since the *mayak* in the Lipiczanska Puscha back in the spring of the year before. Sadly, the joy of our reunion was overshadowed by my father's bad health.

The rest of the house was occupied by Poles or Belarusians. We quickly heard that in Novogrudok, as in the rest of prewar Poland, many gentiles had simply plundered Jewish possessions during the war and took over "abandoned" Jewish homes. I could see the suspicion in their eyes as I stood in Nonye's former home. It wasn't surprising to learn later that, from 1944 on, there were bitter and often violent disputes over Jewish property.

But Jews were not only made to feel unwelcome after the liberation; many were made to fear for their lives. The Soviet authorities could not adequately protect us. Maeshe was the only one of my family to return to Zhetel where he stayed only for a few days. He told us there were almost no Jews left, nearly all their houses occupied by non-Jews, and that the squatters had reacted to him with hatred. Returning Jews from all over the region would later recall a common gentile reaction of surprise tinged with disapproval: "How come you're still alive?" Others report being taunted by the German word *Jude,* simply meaning Jew, but now used as an ethnic slur to evoke the painful memory of the recent Nazi barbarity.

But our attention focused on Tateh. In addition to his chronic bronchitis, which caused him trouble breathing, he also suffered from kidney failure and heart problems. It was an agonizing decision for Nonye and me to leave him. But we moved on to Baranovich. I knew that even in these unsettled times, Sara and Macshe would get him the best care possible.

IN MID-1944, even as the war still raged, Stalin once again annexed our region, making it part of the Byelorussian Soviet Socialist Republic. We couldn't always follow the international news but we knew the upshot of the Yalta Conference of the Big Three: Roosevelt, Churchill, and Stalin. In February 1944, the U. S. and Britain had allowed the USSR to keep the whole *kresy*, the eastern third of pre-war Poland that it had seized in September 1939 following the Molotov-Ribbentrop Pact. The deal meant that Poland would be reconstituted, but moved a hundred miles to the west. It would be only a little smaller than it was before the war, "compensated" for its loss of the *kresy* by gaining "recovered" lands that had belonged to Germany for the past century and a half. But the new Poland would also be a mere satellite of the Soviet Union, which wielded much more influence on the ground than the nationalist Polish Government-in-Exile, still in London.

As in the fall of 1939, the new Byelorussian Soviet Socialist Republic set up institutions identical to those in the rest of the USSR. Nonye, having already worked for the Soviet government as a tax collector, and demonstrating loyalty as a company commander in a Soviet partisan detachment, was a prime candidate to win a leadership position. He became the chief inspector for tax collection in Baranovich.

I was given a government job, too. I worked for the Baranovich branch of a social service agency that functioned throughout the USSR. To replenish the population, the government awarded one-time grants and monthly subsidies to mothers with multiple children. They gave particular recognition, and much more financial aid—the same pension as a war veteran—to those with ten or more kids. These women were called "mother-heroines" and received a medal and a certificate conferred by the Presidium of the Supreme Soviet of the Soviet Union. Both were awarded when the tenth child reached its first birthday, providing that the other nine children (natural or adopted) remained alive too. I was an inspector visiting the homes of those women whose difficult, demanding lives I could scarcely comprehend.

Even with our plum jobs in the Soviet system, Nonye and I knew we had no future in East-Central Europe. We both set the goal of making *aliyah*, immigrating to Palestine, which we called Eretz Israel, and helping to build up a Jewish state. For me, it was a new way of thinking, for the war had changed me from a Yiddishist to a Zionist. I saw now that the hatred against us ran so deep that we had to have our own country. How could I envision a Yiddish-speaking community in Poland or Belorussia when the overwhelming majority of the Yiddish speakers had been murdered?

The war, and the immense losses he suffered, had changed Nonye, too. Yes, he had been a Zionist all along. But he now felt that the socialist Zionism of his youth group, Hashomer Hatzair, had been too accommodating to the Arabs and British, and not sufficiently militant. Instead, he embraced its ideological opposite—the rightwing Betar movement, founded by Vladimir Jabotinsky, and later headed by Menachem Begin. Even while he worked as chief tax inspector of Baranovich, Nonye tried to win over to Betar the town's few Jewish survivors. And he wanted us both to make *aliyah* under their auspices.

That was a line I couldn't cross. Growing up as a Yiddishist with Bundist sympathies, Betar and its underground military organization Irgun always represented Zionism at its most extreme, and my friends and I didn't make much of a distinction between these Revisionist Zionists and the fascists. Through the late 1930s and 40s, the Irgun carried out attack after attack—kidnappings, assassinations, bombings—against the British and Arabs in Palestine, which later culminated in the massive explosion at Jerusalem's King David Hotel in 1946, killing ninety-one people.

I was ready to make *aliyah* but firmly said no to Betar. The virulent anti-Semitism surrounding us pushed me from the land of my youth, and the lure of Eretz Israel pulled me to a new homeland, but Nonye and I remained at odds about which movement would get us there. I was drawn more to Bricha, a left-leaning underground organization that brought Jews to Palestine.

In the end, our ideological differences didn't matter much because *aliyah* was blocked. The British White Paper of 1939, which drastically limited Jewish immigration, was still in effect after the war ended. Hopes rose when the Labor Party came to power in London in July 1945, but Zionists were deeply disappointed when Prime Minister Clement Attlee and Foreign Minister Ernest Bevin gave in to the Arab states because the UK desperately needed their oil. The British would allow only a handful of Jewish refugees to enter Palestine legally, not the immediate entry of one hundred thousand, which David Ben-Gurion demanded. Of course there was illegal immigration, the famous *Aliyah Bet*. But that entailed a rigorous journey over the Alps to an Italian port and then risked interdiction by British naval vessels in the Mediterranean. Captured refugees, who had already endured so much in the past few years, were then interned in Cyprus under deplorable conditions.

Nonye had two uncles and two aunts in San Francisco, so we also considered immigrating to the United States as a temporary haven before making *aliyah*. But we were shut out of America as well. Strict immigration quotas imposed in the prewar decades—largely resulting from anti-Semitism among the public and some government officials—would not be significantly lifted until 1948.

So where were the roughly quarter million of prewar Poland's surviving Jews, the *Sh'erit Hapletah*, the "surviving remnant," to go? From the point of view of our colleagues in the Soviet bureaucracy, there was no reason to emigrate at all given our fluency in Russian, our good jobs, and Nonye's status as a heroic partisan. But we were not persuaded to change our minds.

First, we took the train west across the Soviet border into Poland and could feel the anti-Semitism in the air. On June 12, 1945, in the town of Rzeszow where a nine-year-old Catholic girl was found dead, the age-old accusation of ritual murder led to mob violence. A month later in Krakow, a pogrom instigated by this blood libel was even worse. Several Jews were killed.

We stopped in Lodz, which had become a gathering point and information center for Jewish refugees. And the attitude of the non-Jews there, compared with other parts of Poland, was relatively tolerant. But after a few days of making inquiries, while we lodged in a private home, we saw no practical means of leaving Europe. Our next stop was Prague, which had much more of a democratic tradition than Poland and was rumored to be welcoming to Jewish refugees. Soviet border guards sent us back to Poland on our first try, but we finally reached the Czech capital.

Indeed, there was compassion for Jewish survivors on the part of the local population, and we stayed for a few weeks. But, again, we could find no way to emigrate.

Thankfully, UNRRA, the United Nations' Rescue and Rehabilitation Administration, had set up a network of almost two hundred Displaced Persons camps in Germany, Austria, and Italy. The first one opened before the end of the war and they functioned until the early 1950s. Not an ideal situation, but at least a short-term shelter until Israel or America came within reach. A DP camp was our only choice.

LUCKILY THE ONE recommended to us in Prague turned out to be among the best in the whole system. It was in Austria so we would be in easy range of an Italian port on the Adriatic Sea when the time came to make *aliyah*. The large majority of the DP camps were in Germany but I couldn't stomach the idea of living there even under the administration of UNRRA and the protection of the Allies. True, Austria had been a willing partner of the Reich, and Hitler had been born and raised there, but somehow it didn't stir in me the same revulsion as did Germany.

Badgastein, about fifty miles south of Salzburg, was just within the American zone of occupation. A resort town high in the Austrian Alps and on the rim of a national park, it had fresh mountain air, thermal springs, and a beautiful waterfall near its main street. In the nineteenth century it was considered so fashionable that heads of state and even royalty frequently visited.

UNRRA had rented five of the main hotels and converted them into dormitories for Jewish refugees. Nonye and I were assigned to the stately Straubinger, which held about a thousand DPs. To be sure, the elegant rooms were stripped bare in the makeover.

The paintings were taken down from the walls and even the carpets were pulled up from the floors. Plain, wooden bunk beds, several to a room, replaced the large, luxurious feather beds that had comforted well-to-do vacationers in better times.

The Badgastein camp was so overcrowded that Nonye and I didn't even have our own room; we shared it with two single young men. We put curtains around our bed for privacy. But we could enjoy the large tiled bathtubs in the basement, almost little swimming pools, and we spent many hours hiking the forest paths and taking in their breathtaking views of meadows and mountains.

UNRRA provided free medical and dental care at another hotel where relief organizations like the Joint Distribution Committee distributed winter clothing. A pension, Bad Ischl, was designated for those in need of special medical treatment, usually for lung

Nonye and I soon after our arrival in Badgastein

illness or malnutrition. In addition, a school for children opened at the Hotel Victoria, which offered courses in English for adults too.

I got another full-time job in Badgastein, assisting an UNRRA social worker, a dedicated American woman whom I knew only as Mrs. Adams. She was helping the refugees, many of who had been in death camps only a few months earlier, begin their long, hard road to recovery. Among other duties, I served as her translator, using the English I'd learned at the Real-Gymnasium to enable her to communicate with speakers of Polish, Russian, and Yiddish. Of course, we former partisans, despite all that we had endured in the ghetto and forest, were generally healthier, physically and mentally, than those who had been in the Nazi camps. Working with Mrs. Adams, I saw people who had been so crushed by what they'd endured that I wondered if they could ever again lead normal lives.

With the UNRRA staff in Badgastein. I am second from the left in the first row; Mrs. Adams is third from the left

I spent a lot of my time with former partisans as well. One day I got the idea to interview men and women about my age, to record their partisan experiences or those of partisans they knew who had been killed in action. A few had escaped to the Lipiczanska Puscha so their stories were very familiar to me. I thought also that the partisan contribution to the war effort might get lost if someone didn't write it down. In the bustling DP camp it wasn't easy finding a quiet, private place to talk. In the end, I settled on my hotel's dining room, in between mealtimes when the big hall was empty.

I wrote down their accounts in the language they were told to me, Yiddish. But most speakers included some Russian, Lithuanian, Polish, and even German words too, which I transliterated into Yiddish. I didn't change any of the facts told to me, but I enriched the vocabulary and sometimes edited the narrative to create clear, compelling stories. It put me back in touch with the Yiddish literature that had been such a big part of my life before the war. Hand-written in a copybook, each memoir is one to three pages and I treasure them to this day. (Eight are included in the appendix to this volume.)

One of the stories I entitled the "Death of the Blind Partisan." It was related to me by a nurse who had witnessed three young fighters returning to camp after a terrible accident, an explosion that left one deaf, one blind, and one with burns covering his whole body. It so moved me that I took special care that the Yiddish I wrote was worthy of the story.

For several days and nights the nurse sat next to the blind one, in agony over the thought that he might never recover his sight: "I remember that the world is so beautiful. In the battlefield... I bravely resisted death—today I blew up eight trains and after the ninth I myself was made a casualty... *Ach*, my beloved mother—

where are you? Will I ever see you again?" My informant told me that she tried to comfort him. "Bitter tears came rolling down my face," she said, "but the invalid wasn't able to see them. Only yesterday he was painting promising plans for the future, which he had seen in rose colors." The partisan soon died from his wounds, "ending a life that was no longer shining."

IN A REVERSAL of our roles in the forest, Nonye had a lot more leisure time in Badgastein than I did. He found that sports helped him make the transition to the postwar world. He played a lot of volleyball, a game introduced to Europe by American soldiers in World War I and popular there ever since. The DP camps in Austria had their own league of volleyball teams. Nonye, a good spiker who hit the ball fast and hard over the net, played for Badgastein as far away as Vienna, a four hundred-mile round trip.

He seemed to tire easily, though. I was not too worried, but eventually we went to an Austrian cardiologist. The doctor found a heart murmur, related to rheumatic heart disease that had stricken Nonye as a child. He was only in his mid-twenties when we learned about this and at the time neither of us thought much would come of it.

Nonye also spent a lot of time in conversation with the other DPs about the future. From the moment we arrived in the summer of 1945, *aliyah* seemed to be on every Jew's mind. There were noisy demonstrations against Britain's intransigence and much talk about illegal immigration to Palestine. The rivalry between Bricha and Betar was especially fierce as left- and rightwing Zionists competed for members among the DPs. In November 1945 an agreement in our camp was finally reached among the factions and tensions eased.

My husband soon
after our arrival in
Badgastein

At a Zionist demonstration in Badgastein, Nonye marching
under the sign demanding the creation of a Jewish state

There were also some Zionist youth groups that spanned the whole political spectrum. One was called PaChaCh, derived from three different words: the partisans, and then *chayal* and *chalutz*, Hebrew for soldier and pioneer respectively. Because of my work with Mrs. Adams and my interviews of former Jewish fighters I was too busy to be a member, but I followed its activities. Nonye, meanwhile, marched in demonstrations demanding an independent Jewish state in Palestine.

The American officials and soldiers were friendly towards us, but relations between the Jewish refugees and the local population were not good. Austrians had been constantly subjected to Nazi propaganda since the *Anschluss*, or union, of the two countries in 1938, so their image of the Jew was at a low point even before many tens of thousands of DPs arrived. Now that the war was over, food and other commodities were rationed and the locals actually envied us because we were adequately fed at the UNRRA camps. We also benefited from the International Red Cross and several Jewish relief organizations. In fact, we often had extra food and clothing that we sold on the huge black market—Badgastein was one of Austria's main centers of the illicit trading. This added further to the locals' perception that the Jews were unfairly privileged.

There was a brisk trade every morning right in front of the Straubinger Hotel where many Jews, including Nonye once in a while, sold surplus items. Of course it wasn't only Jews who made money on the black market. American soldiers, non-Jewish refugees, and quite a few locals profited as well. Yet public opinion surveys at the time revealed that almost half the population blamed the Jewish DPs for shortages. We were seen as "parasites (who)... have too good a life in the camps (and) trade their food illicitly." In Badgastein the hostility between the DPs and the locals led to violence a couple of times when fights broke out at a vegetable market and a bar.

But Nonye and I had little contact with the Austrians and I look back on my Alpine experience as a period of revitalization. After a while, Maeshe arrived in Badgastein and stayed with us (a fifth person in our room at the Straubinger) leaving Sara in Novogrudok to care for father. Already eighteen, Maeshe had plans to continue his education. It was good to be with him again.

Then came terrible news. One day late in 1945 another DP told me that she'd heard my father had passed away. I had tried to prepare myself for this for a long time but was still devastated when I heard her words. We three siblings had survived, but now both of our parents were gone. If Nonye and I ever had children, they would have no grandparents.

I didn't want to believe it, and went into a state of denial. Maybe the woman was mistaken. I recall walking in the camp a few days later and seeing another woman across the street who had just come from Novogrudok and I purposely avoided going up to her to ask about my father out of fear that she'd confirm the worst.

But it was all too true. Sara soon arrived in Badgastein and gave us the details of father's last days. Toward the end, his skin was so pale that he kept his hands under the bed covers, so she wouldn't worry that death was near. Sara also told us that, through her, he had said goodbye to all three of us. At least we were now together to mourn him.

My brother and sister soon left Badgastein for the university in Munich. Sara had attended the gymnasium in Novogrudok and had enough course credits to be accepted. The war had prevented Maeshe from studying at an academic high school but, after com-

My family reunited in Badgastein. In the photo on the right, Sara is to my right. In the group photo, from the right, Maeshe, Sara, Nonye, and me

pleting an intensive six-week course, he passed an equivalency test that granted him admission as well. Among a group of many young survivors, they enrolled in the famed Technische Universitaet, studying chemistry. Both would remain in Munich for the next four years.

Nonye and I stayed in Badgastein almost until its closure in the late summer of 1947. The news from Poland gave us every indication that the country of our youth remained viciously anti-Semitic. In mid-1946, the town of Kielce, about midway between Warsaw and Krakow, was rocked by wild rumors of Jewish ritual murder. What followed was an assault on a far greater scale than the blood libel incidents the previous summer in Rzeszow and Krakow. In Kielce, a savage pogrom took the lives of over forty Jews and wounded almost a hundred more. Among the dead were three Jewish veterans of the Polish army and a woman and her unborn baby. There were credible reports that the local police participated in this atrocity.

AS MUCH AS we wanted to leave Europe, we would remain in limbo in Austria until 1949. After Badgastein was shut down we were transferred to Parsch, a suburb of Salzburg, the headquarters of the American zone. Parsch had been home to a former German Army base and that's where we were now housed. Comprised of three unremarkable brick buildings, and three wooden barracks, the setting was much more typical of DP camps than the resort town we'd enjoyed for two years. But we weren't that sorry to leave Badgastein despite its natural beauty. After all, we'd wanted this period in our lives to be a temporary asylum and living conditions were not our main concern. But some of the DPs reacted violently when required to change camps; before departing they smashed furniture in the hotel lobbies.

Known as New Palestine, Parsch held far fewer DPs than Badgastein, about four hundred fifty people, mostly Polish Jews. Despite the plain surroundings, we enjoyed a lending library, theater evenings, and a camp newspaper. As in Badgastein, there was a school, and sports for kids and adults. Nonye again joined the volleyball team.

While in Parsch, I worked for the Sochnut, the Jewish Agency for Palestine, commuting by bus from the DP camp to its offices in nearby Salzburg. The Sochnut was highly active in Austria after the war with about one hundred fifty *shlichim*, or emissaries, from Palestine in the country. As in Badgastein, my fluency in four languages was put to good use. We tried to find Jewish survivors, arrange family reunions, and above all prepare refugees for immigration to Eretz Israel. For that purpose we worked closely with the Joint Distribution Committee and especially with the underground Bricha, which, often through well-placed bribes, arranged for illegal border crossings. By now, the differences Nonye and I had about the merits of Betar and Bricha were in the past. He and I both passionately supported *aliyah*, legal or undercover, and the rightwing-leftwing split in Zionist politics was no longer important to us.

But I wasn't long in Parsch before I was overwhelmed by something entirely different—in mid-1947 I became pregnant.

Nonye was just as overjoyed by the news as I was. Creating new life is almost always awe-inspiring, but childbirth in the DP camps was in a category all its own. We were bringing forth a new generation that would bear the names of our slaughtered parents and ensure Jewish continuity. You saw pregnant women everywhere; the DP camps must have had one of the highest birth rates in the world. Nonye had often spoken to me about his yearning for a son, whom we'd name Yitzchak, or Isaac, for his father who had been killed in his place during the roundup of July 1941. He longed for a "little Isaac," an *Itzikel* as he said in Yiddish. On April 6, 1948, a healthy baby boy, Yitzchak Shelubski, was born in a Salzburg hospital.

It was a very difficult delivery and I shed a great deal of blood, leading to a life-threatening situation. Only later did we find out that my Austrian obstetrician had lost several other new mothers to postpartum hemorrhage and that if I'd died too, his license to practice medicine would have been revoked.

I had anemia in the hospital and was so frail that I couldn't walk for weeks although I did breast-feed my baby. We hired a local nurse to stay in our room and be a nanny for Yitzchak—and

Nonye holding our
Itzikel in Parsch

take care of me. It took a long time to recuperate but thankfully she was skilled and devoted, and got us through. She certainly showed me another side of the Austrian character.

Once I had fully recovered and our baby was a few months old we began a journey to show him to his aunt and uncle in Munich, about seventy miles away. But when our train approached Germany a wave of loathing came over me and I simply couldn't bring myself to enter the land that had spawned Nazism and destroyed so much that I held dear. Not with my Itzikel. Had he been born a few years earlier, they would not have hesitated to murder him too. Nonye went on to visit Sara and Maeshe and give them my love. But I turned back at the border—holding my baby in my arms.

EVEN IN THE midst of my health crisis, we followed events in Israel closely. The state was born the month after our son came into the world. There was a wild celebration that night that spilled over from the camp into the residential area of Parsch. But with Ben-Gurion's declaration of statehood, four Arab countries invaded the newborn country. I got healthier, but the fighting meant that we would have to delay *aliyah* again. We simply couldn't take an infant into a war zone. As it turned out, over six thousand Jews would die in the War of Independence, about 1 percent of the Jewish population.

At the same time we began to be bombarded by letters from both of our families urging us to come to America. And even in Badgastein, well before I was pregnant with Yitzchak, I was open to immigrating to the States. Nonye and I felt a deep longing to leave the DP camps and if America were a viable option we'd take it enthusiastically.

Nonye was a sole survivor but two of his mother's brothers and two of her sisters had immigrated to the U.S. before the war and wanted us to join them in San Francisco. Nonye's Aunt Mildred had married a man named Yisroel, whose Yiddish was excellent, and I carried on a long correspondence with him in particular.

I had two uncles and an aunt (my father's brothers and sister) in Baltimore and they were no less insistent. They were still shocked that their sister, Nechamke; her husband, the expert tailor known as *Der Gott;* and two of their three sons had been murdered. And they grieved over my father who had died soon after the war. My American family longed to see my baby, my husband, and me.

We still considered Israel our ultimate goal, but in June 1948 the United States changed its immigration policy toward us survivors. With President Truman's reluctant backing (he'd actually wanted something much more sweeping), Congress passed the Displaced Persons Act, which accelerated the immigration of two hundred thousand survivors of Nazism over the next four years. Nonye, Yitzchak, and I were among that fortunate group. Nonye's Uncle Max, who owned a thriving furniture store in San Francisco's Mission District, was our American sponsor.

We sailed from Bremerhaven on the North Sea in January 1949. This time I did enter Germany, and traveled across the whole country to get to the port, but told myself it was for the best possible reason.

What do I remember most from the voyage that remade my life? A wretched bout of seasickness. It hit most of the passengers; each day there were fewer and fewer people around the ship's banquet tables at mealtimes. But little Yitzchak and Nonye were spared and my husband took care of our baby and me. I was miserable with diarrhea and nausea until we docked at Ellis Island. But even during my worst physical distress while aboard ship, I knew it was a small price to pay.

SIX

An American Family

As soon as we came ashore, I felt better. My first experience in the Golden Land was one of healing, a good sign I thought.

After going through Ellis Island, we were met in New York by my husband's distant cousin Joe Pine, who warmly embraced us and drove us to his home in New Rochelle, a suburb just north of the city. I was amazed at the skyscrapers we viewed through his car windows, taller than any buildings I could have imagined. But there was so much going through my mind that January day, about the future of my young family in a new country, that even the dazzling skyline could not claim my full attention.

During the few weeks we stayed with the Pines we visited New York City only a couple of times. This is because Joe, a generation older than us, his wife, and his daughter wanted to talk about what had happened in Europe rather than show us the sights of Manhattan. He was a butcher—his wife worked in the store with him—and every evening they'd bring home freshly cut meat for dinner. Afterwards, we'd sit around in their large, well-furnished home, and talk long into the night. Fortunately, the whole Pine family knew Yiddish.

In 1949, American Jews were just beginning to grasp the enormity of the Holocaust and Joe had two eyewitnesses in his living room—relatives at that—speaking frankly about what they knew. He and his family wanted to know everything, and they were aghast when we told them of the ghettoes, the mass executions, and the death camps, much of which we'd learned from fellow DPs. But they were also awestruck when we informed them about how we partisans had fought back—derailing trains, ambushing enemy troops, and saving civilians.

We went next to an American member of my family, my father's sister, Sophie, who lived in Baltimore with her second husband. My father had two brothers in that city, too, Irvin and Morris. Like Joe Pine, Sophie and her family were doting hosts who took care of our every need while they heard of our ordeal in Europe. They gave us a room upstairs in their attractive row house, and I still recall how they washed Yitzchak's diapers every night, leaving them clean, dry, and neatly folded in front of our door in the morning.

Aunt Sophie and my uncles, who often came over to be with us, had known of their siblings' and nephews' deaths, but to hear me, their niece, recount the details gave them a sense of closure even as it added to their pain. My role as a witness of the Shoah began soon after my arrival in America; the responsibility I feel to tell the story has never ended.

It was a wrenching few weeks, but Sophie left me with some hope for my future. She was a real *balabusta*, a flawless homemaker, and when I admired her handsome furniture, carpets, and wall hangings, she said to me, "Don't worry, Mirele, you'll have something even better."

We could very well have remained permanently on the East Coast—we certainly were welcomed with open arms—but Nonye's uncles and aunts in San Francisco beckoned us to come across the country and settle with them. We had heard it was an almost magical place with spectacular bridges and romantic bay views. Perhaps most important, they offered their nephew a job.

WE WENT BY train and I still recall the little compartment we had. It had two benches, one on either side; Nonye and I slept on one

With my family in Baltimore in January 1949, less than a month after my arrival in America. In the top row, left to right: Jack Yarmosky (my Aunt Sophie's son); Nonye holding our baby, Yitzchak; Meyer Oberfeld (Sophie's second husband); David Schultz (Sophie's son-in-law); and my uncle Irvin Rosnow. In the bottom row: myself; Uncle Irvin's wife, Rebecca, with their daughter, Nancy, on her lap; Aunt Sophie; my cousin Anne Yarmosky (Sophie's daughter); and my cousin Jack Yarmosky's wife, Shoshana and Yitzchak, whom I was still nursing, on the other. Day after day we saw the great expanse of America out our window, the plains and the mountains, and I was taken aback by the changes in scenery in this nation that spanned a continent.

But it was San Francisco that made the greatest impact on me. Nonye's Aunt Mildred and Uncle Irvin (Yisroel, with whom I'd corresponded, had anglicized his name) picked us up in Oakland, the western terminal of the transcontinental railroad. He drove us over the Bay Bridge to their home. With the hilly city bathed in sunshine in front of us, and the Golden Gate Bridge in the distance I thought I was in heaven.

Irvin had a barbershop on Market Street and after he went to work, Mildred would take their daughter, Myrna, to school while my family remained in their house on Hayes Street. It was hardly the most scenic part of town, but I loved the crisp ocean breeze, the grand Victorian homes, and the easy-going nature of the people on the streets. Often I was content just to look out the window and count my blessings. In only a few years, Nonye and I had gone from one of the worst places on earth to one of the best.

One day, soon after we arrived, Irvin called from the store and said a letter had come from my brother and sister, still at the Technische Universitaet in Munich. I was so eager to get it that I couldn't wait for him to bring it home; I walked more than a mile through Hayes Valley to pick it up. Tearing it open on the spot, I learned that my brother and sister were completing their studies in Germany and planned to immigrate to America. They hoped to join me in San Francisco in less than a year. I was elated and ran all the way home to share the news with Nonye.

We soon moved into a little apartment of our own, a one-bedroom on Frederick Street, just across from the southeastern end of Golden Gate Park, where I would take Yitzchak in his stroller and where he played in the sand. I was in that marvelous park all the time; it was almost a second home. If people couldn't find me, they looked for me there. The park gave us the room to move freely and enjoy the fresh air we'd grown accustomed to in the forest and the Austrian Alps. But our apartment itself, with a tiny kitchen, was cramped. All three of us slept in the same room, and for a time, we put up Morris (Maeshe had changed his name) and Sara too. Yet I kept it so clean that the landlord would often show our apartment to prospective tenants in the building.

After a couple of years on Frederick Street, we moved to a more spacious apartment only a few blocks away on 2nd Avenue. A three-bedroom flat with a big kitchen, it was the upper unit of a duplex, so close to Kezar Stadium, where the 49ers played, that on game days we could hear the crowd cheering.

The bigger home was needed because our family was growing with the birth of our daughter Elaine and later another son, Mark. Right near us on 2nd Avenue was Parnassus Hill and leading to it one of the steepest streets in San Francisco—the sidewalks were actually stair steps. Every time I went up and down that block, carrying groceries or a child, I'd be out of breath. Yet even then I thought I was in heaven.

The immigrant neighborhood where we lived was a highly diverse home to Hispanics, Italians, Poles, and a few Jews and blacks. Most were warm and friendly but I was sometimes in for a rude awakening. One Polish woman, whose husband had converted from Judaism to Catholicism to marry her, was an anti-Semite who uttered racist slurs in my presence against both Jews and blacks. Finally, I couldn't take it anymore and had it out with her. "This is America where everyone is equal," I let her know in

With baby Elaine

From left, Elaine, Mark, and Irwin

no uncertain terms. After that, she backed off and became much more respectful.

FOR ALL OF the assertiveness that exchange implied, in the early 1950s I didn't want my children to be known as Jews just from their given names. So Yitzchak became not Isaac, but rather Irwin (we wanted to make a distinction from Uncle Irvin in Baltimore and Uncle Irvin in San Francisco, although at first I had trouble pronouncing Irwin). Mark's middle name is Seymour in memory of Norman's brother, Simcha, who was killed by the Nazis. Our daughter was named in memory of Norman's mother, Elke, and my mother, Chana, but we named her Elaine Ann. The irony, Mark has pointed out, is that the names Seymour and Irwin are so common among Jews born two generations ago, that rather than hiding their identity, the monikers are actually a giveaway.

Nonye changed his last name as well as his first like many *greeneh*, as the new East European Jewish immigrants described themselves, a term equivalent to greenhorn in English. His name was Nuchem and he became Norman. We also shortened Shelubski to Shelub once we found that people didn't know if the last syllable was spelled "sky" or "ski." As for me, I kept my first name. I could have Americanized it by making it Myra, but I preferred the sound of "Mee-ra," and have kept that pronunciation my whole life.

Of course going from Nuchem Shelubski to Norman Shelub was hardly enough to prevent my husband from being immediately pegged as a *greeneh*. The major stumbling block was the English language, which I had learned well at the Real-Gymnasium and used in the Badgastein DP camp, but with which he struggled in America. In the 1950s, he studied nights at the nearby

Polytechnic High School and even tried memorizing a dictionary to improve his vocabulary, which actually became quite rich.
He had no problem being understood, and could even throw out
witty one-liners, but spoke with a thick accent. Fortunately, we
could joke good-naturedly about his pronunciation and he never
took offense. Once, when we were all riding in a car, he spotted
the sign "Ice Cream" over a store window and called it "Itchy
Cream." He never made that mistake again, but it remained a
funny family story for years to come.

By 1959, we left our rented flat and bought a three-bedroom
home on Middlefield Drive in a neighborhood of many Jewish
immigrants, just beyond the outer Sunset in the southwestern
part of San Francisco. For $27,500 we didn't get anything fancy:
a small, attached, postwar house with a stucco exterior. But it
meant that in just a decade we'd moved up considerably: from
staying with relatives, to getting our own apartment, to renting
a much larger flat, and now becoming homeowners. Norman lay
awake at night, anxious about the $300-a-month payment for the
mortgage and taxes, but I didn't worry; I knew we could handle
it. Only a few years later I even wanted a much larger, freestand-
ing house—I had one picked out near us on Gellert Drive close to
Lake Merced—but we never got it.

I wasn't sorry to leave 2nd Avenue despite its advantage of
being so near to Golden Gate Park because now I lived closer to
many of my immigrant friends in a neighborhood that was much
more Jewish. And on 2nd Avenue I'd been concerned that Irwin
was falling in with the wrong crowd. He had always been a *bondit*,
a little rascal. In the park he'd break away from me while I tended
to my younger children and ride his bike recklessly, sometimes
injuring himself. By the age of eleven or twelve, he was actually

the leader of a pack of about six or seven non-Jewish boys and girls that frequently got into trouble. Even though he was at the top of his class academically, his elementary school disciplined him frequently. I hoped that the new neighborhood would give him a fresh start.

Still, we were living the proverbial American Dream. We'd survived the war and even fought back, and now we were raising a family in a home of our own.

AS MUCH AS we loved San Francisco, Norman's job had been the main reason we'd crossed the continent. One of his uncles, Max Shaff, was very successful. He had immigrated as a teen back in 1906, married into a third-generation San Francisco family, and ran a large furniture store that bore his name on Mission Street between 22nd and 23rd Streets. That's where he put his nephew to work, first in deliveries and warehousing with two likeable guys named Johnny and Caesar, and Norman got along well with these American-born, working class men. He also showed a lot of empathy toward the poorer customers. Irwin, who often went with him making the rounds on Saturdays for deliveries and collections, recalls that when they knocked on the door of a family that owed money, his dad would size up their circumstances. If the parents were avoiding him and the children looked deprived, Norman would turn to Irwin and tell him, "Let's just say they weren't home," in order to give that family another week to pay.

My husband felt good that his job gave him the chance to give a break to the needy once in awhile. But he also felt mistreated by Max and even more so by his far younger uncle, Sydney, whom Max had brought over from Novogrudok in 1937, and who worked in the business as well. Uncle Sydney, only nine years older than Norman, often assigned him menial and even demeaning tasks. Max appreciated Norman's skills and eventually promoted him to sales (although at a flat salary without commissions), but Sydney, with more seniority and a higher rank in the store, still lorded it over him. It especially rankled Norman because his uncle barely had an elementary school education, while he had graduated from the gymnasium in Poland and even spent a year at the university in Vilna. And of course only a few years earlier Norman had been the one giving orders—to fifty men, many of them older than him—as Commander *Roti* of a partisan group in the Naliboki Forest. Even Max sometimes made fun of Sydney's ignorance, but that only caused the younger brother to resent Norman and his higher education even more. To make matters worse, after we moved to Middlefield Drive, Sydney, who lived just a few blocks away, often commuted by car with Norman. So their bickering began well before the workday started and continued after the store had closed for the night.

Beyond that, Norman earned very little at Shaff's and we had to struggle to make ends meet for our growing family. Yes, Max had sponsored us when we immigrated to America, but we thought that our rich uncle would do even more for his nephew and his young family, especially given that Norman was a sole survivor. After a few years, frustrated by his low wages, my husband joined the Teamsters' Union to earn more money and receive healthcare benefits. At first, Max tried to discourage him, claiming that the union dues would eat up any increase in pay. But Norman would not be deterred and Max reluctantly gave his approval. As it turned out, his salary and benefits increased a great deal once he became a union member, and the financial worries of the Shelub family eased quite a bit.

Still, Norman and I both wanted to supplement his earnings at Shaff's. We knew that starting with nothing but our wits and skills in a new country meant that we had to work harder than others, and we were always talking about new entrepreneurial ventures. At first, when we lived on 2nd Avenue, I made a few dollars just by selling nylon stockings to other women I met in Golden Gate Park

By the late 1950s, something much better emerged. My old friend from the partisans Melech Zuckerkopf, now Max Cukier, had been living in Los Angeles, running a successful import business. One of his specialties was fine hand-blown Italian glassware: goblets, figurines, vases, liqueur sets, and many other lovely pieces. We decided that I would be his representative in the Bay Area. I even had a name for my little operation, M & S Imports, and hired an accountant to keep the books and file the business taxes.

Max would send the goods to our home and I still recall the big, yellow freight trucks that stopped outside the front door. Other times Norman and I would drive to LA, visit Max and other friends from Poland, and bring back samples in the trunk of our car. We stored it all in the basement of our new house on Middlefield Drive and Norman even built a little warehouse with shelves for samples and undelivered orders. I kept detailed charts to track the inventory. Often my tired husband and I labored late into the night, unpacking the cartons and sorting out the merchandise for delivery to local merchants. It was hard work. Frequently, there was breakage of the delicate items, even though they'd been packed in hay. Another problem was that Max often mixed up the orders. We'd have to search for glassware intended for one buyer in boxes marked for another, or replace what the customer ordered with something similar but not quite what he'd asked for. We could only hope it would be accepted.

It also took a while to figure out how to wholesale the product. At first I offered the blown glass to the big Emporium department store downtown. I walked in and went up in the elevator to pitch my wares to the buyer. She was gracious, and listened to my whole speech, but then told me they could not take goods from anyone but their established suppliers. I must have looked dejected because she also gave me some free advice: try selling to the many small florists and gift shops in the city. She was right; I soon had success with shops on Haight Street near our former flat on 2nd Avenue, and small stores in San Rafael and Sausalito as well as shopping centers like Sharp Park in Pacifica. Often I made cold calls to bring in more customers. I worked about half a day, three days a week, and though we never got rich from my little business, my earnings helped send our kids to their many extra-curricular activities and pay for our family vacations.

Norman also had a sideline. He had a knack for fixing appliances and, through mail order courses, my enterprising husband learned how to repair radios and TVs. Exhausted as he was after a day's work at Shaff's, he'd stop off at people's homes at night and fix their sets or bring them home to repair in the house. That was a benefit to our kids who often had half a dozen televisions in easy reach. Whenever I worried they were not getting enough sunshine, I'd shout, "Go outside and play!" But they'd just sneak into another room and finish watching the program on a newly fixed set.

So we worked night and day to better our situation, and while our kids sensed our economic struggles, they never felt any deprivation. They enjoyed every after-school pursuit they chose except one: we put our foot down when Elaine wanted to take up horseback riding. "When you find a three-legged horse, we'll think about it," quipped Norman.

And my children were always well dressed and well fed. I'd routinely whip up a big breakfast for them, including French toast with maple syrup, or scrambled eggs, along with oatmeal, and hand-squeezed orange juice; make them sandwiches to take to school for lunch, often tuna fish on rye with an egg and lots of carrots, celery and cherry tomatoes; and of course cook a big dinner. I did a lot of baking too and they still remember my coffee cakes, three-seed cake, and chocolate tortes.

NORMAN'S GOAL WAS to open his own full-time business—he had seen many other survivors take risks and succeed as entrepreneurs—but eighteen years would pass until the opportunity arrived. As tight as our budget was when he worked at Shaff's, we somehow managed to squirrel away a little every month, but he was very cautious about committing his modest savings to a new venture. When the time finally came, in 1967, he was proud to walk into Shaff's and announce his resignation. Max had passed away by then and his daughter, Merle, was in charge. Norman told me that the first words out of her mouth were, "How are you going to make a living?" For him it was final proof that his uncles, and now his cousin, thought they were doing him a favor by letting him work in their store. He needed to be on his own and this was one of the happiest days of his life. He felt liberated.

Our big break was a business new to us—fast food. It began through our friendship with two local survivors, Ben and Ann Zeitlin. They had a small deli on Haight Street and sold food to the hippies who were descending on the area from all over the country, especially in 1967, the Summer of Love. The Zeitlins also knew Bill Graham and sold refreshments at the rock concerts he held on Mount Tamalpais. They had good connections with the suppliers, knew the food industry well, and were very successful.

Norman suggested that the four of us go into business together and serve a different clientele, indeed the opposite of the hippies—the workers in the downtown financial district. The Zeitlins agreed and we opened a sandwich shop on Sansome Street, a small store between two banks, and right across from the imposing Pacific Stock Exchange. We committed the savings we'd built up from all of our jobs over the years. It wasn't a lot of money, but at least we didn't have to take out a loan for our share of the new venture that we named the Big Board.

We put in long hours. The financial employees started the day near dawn because the stock market opened in New York at 6:30 Pacific Time, so we had to get up around 4 AM to get the store ready for the breakfast crowd. At night we often had to stop on the way home and negotiate the price of a delivery with a supplier.

But it was worth it. The Big Board did well, and for the first time in our lives we were making a good living. We gave up our part-time jobs: I no longer sold the glassware and Norman stopped repairing radios and TVs. It was a cash business so at night Norman often came home with stacks of bills. He sometimes arrayed the money on our bed, not just to count it, but also to admire it. I rarely saw him so happy. In fact, we even went out to a restaurant for dinner on Friday nights. It was nothing fancy, often a diner like the Copper Penny, but for us it was a real treat.

Sadly, though, we soon had a falling out with the Zeitlins, who could be quite bossy. Our partners, especially Ben, believed they really didn't need us, that they could run the store very well on their own, and that with our lack of experience in the food business we were a drag on the operation. They thought they could simply hire someone to do our work, and without us keep twice as much of

Moving up

the profit. We had a number of arguments and one time Ben got so angry and frustrated that he threw a plate of food on the floor.

Norman and I urged the Zeitlins to take a vacation to cool off. They agreed and enjoyed their time away, but once they returned our struggles got even worse. Less than three years after we opened, we split up. The cook bought out our share, and we made a small profit, but now we were on our own and needed another source of income.

We decided to remain in the food business—after all, despite the Zeitlins' railing about our inexperience, we'd learned a lot in the past three years. We would open another sandwich shop, called Norm's, where we would be the only owners. Little did we know what a challenge it would be.

We stayed in the financial district. Norman found a good-sized space with about sixty seats on the ground floor of One Embarcadero Center, the first structure of a huge commercial complex that would eventually include five office towers and two hotels. It was a prime location near the piers on the Bay. Before we took the plunge, I did a lot of market research, standing in front of the elevator of the building and asking workers if they'd patronize a sandwich shop there. The answer was an emphatic "Yes," and my canvassing gave me a lot of confidence that we were on the right track.

Norman, though, required a lot of coaxing. Although he needed to work—many months had gone by since we'd left the Big Board—he was feeling less secure at this point than when we'd partnered with the Zeitlins. His experience in the Holocaust had taught him that catastrophe could hit with no notice. He had not only lost his entire family, but he himself could have been killed in the forest at any moment. Financial ruin was a different kind of calamity, of course, but he worried that if he lost his little nest egg in this gamble, his family could be destitute. Elaine was in college and Irwin in medical school so he feared he might not be able to help them with their tuition. Mark was living at home, but would Norman even be able to support him and me?

He had just turned fifty and knew he had heart problems, which I believe worsened at this time due to all the stress. Restaurants are among the riskiest businesses and if things went wrong, he feared he wouldn't have the years needed to replace his savings. One of his most anxious days was when he went to a trusted attorney to ask him to review the contracts to be signed to begin the project. If the venture failed, Norman asked him, could he lose not only his life savings, but also his house? The lawyer answered yes, it was a possibility.

But we decided to go ahead and as it turned out, a raft of problems fell on our heads, only adding to my husband's distress. As so often happens, there were delays in the construction and cost overruns in the budget. After a while, he just couldn't see an end to the outflow of money. At one point, Norman literally became sick after meeting an architect who proposed a fancy ceiling for the store; he finally got the interior designer to scrap that. When I tried to ease his worries by reminding him that my market research had shown a great need for Norm's Sandwich Shop, he shot back, "Sure there'll be lots of customers, but that's because you'll be giving everything away for nothing."

Meanwhile, we got advice from our loved ones about what to do. Sara and her husband, Joe Starr, an American-born physical therapist, counseled us to walk away and cut our losses before things got even worse and we'd be forced into bankruptcy. But my brother, now a pharmacist across the Bay near Walnut Creek, was of the opposite opinion. He said that since we'd already invested so much time and money we needed to see it through to the end.

Ultimately, the increasing pressure proved too much for Norman. He ceased functioning and was unable to participate at all in the restaurant's opening, a huge burden that fell entirely on my shoulders. Looking back on it now, I'm not sure how I managed to do it alone—the whirlwind of the opening day remains a blur to me—but the cook and I got there very early every morning, unlocked the door, and went to work. I didn't know any other way than to face this crisis head-on.

From the start, Norm's was mobbed not just with office workers in suits and ties, but also construction workers in overalls who often ordered heaping pastrami sandwiches. We served almost every other kind of sandwich too, salads, and desserts. Especially popular were our almond-flavored bear claws. Every day, two long lines of people waited to order. Many ate inside but our take-out business was even bigger.

Nothing could have been better for Norman's recovery. As soon as he saw the crowds waiting outside, he snapped out of his funk and was 100 percent his old self.

We had two cash registers, Norman was at one and I was at the other, and it seemed like we never stopped ringing up sales. But it wasn't just the money that lifted Norman's spirits. He loved the interchange with people, especially the Jewish patrons. If a customer looked Jewish, he'd often ask the question "Amcha?"—Hebrew and Yiddish for "Your people." It had been a codeword used in Europe to help survivors identify fellow Jews. Of course, most San Francisco Jews had no idea what he meant, but when one did respond affirmatively, he was thrilled to have found a kindred soul.

He also frequently gave extra helpings to Jew and non-Jew alike, like secretaries who he could tell were working for a pittance. The shop soon gained a special reputation as a charming mom-and-pop operation run by two immigrants who liked to chat up the clientele. When the police stopped by for lunch, Norman never accepted any payment. Asked about it, he offered some Old World wisdom: "These are the people that are going to protect me. I want them always to be my friends—that's more important than collecting a dollar fifty for a sandwich."

The thriving business was also a family affair. When we went on the road we'd leave Norm's Sandwich Shop in the hands of Irwin, Elaine, and Mark. By the way, I later heard that Irwin and Elaine ate many of the irresistible bear claws and cheese Danishes while we were away. One time they accidentally over-ordered the bear claws, so they took about a dozen of them home—and with half a gallon of milk that was their dinner.

We employed a colorful cast of characters at Norm's. There was the busboy, Ray, an edgy guy in his forties, who told everyone he was our distant cousin. In fact, he was not even Jewish. At times, he could be a real *shlemiel*, a bungling fool. When my son Mark graduated *magna cum laude* from Yale, I was so proud that I brought his diploma to the store to show everyone and Ray inadvertently threw it away.

Our cook, a Puerto Rican named George, was another eccentric personality. He and Ray fought all the time—not about anything of real substance, but rather some minor mix-up in the kitchen. To be sure, we were flooded with orders and the food had to be prepared quickly, the store was noisy and the workers had to yell to be heard. So amidst all the clamor, some friction among the staff was to be expected. But it seemed like these two took it further and were looking for any excuse to jump down each other's throats. Time after time I had to be the peacemaker; I sat them down and told them that they had to work together and couldn't constantly argue.

WE WERE LUCKIER than most survivors—we had a big family in America. As long and as hard as we worked to earn a livelihood, we never stinted on the time we spent with them or with our friends. At our home on Middlefield Drive we renovated the basement—a wood-paneled "finished basement" was a middle class status symbol in those days—and put in a bar. It was the perfect place for parties of up to twenty people, mostly other *greeneh*, with lots of music and dancing, and we even threw some masquerade balls. I'd cook for three days before these monthly galas.

Early on, when the kids were young, we usually enjoyed Rosh Hashanah, Chanukah, and Thanksgiving with Sara and Joe and their two kids, and later on with Morris and his wife, Gina, and their three children. There were six adults and eight kids on my side of the family and it gave me a warm feeling to see my kin reconstituted in America and able to get together frequently. The Passover Seder, hosted by Norman's Aunt Fanny and Uncle Oscar, was even larger with twenty-five to thirty people.

We also spent time with Norman's Aunt Mildred and Uncle Irvin. Their daughter, Myrna, and her husband, Jim Bennett, decided to live as Orthodox Jews and they made *aliyah* soon after the Six Day War, eventually settling in Haifa. As they planned, all three of their sons were born in the Holy Land and the youngest, Naftali, would become a leading Israeli political figure. In early 2013, the rightwing party he heads, the Jewish Home, won twelve seats in the Knesset and represents a key element in the governing coalition. Naftali Bennett was appointed to three Cabinet posts at the same time: Minister of Religious Services; Minister of Trade, Industry and Labor; and Minister for Jerusalem and Foreign Affairs. He is firmly opposed to a Palestinian state and believes that Israel should annex much of the West Bank. The irony is that his grandfather, Irvin, was a leftist and a non-believer and Naftali's mother grew up in a home of minimal Jewish observance. Irwin sent congratulations to Myrna after Bennett's strong showing in the recent elections, but Mark jokes that we ought to have sent a picture of Aunt Mildred and Uncle Irvin to remind Naftali where he came from. His politics aside, we're naturally proud that Norman's second cousin has risen so high. In another ironic twist, Mildred and Irvin actually made *aliyah* late in life, although it was not out of Zionist convictions but rather the desire to be near their family.

Norman and I were dedicated Zionists but we loved San Francisco so much we never considered *aliyah*. And we were eager to see the sights of our adopted land. When he worked at Shaff's, Norman had a few weeks of vacation every year so we'd load the kids in the car and go touring. We visited national parks like Yosemite, Yellowstone, and Sequoia; enjoyed Lake Tahoe, Crater Lake, and the Grand Canyon; and explored big cities like Las Vegas, Los Angeles, and Vancouver. These were low-cost trips; we stayed in inexpensive motels and ate in fast-food places. Once the lodging Norman insisted upon was so run-down that I preferred to sleep in the car. Yet it meant a lot to us to show our children the scenic wonders of the West.

One time we went back East. In 1964, the five of us flew to New York for the huge, futuristic World's Fair and to visit friends and relatives there and in Baltimore. Norman had given the kids and me a choice: the cross-country trip or the much larger house on Gellert Drive. We chose the former because we loved travel so much and we loved being with one another. Giving my kids an unforgettable experience outweighed everything else. To save money, we took to the air in a propeller plane, not a jet, and had to make multiple stops.

The Fair, symbolized by a giant, stainless steel model of the world called the Unisphere, unveiled mainframe computers and Space Age technology and our children thoroughly enjoyed it. Also in Queens, we spent a day with Zus Bielski and his wife, Sonia, at their apartment. He had come to New York from Israel eight years earlier and, with his brother Tevye, now ran a small taxi service and trucking company. But my husband's former comrade-in-arms spoke little of his wartime exploits in the forest. Instead, he talked a lot about his sons' exploits on the football field, and their injuries. It was a time for many survivors, even a Bielski, when the American present eclipsed the European past.

Even so, only a few days later, we went to a big party of former partisans in Brooklyn where the old days were discussed and Norman was hailed as a hero.

Then we visited my family members in Baltimore, whom Norman and I hadn't seen since our first months in America fifteen years earlier. We stayed with Aunt Sophie, who had hosted us so warmly in 1949—and was just as kind this time—and with Sophie's son and his Israeli wife, who had four sons. We also spent time with Sophie's daughter and her two sons. Building bonds with this wonderful family was important to all of us and we've been close to them ever since.

We vacationed much closer to home for a month every summer near the Russian River not far from the town of Guerneville. The natural beauty and idyllic setting reminded me a bit of the rural villages near Vilna that I had visited with my aunt, the dentist, during summers in the mid-1930s. Sometimes I'd walk through the fresh, earthy-smelling forests with Elaine, often for a couple of miles, and tell her stories of my youth in Zhetel and Vilna.

At first we rented a modest cabin from a Russian woman everyone called Babushka (grandmother in Russian) and on Sundays people from the entire area came over for her delicious piroshkis. We loved hiking in the eight hundred-acre Armstrong state park, with its hundreds of towering Redwood trees. Talent shows and dance contests could be enjoyed at a clubhouse in Guerneville; one time Mark and Elaine won first prize for dancing the Twist. We also played ping-pong, basketball, and volleyball. But what Mark liked most was the miniature golf course and he often won a free game with a hole-in-one on the 18th hole. He also frequented the corner drug store where he'd read its science fiction books for hours. Irwin could usually be found on Johnson's Beach at the river although I know there's one time he'd like to forget—when he got a horrible sunburn that caused him pain for days.

Norman would drive up for the weekends. I guess this was similar to the pattern of New York Jews where the husband had to work during the week, but could take off for the Catskills on Friday afternoon. He would often bring a tall round tin of sweets with him and because he was so frugal in these years, they were usually broken cookies that he could get at a discount. But they came from a fabulous Italian bakery near his workplace where he knew the bakers, and were absolutely delicious. He also brought toys for the kids and spent a lot of time with them. Elaine still remembers how they'd get in the water together and she'd stand up on his shoulders, feeling tall, adventurous and safe at the same time. All of us couldn't wait for his weekend visits.

Often Morris would come up and stay with us as well. My brother was dating frequently and sometimes brought a young woman with him. In the repose of the Redwoods he'd take me aside and privately ask my opinion of her. What I didn't know at the time was that my children were sizing up potential new aunts. He didn't marry until 1963, at the age of thirty-six, when he wed the worldly Gina Einstein (a distant relative of the famed physicist) who worked as an occupational therapist. She was born in Germany, raised in Israel, and then spent a year in Italy before coming to America with her family in her late teens.

By the 1960s, we could afford to upgrade our accommodations at the Russian River. We left Babushka's cabin for the Imperial Lodge, but our modest unit, with two rooms and three beds, was fairly plain and we often joked about the name. I doubt the electricity was up to code. When you touched the refrigerator, you often felt an electric shock.

Irwin was more independent than his younger sister and brother, and by the time he was in his late teens he came to the Imperial Lodge and left on his own, preferring his school friends to the quiet countryside. But when he did stay, he'd often take long evening walks with Norman, who was much more relaxed on the Russian River than in San Francisco. This is how Irwin first learned about some of the more grisly details of his father's daring deeds in the partisans. Norman and I hadn't spoken much to the kids about our wartime experiences; they knew that we were born and raised in Poland, fought in the resistance, and weren't in the death camps but not much more than that. And we'd told them little about the horrors of the Holocaust. But now, with Irwin, Norman unburdened himself.

One story he'd heard from a friend in the Badgastein DP camp had tormented him ever since; he even kept it from me. The man's baby had been killed before his eyes, the infant tossed in the air and speared by a Nazi officer's bayonet. Irwin heard that several times, even before he was a teenager, and the image never left him. Norman also told Irwin of being wounded in battle in the Lipiczanska Puscha before I had arrived. The bullet went through his upper left arm near the inner biceps; just a few inches to the right and that bullet would have entered his heart. I didn't know that story either. During the war, he didn't want to add to the anxiety I felt every time he rode out of camp on a mission. After the war, he wanted to put the traumatic incidents out of his mind—except when talking with his firstborn at the Russian River.

When Norman recounted for him the bold operations of his various partisan groups, Irwin naturally asked if he'd been afraid of death. Norman always answered that he "just didn't care." His fearlessness stemmed neither from bravery nor vengeance, he said, but rather from the profound losses he'd already suffered: the murder of his father, his mother, and his brother. His own life, he calmly stated, meant very little to him.

But close as they were at the Russian River, at home Irwin often got into fierce political arguments with Norman, some of them so heated that they wouldn't speak for days afterwards. Irv, as his friends call him, was at UC Berkeley in the mid- and late 60s, a period of vehement intergenerational disagreements in many families. He majored in western traditions of political and social theory, was on the left, and supported, although did not participate in the campus rallies and demonstrations. Norman strongly felt otherwise than his idealistic son. Very hardheaded, he saw the student movement as a rabble of spoiled kids naively thinking they could change the world. On top of that they were studying and living off their parents' money. Simply put, Norman thought Irwin had his head in the clouds.

But the two of them were like-minded on the Vietnam War, if for different reasons. Watching the news every night over din-ner—Walter Cronkite *and* Huntley and Brinkley in order to get more than one perspective—they both strongly believed that the war was a massive blunder. Norman drew upon his own wartime experiences to conclude that the Unites States could never win because the peasants were allied with the Viet Cong. He compared it to the Belarusian forests in the early 1940s when many of the peasants supported the partisans with food, supplies, and infor-mation about the movements of German troops. "That's how we held out," he said.

But if they came together regarding the Vietnam War, a deep rift developed in 1974, when Irwin, then a resident at the UC Davis School of Medicine, announced his engagement to a non-

Jew, Cheryl Douglas. We liked her but had had our hearts set on our daughter-in-law being Jewish. Intermarriage was far less common than it is now and Norman in particular was dismayed by the news. Irwin still remembers his father saying, "Did I go through the war for you to do this?" an utterance that hurts him to this day. Elaine also recalls her father's strong disapproval whenever she dated a non-Jew, which was quite often. Irwin and Cheryl never had a formal wedding with clergy, but rather got married in a civil ceremony.

A few of my friends were also disappointed. Irwin was sort of a darling among our circle of *greeneh* and not only because he'd become a doctor. He had been born in a DP camp and knew a lot of Yiddish, he had learned Hebrew well during a year in Israel, and upon returning had taught the Confirmation class at our synagogue, Ner Tamid. Intermarriage was the last thing they expected.

But in the end we realized that it was his decision to make, and we could easily see that Irwin and Cheryl were deeply in love. We soon reconciled and, shortly after they were married, threw a big party for them at our home. Irwin recalls that before the marriage, Norman said he'd be willing to give his approval if Cheryl converted to Judaism, but she declined, feeling that it would be insincere to convert just to get parental consent to be married, that it would lack true conviction or commitment. She did convert wholeheartedly about five years later, based on study and shared Jewish experiences with Irwin.

Looking back on it now, I'm happy that they married because *they've* been so happy. As time went on, I came to adore Cheryl, a wonderful wife and mother. She and Irwin have two sons, and for Norman and me becoming grandparents was the greatest miracle that could have happened.

The boys, like Irwin, Elaine, and Mark, became professionals. Nathan is an attorney and Aaron a doctor. He went to medical school in Israel where he met his future wife, an Israeli named Iris. They have two young sons, so I have two great-grandchildren, Daniel and Ron. I sometimes joke that they ought to be filling out their applications to medical school any day now.

I'M PROUD OF the educational achievements of my children and grandchildren. From the beginning, Norman and I tried to instill in our kids a love of learning. We taught them how to read very, very early. By the time Irwin was in first grade, Norman gave him a book about Greco-Roman civilization and they read it together at the Russian River. In second grade he received a book from his father on the Trachtenberg System, developed by a concentration camp inmate trying to keep his mind active. It's a method allowing someone to perform arithmetic computations in his head without pen and paper. Irwin mastered the Trachtenberg System,

Norman and grandson Aaron

and as a result his elementary school teachers handed the seven-year-old the fifth-grade math book—in front of a class of fifth-graders who had been complaining about its difficulty.

But it was not only learning for its own sake. They also sensed the economic insecurity we faced and realized early on that higher education and a profession would ensure them a good living. When Irwin was in third grade, for example, Norman decided that our son should have a background in electrical engineering, and enrolled him in a program for kids in elementary and junior high school at Lux Lab in San Francisco Polytechnic High School. Later he sent Mark there, too.

All three of my children went to Lowell High School, its new campus conveniently located a few blocks from our home. It's a selective-enrollment public school, known for its academic excellence, with acceptance at that time based on junior high school grades. And there was no question that we would pay the tuition and board for the best college they could attend: Yale for Mark, UC Berkeley for Irwin, and UC Davis for Elaine.

Irwin became a physician, and recently retired from Seton Medical Center in Daly City where he served as Chief Medical Officer. Mark also went to medical school, at UCLA, and practices physical medicine and rehabilitation in Oakland. In college neither of them majored in the sciences and Irwin in particular felt that medicine was not his true calling, but Norman strongly encouraged them to become doctors. "You'll always be needed," he'd say, and his partisan experience affected his thinking. A philosopher, he told them, was useless in the forest; a doctor was invaluable. Norman did everything he could to convince his sons and even sent Irwin on a trip to Southern California to see the practice of a survivor friend who had become a successful physician.

Irwin had always wanted to solve problems. When he saw that the doctor was analyzing different kinds of data—what tests showed, what the patient told him, what the examination revealed—to solve a unique problem, he came to view the profession differently. Medicine, thought Irwin, could be an intellectual challenge after all. And he saw the physician use his hands: he palpated, used a percussion hammer, and utilized a stethoscope. Irwin realized that in medical school he could improve his manual dexterity—which had not been his strong suit, much to Norman's chagrin. Beyond that, he anticipated the social connections he could make with his patients who in those days talked to their doctors with candor they reserved for almost no one else. Driving home, he decided to apply to medical school. He could please his father and himself.

Norman also had Elaine's profession picked out for her: pharmacist. He thought it would enable her to make good money, work part-time when she was ready to care for a family, and still have a measure of respect in the community. But Elaine had a mind of her own and, despite her father's displeasure, earned a Master of Social Work at the University of Chicago. Her career has taken her to the East, the Mid-west, and California as a medical social worker, as the director of social work at Kaiser, and as a management consultant and senior account administrator for firms managing major corporations' health care systems.

But for all the emphasis we put on education, I don't want to leave the impression that it was all work and no play in the Shelub household. The kids had all sorts of hobbies. Mark was an avid reader as a young child, everything from science fiction to great Russian literature. His imagination was always on display: he could build intricate model forts out of Popsicle sticks;

he could fashion model buildings by delicately balancing playing cards; he raised species of fish that were difficult to mate.

And my children loved sports. Irwin and Mark were on the varsity basketball team of the neighborhood junior high school they attended, Aptos, and I went to every home game. Irwin, the only white boy among the starting players, was a high scorer and led his team to the city championship game, although they lost that contest. He probably would have played for Lowell as well, were it not for an ankle fracture he sustained playing football, another of his childhood passions.

As for Elaine, I don't know where she found the time for all of her activities. She went to the well-known Anna Perkova Dance School, learned tap, ballet, acrobatic, and modern dance, and participated in public performances every May Day; I sewed all her costumes, usually with satin tops and four layers of pink, netted tutu skirts. She joined the famed Merrionettes Swim Club and took part in physically demanding synchronized swimming meets. She took weekly figure skating classes, which also involved

Norman and Mark

competitions and shows. On top of that, Elaine was class president of Aptos and it didn't surprise us when she also won the school's Scholarship and Athletics award.

All three of my kids took weekly piano lessons for many years, practiced in our home, and performed in recitals. We joked about how often I *shlepped* them to all these things—driving from one lesson to another Elaine often had to change into a leotard in the car. But Norman and I wanted to give our children every opportunity and were deeply satisfied in seeing how were well rounded they were becoming.

We also wanted them to have a strong Jewish identity, although with everything he had gone through in Europe, Norman could not embrace traditional Judaism. He had a rock-solid bond to the Jewish people, but not to religious practice. I was not an ardent believer then either, although I did not voice skepticism the way he sometimes did. I guess I was superstitious enough to think that openly doubting God's existence might bring a curse down on our heads.

But Norman did not believe entirely in the material or physical world. He was a spiritualist, thinking that it might be possible to communicate with his relatives murdered by the Nazis. He experimented with automatic writing and hypnotism and delved into Rosicrucianism, an occult sect claiming to possess ancient, esoteric wisdom. Using spiritualism, Norman also sought to make contact with the living. He clung to the very remote possibility that his brother had somehow survived and that he could reach him through extra sensory perception. I was somewhat familiar with telepathy having participated (admittedly with skepticism) in séances amidst the despair of the Zhetel ghetto.

Yet Norman and I strongly felt ethnically and culturally Jewish and Irwin says that growing up he heard more Yiddish than English in our house. However, that was before a pediatrician told us, contrary to the bilingualism in vogue today, that he'd be better adjusted if we spoke only English. But even then our speech was peppered with *Mameh Loshen* and he learned the language. If Norman and I wanted to talk to one another without our children understanding, we spoke Polish.

Early on we wanted to join a synagogue, not so much for the services, but to meet other Jews. We chose the Conservative Congregation Beth Sholom, across Golden Gate Park, and were quite impressed with its rabbi, Saul White, a protégé of the Zionist and social activist Rabbi Stephen Wise. White was a former boxer and had a lot of fight still in him. Born in Russian Poland, he had stood up to San Francisco's passive German-Jewish establishment

Norman and I in front of Marc Chagall's mosaic *Four Seasons* in Chicago

in the 1940s and demanded a strong local response—mass meetings and demonstrations—protesting the extermination of the Jews. He wholeheartedly endorsed Zionism (unlike most of the city's old line German-Jewish families who belonged to Congregation Emanu-El) and openly bewailed the weakness of Jewish education in the Bay Area. In the 1950s he stridently called for more *Yiddishkeit* in San Francisco, and his sermons, delivered with the passion of a Hebrew prophet, resonated with us. All these years later, Elaine remembers him as "mesmerizing" and fondly recalls the Bible stories he gently told to the little kids. Irwin went to Sunday school at Beth Sholom and became friendly with Rabbi White's son, David, his classmate, who was destined for the rabbinate himself. But my first-born did not attend Beth Sholom's Hebrew School. After public school, the rambunctious kid would play basketball with his friends rather than go to the synagogue classrooms. We had to hire a tutor to come to our house to teach him enough Hebrew for his Bar Mitzvah. Once, Irwin didn't let him in. I was away that day, so he pretended no one was home. He didn't answer the bell and when a frustrated Mr. Schwitzky knocked, Irwin didn't open the door.

As much as she admired Rabbi White, Elaine, too, was unenthusiastic about Judaism when she was growing up. As an adult she would become more interested, study Talmud with the "Zen rabbi," Alan Lew, at Beth Sholom, and try to incorporate Jewish ethics into her life. But in her youth her many other pursuits were higher priorities.

When we moved to Middlefield Drive, across the city from Beth Sholom, we joined another *shul*, Ner Tamid, much closer to us, where many of my friends were congregants. I've been an active member to this day. Here, too, a learned East European-born rabbi was at the helm of a Conservative congregation, Rabbi William Dalin of Lithuania, who had studied with some of the greatest Talmudic scholars of his time. He had been the founding rabbi of the synagogue in 1950. The *shul* had many immigrant families like us, and a vibrant Hebrew School, which Mark attended while Elaine went to the Sunday school.

Elaine's confirmation and Irwin's and Mark's Bar Mitzvahs were held at Ner Tamid and Irwin's party afterwards was quite unusual. The master of ceremonies was a Jewish celebrity who lived next door to us on Middlefield Drive. Ira Blue was a late-night radio talk show host but, more important to Irwin, he was the sportscaster of the San Francisco 49er home games on KGO radio. Through Blue, Irwin met some of the great 49er players of that era: Y.A. Tittle, R.C. Owens, and Hugh McElhenny. Certainly for Irwin and Elaine, the sporting life was more important than Jewish life when they were growing up and we had to accept it. After all, we weren't in Poland anymore.

SEVEN

Sorrow and Hope

By the late 1960s, we were worried about Norman's health. It seemed that whenever he exerted himself he had difficulty breathing. In the summer of 1968, he visited Mark at a basketball camp in Squaw Valley and started a game of tennis but soon ran out of breath and had to stop. Two years later, the pressure of opening a new business may have further weakened his heart. When we'd walk from the store to the parking lot on the pier, only about a hundred yards, he had to stop several times because he got so worn out.

We went to cardiologists at the Kaiser Medical Center and they put him on a low fat, low cholesterol diet, which he followed fairly well. But he didn't get any better and by the mid-1970s began to feel pain in his chest as well as breathlessness.

The diagnosis was mitral stenosis. As Irwin explained it to me, a narrowing of the heart's mitral valve opening had resulted in reduced blood flow from the left atrium to the left ventricle. The doctors at Kaiser confirmed what the physician in the Badgastein DP camp had said thirty years earlier: Norman's rheumatic heart disease was probably a residual effect of the scarlet fever he'd had as a child, caused by a strep infection. Indeed, he'd had a heart murmur since he was a boy, although he had not shown symptoms until well into adulthood.

In late 1975, he suffered a heart attack and cardiac arrest after undergoing a biopsy of his prostate gland, when a nurse gave him the wrong medication. Fortunately he was still in the hospital and, luckier still, the Chief of Medicine happened to be seeing the patient next to him and rapidly resuscitated Norman. But now the doctors recognized that in addition to the mitral stenosis, he was suffering from progressive coronary heart disease.

Drug therapy didn't help and, not surprisingly, hypnosis failed too. Norman, ever the spiritualist, hoped that by imagining a healthy heart he might be able to bring it about. By 1977, he couldn't even walk. The doctor felt Norman's mitral valve was so badly damaged that it needed to be replaced and that he also required a coronary artery bypass. That meant open-heart surgery, frightening today, but even more so almost forty years ago. There was considerable risk involved, a 15 percent chance of death we were told. His heartbeat would have to be stopped during the operation and he would be placed on a heart-lung machine to deliver blood and oxygen to his body.

Naturally, our family agonized over the decision. I was reluctant, but we chose surgery, agreeing in the end that it was a gamble we had to take. Without it, we were advised he would soon die. An echocardiogram was performed on my husband, using the latest techniques available at the time, and the doctor, a pioneer in this field, told Irwin that he had never seen such a severe case of mitral stenosis. Norman calmly resigned himself to going under the knife. He simply said, "I'm ready for it."

He would be in the hands of one of the leading heart surgeons in the world, Dr. Norman Shumway at the Stanford University School of Medicine, where he had performed his famous heart transplant. Irwin arranged his father's operation through one of Shumway's former students, a cardio-vascular surgeon and head of that department at UC Davis where my son was then chief medical resident. Also, the anesthesiologist in the operating room was a close friend of Irwin's.

But my husband died a day and a half after the operation even with treatment from such a renowned specialist. His left ventricle, the main pumping chamber of the heart, was just too weak to maintain the flow of blood once the new valve was put in place. It's called pump failure.

He was fifty-seven. I was fifty-five and felt my life was over too. It was the only time I can remember being at a loss about what to do. We had lived through so much together: the war, the partisans, and the DP camps, of course, but also immigrating to the United States, raising three children, and starting two businesses. And that still doesn't describe what we had. The whole time we were deeply in love—it was our lifeblood. We were affectionate in front of our kids and in public even in middle age. People often marveled at the tenderness we showed each other, which many married couples lack. Even when we argued, it was as lovers. I knew I could never share my life with another man and I didn't know how I'd carry on.

But as I did in other crises, I somehow persevered. My family was of great comfort. Even my grandson Aaron, only two years old and just learning to speak, came up to me and said, "Don't worry Grandma, everything's going to be OK." My three children, themselves shattered, supported me in every way. My daughter-in-law, Cheryl, was also a godsend in my time of grief and we bonded as never before. For all of us, just being in the house caused not only overwhelming sorrow but also disorientation. Where is Pop? How could he not be here?

Yet we did our best to adjust and the whole family made the decision that I should continue to operate Norm's to maintain some stability. After about a month of mourning—when Ray and George, also grieving for Norman, managed everything—I returned to the shop and ran things there for another six years, until 1983. At first, some of the vendors were so heartless as to try to take advantage of me by jacking up their prices, but I was not shy about confronting them and they usually backed down. When I closed Norm's it was primarily because the lease on our well-located space on the ground floor was due to expire, and the owners had offered us a third-floor unit that I thought was nowhere near as good.

But there was another reason I wanted to shut down Norm's. I'd simply had enough of the long hours and endless demands of the food business, my line of work for the past sixteen years. Elaine, who had almost gone for an MBA after getting her MSW at the University of Chicago, was now ready for another career and wanted to open a new food store with me. She had not only operated Norm's with her brothers when Norman and I were on vacation, but had also come in every Friday when she was at college. Even so, I had to turn her down. I chose instead to finish my education that had been interrupted by the war. At age sixty-two, I decided to go back to school.

I HAD ALWAYS encouraged my kids to pursue higher education and now they encouraged me. I wasn't sure what I wanted to study, but I knew where, San Francisco State University, less than a mile from my home.

My path to acceptance was not a typical one. First I needed to pass a GED (General Educational Development) exam, which would give me a high school equivalency certificate. Mark helped me prepare for it. Although I had taken some extension courses, I hadn't been a matriculated student since 1941. He took me to an office on Market Street where I sat for the exam and passed. But I still had to clear another hurdle, the entrance exam administered by the university. I passed that one too, was accepted, and entered in the fall of 1984.

I decided to major in history and although I was still grieving over Norman—I miss him terribly even today—I was reinvigorated by my four years of college. For some of my term papers I wrote about growing up in Zhetel, the occupation of Poland by the Soviets and Nazis, and my life in the partisans. I had lived through much of the history I was studying.

Sitting in class among young people caused me no awkwardness; rather, my spirits were lifted by their enthusiasm and curiosity. Many of the instructors were outstanding, such as Jules Tygiel who taught California history, and Rabbi Gary Greenebaum, Director of the campus Hillel Foundation. Professor Anthony D'Agostino, who taught modern Russian history, took a liking to me and, having heard about my experience with the Big Board and Norm's, suggested we open a food store together. But I declined his request just as I had Elaine's; I wanted to focus on my studies and see where that would lead.

I graduated *magna cum laude* in 1988 and my family held a

Nathan left and Aaron at my graduation from San Francisco State

party for me. I still remember the hoorays of my grandchildren: "Grandma, you made it!"

I took some time off and then reentered San Francisco State for post-graduate work, an MA in Counseling, which I received in 1994. Wanting to take advantage of my fluency in Russian, I thought I could help the large community of Jewish émigrés who had come to San Francisco from the Soviet Union in the 1970s and 80s. It seemed like a natural path for me, having grown up in a shtetl where Jews cared for one another through many mutual aid organizations. I applied to the Jewish Family and Children's Services and was first turned down. But I persisted and continued the volunteer counseling work I had been doing as a graduate student in that agency's L'Chaim Adult Health Center for Soviet émigrés. Within a year the JFCS hired me and I've worked there ever since. Even now, I help the "old folks" although I've cut down from five days a week to three.

I usually visit homebound clients and, while I draw upon my training, I've found that just conversing with them in their native language heartens them a lot. They often prepare a snack and my hour-long visits seem to ease their loneliness, anxiety, and depression. My clientele is mostly in their seventies or eighties (I've seen some of the same people since I began my career), and a number of them are ill or disabled. After immigration most had great difficulty getting a job in their profession, and some had trouble learning English and becoming American citizens. Many feel alienated from their adult children, of course far more Americanized than they are. As we talk, I try to gain insight into their needs in order to help them deal with daunting bureaucracies such as social security, insurance companies, Medicare, and the IRS. I even tutored one woman on the civics questions she'd be asked on her citizenship test.

My supervisor, the geriatric specialist Stella Raukhman, says that I'm their "life line." I try to empathize with my clients and some of them probably see me as an example of an immigrant who ultimately succeeded in America, in business and the non-profit sector, despite economic challenges and the untimely loss of a spouse. For my volunteer activities, I was awarded the JFCS' coveted Fammy Award for "extraordinary caring and community service" in 1995, and five years later that institution honored me again for my professional work.

After leaving the food business I had more time for another consuming interest—studying and teaching Yiddish. It has been part of my soul and the foundation of my Jewish identity from my mother's cradlesongs, to the Sholem Aleichem School and Real-Gymnasium, to the partisan hymn. In the mid-1980s, I delved into Yiddish literature at summer programs at Oxford and Columbia Universities. In 2004, I went with Mark to study at the Vilnius Yiddish Institute.

But nothing has been as satisfying as teaching Yiddish, my goal from the time I was a schoolgirl. During the late 80s, I taught at San Francisco State University. A typical introductory class had about twenty students, most of them young people who wanted to learn enough to speak to their grandparents. But elsewhere I was asked to conduct more advanced courses on Yiddish litera-ture: at my *shul*, Ner Tamid; the Holocaust Center, then down-town at the Jewish Community Federation; the College of Jewish Studies, a school for adult Jewish education just off Park Presidio Boulevard; and the Jewish Community Center on Brotherhood Way, not far from my home.

The advanced courses drew students of all ages, some already well versed in Yiddish, to whom I could teach the writings of the great authors who had always moved me to laughter and tears. I taught a lot of Sholem Aleichem— known to everyone as the Yiddish Mark Twain—whose stories inspired the musical *Fiddler on the Roof*. I love his whimsical, comedic style and the way his descriptions of life in the shtetl capture personality types and social interactions I can remember from my youth.

I also taught more serious writers like I. L. Peretz, author of the classic short story "Bontshe Shvayg" ("Bontshe the Silent"). The title character is a meek and uncomplaining man, downtrodden on earth as he suffers one misfortune after another, but exalted in heaven for his humility. Offered any reward by the angels, he chooses nothing more than a "warm roll and fresh butter." I shared with my students the renowned Mendele Mocher Sforim and Sholem Ash as well, but in my advanced courses I also taught some authors from the Yung-Vilne circle such as Chaim Grade and Avrum Sutzkever. The leftist literary group that had emerged when I lived in that city as a student in the 1930s made a lasting impact on me. I frequently read the works of Yung-Vilne today. And in my home I speak *Mameh Loshen* with Mark.

I was also drawn more to Judaism. While Norman was alive we didn't keep kosher and barely marked the Sabbath. But with Mark, who moved back to the Bay Area from Los Angeles in the early 1990s, I have experienced the balm and beauty of Jewish religious life.

Mark had been deeply affected by a year he spent in Israel in 1981–82 after he graduated from medical school. At first he stayed on a secular kibbutz where he attended an *ulpan*, or Hebrew language course. Then he spent a few months at a highly regarded Orthodox Yeshiva in Jerusalem, Ohr Sameach. The non-religious kibbutzniks thought he had lost his mind when he told them he was entering a Yeshiva, but he studied under extraordinary teachers like Rabbi Dovid Gottlieb, who holds a Ph.D. in mathematical logic from Brandeis University and was a professor of philosophy at Johns Hopkins University. Mark also volunteered in an Israeli hospital, where he further improved his Hebrew. He returned with a commitment to live a more Jewish life.

He did his medical residency in Los Angeles and had opportunities there to embrace Judaism—more than he would have had in the Bay Area. Today, my devoted son visits me often and my home is kosher. When we go out for a meal, I am especially fond of a kosher Chinese restaurant in the Sunset District. I also keep Shabbat by regularly attending Friday evening and Saturday morning services with Mark at Ner Tamid, the Richmond Torah Center, or another San Francisco synagogue. Ner Tamid has changed considerably over the past generation; it now serves mostly older folks rather than young families and no longer runs a Hebrew School. But it has another inspiring rabbi, Moshe Levin, and a gifted cantor, Rudy Hasid. Rebbitsen and Rabbi Hecht at the Richmond Torah Center host lovely Shabbat services and meals. Rabbi Ahron Hecht is a superb teacher, and Mark has been attending his classes for many years. All week I look forward to Friday evening when I usher in a twenty-four hour period of prayer, rest, and reflection.

AFTER NORMAN'S DEATH, I traveled overseas a lot. But even before he passed away we took several trips to Hawaii together, to the Big Island and Maui, and went abroad twice, a summer vacation in Western Europe, and a journey to Israel before we opened Norm's.

The visit to Israel was profound. It was the first time for both us and, although I've returned eight times since, it was the only trip to Eretz Yisrael that Norman would ever take. Given his life-long passion for Zionism, he was awestruck by the way the Israelis had built up the land only a little more than two decades after independence. I too was uplifted by how much they'd accomplished. It was only three years after the Six Day War, when they'd conquered the Sinai Peninsula and the Gaza Strip, the Golan Heights, and the West Bank including the Old City of Jerusalem, so they also had a sense of hard-won security.

Most emotional for us were our meetings with friends and relatives whom we hadn't seen in over a third of a century. We were treated like a king and queen; the Zhetlers fawned over me, the Novogrudokers fell all over Norman. We met with Rishe Kaplinski, my best childhood friend, in a living room full of people and I learned the fate of many of my classmates and comrades. Rishe and the other Israelis were animated at the gathering, and self-confident about their lives in the Jewish state. Referring to crime in America, one of them said to us, "You're afraid to go out in the evening, and we're not." Norman's cousin Seymour was there, too, the son of his Aunt Fanny. Like his cousin Myrna, Seymour had made *aliyah*. He drove a taxi for a living but seemed very content with his life in Israel. We also met with Myrna, her husband, Jim, and their three sons, including two-year-old Naftali who was destined for big things.

In Tel Aviv, we saw the artist Alexander Bogen, the stepson of my Uncle Sroel Ber with whom I'd lived in Vilna for three years of my studies at the Real-Gymnasium. Although he had exhibited some sketches and paintings of partisans at Yad Vashem (he himself had been the commander of a unit), and worked in Israel both as an artist and an art teacher, he was visibly short of cash like many in Israel in those years. We took him and his wife and son out to dinner and also bought a lot of food in the market for them to eat at home. We felt good to spend a little on our Israeli family. It reminded me how much we had appreciated the packages of clothing our American relatives sent to Zhetel in the 1930s.

In 1979, two years after Norman was gone, Mark and I went to Vilna, Zhetel, and Novogrudok, my first time back since the war. All three places were in Poland when I was growing up, but of course the borders had radically changed since then; they were now all in the Soviet Union. Vilna was the capital of the Lithuanian Soviet Socialist Republic, and Zhetel and Novogrudok were part of the Byelorussian Soviet Socialist Republic.

We began in Vilna and were taken around by none other than Shmulke Kaplinski, the older brother of my dear friend Rishe, and himself a former partisan. We met him by chance. While we were sitting on a bench, a woman passed by who looked Jewish

With my cousin
Alexander Bogen
in Israel

and I went up to her and began talking in Russian and Yiddish. As soon as I mentioned Shmulke, she was stunned. He was one of her best friends, she said, and led us right to him.

He was thrilled to see us, but of course Shmulke's Vilna was no longer the "Jerusalem of the North." The Jewish population had shrunk from almost one hundred thousand before the war to only five thousand. Far from being the region's center of Jewish learning, it did not have even one full-time rabbi. We went to the Real-Gymnasium and, as I had known, the high school that had been so influential in my life was no longer functioning; the building was being used as some sort of government agency. But I was able to identify my classroom and for a few minutes was transported back to the school's intellectual atmosphere of the late 1930s.

At Shmulke's house we met his wife and were a bit surprised to discover she was an ardent communist. Shmulke, though, seemed a little reserved about collectivism. "We have everything," he told us, but he mouthed the slogan with a smile; we weren't sure if he was being sarcastic. We didn't ask him directly about it, however. Throughout our trip, we had sensed fear on the part of the populace and we didn't want to put him in a compromising position.

He and his son-in-law drove us to Novogrudok and Zhetel. It was also Shmulke's first trip back since the 1930s, even though he had been living only a hundred miles away. The Jewish population of the Byelorussian Soviet Socialist Republic was barely twelve thousand, down an astounding 98 percent from its level before the Nazi invasion. In my hometown, which had been three-quarters Jewish before the war, no Jewish life was left. I could see where the market square had been, but my father's shop and all of the others were gone. So too was our house. As for the locals, again it seemed that dread hung in the air. One woman seemed to recognize me, and she followed us, but appeared afraid to come up and introduce herself. We were speaking Yiddish and wearing western clothing, so perhaps she worried we had come back to lay claim to our possessions. We were almost six thousand miles from home but more than the physical distance, it was the sense of foreboding everywhere we went that reminded me how far we'd come from America.

I traveled with Elaine, too, on trips that were pure pleasure and reminiscent of what we'd loved to do together many years earlier at the Russian River. In the 1990s, we went hiking in the Cotswolds in England and on another occasion we rambled through the state parks in Vermont, up and down hills for miles at a time. Later we went on an Alaskan cruise.

But by 2001 I was ready to see what might have changed in the region of my youth. The heavy hand of communism in 1979

My three children in the late 1980s,
from the right, Irwin, Elaine, and Mark

had limited our access to people and places, but a decade after the breakup of the Soviet Union I went back on a trip planned by Irwin and Cheryl.

Irwin had had a faint Jewish identity growing up. He tells me he was influenced by Uncle Irvin who often whispered in his ear that the only reason to be Jewish was because there were anti-Semites in the world. But like his younger brother, Irwin spent a year in Israel—a junior year abroad program at the Hebrew University of Jerusalem—and it was also a life-changing experience although in a different way than Mark's. He studied Israeli archaeology and Jewish history, becoming an avid Zionist based on his new understanding of Jewish peoplehood.

Most of all, he fell in love with Jerusalem, which became a united city after the Six Day War, only a few weeks before he arrived to begin his summer *ulpan*. He was given a tour of the Old City by Israeli students who as soldiers had just fought to gain the Western Wall but at that time the *Kotel*, as it is called in Hebrew, was just part of a narrow alleyway. He went on tours throughout the country given by army veterans, but he learned the ancient streets of Jerusalem the best, and eventually led tours himself for American visitors. One was the sportscaster Ira Blue, who had been the MC at Irwin's Bar Mitzvah, but more important were Norman's cousin Myrna and her husband Jim Bennett, who soon afterwards confirmed their plans to make *aliyah*.

Four or five weekends that year he also visited Yakov Shelubski at his chicken farm in Pardes Hanna near Tel Aviv. Yakov was Norman's second cousin and his sole surviving relative from Novogrudok. His three children had all died during or soon after the war. He had owned a big lumberyard in Novogrudok and employed Norman's father. Sadly, Yakov died six months before

Norman and I made our first trip to Israel and it was a pity that my husband was never to meet him in his new homeland. At least our son had made the connection.

At the end of that pivotal year, Irwin traveled extensively in communist Eastern Europe, but did not visit Vilna, Zhetel, or Novogrudok. So more than three decades later, after reading a lot of Jewish history, he was ready to explore his roots. He wanted the whole family to join him on this journey of discovery: his wife and two sons (Aaron was already living in Israel and about to enter medical school; Nathan was in college), Mark, Elaine, and me. Only one person was missing, but in a way Norman would be with us.

Irwin and Cheryl prepared for the eight-day expedition for more than a year, not only planning the logistics, but also poring over history books, detailed maps, and genealogical records at Salt Lake City's Family History Library. Cheryl also studied her own family's ancestry and on the way back home she, Irwin, and their sons toured Scotland, the land of her forebears.

From the beginning I was struck by the depth of my family's interest in their origins, and the great empathy they had for the suffering of my generation during the war. We had some superb guides, but I too explained the significance of key sites and translated the discussions we had with locals in Yiddish, Polish, and Russian. Knowing the trip would surely stir up many painful memories, Elaine said at the outset, "I'll hold your hand and if you need to cry, cry." Really, though, we all supported one another. Fortunately, my loved ones didn't have to worry about my stamina. Emotionally draining as the trip was, my energy never flagged. I think my grandson Aaron really meant it when he told Elaine that he couldn't keep up with me.

We started in Vilna and I pointed out my aunt's lovely home where I had lived for three years, right across the street from the opera house. It was through her window, I told my family, that I'd seen the funeral procession carrying Polish president Pilsudski's heart.

Again I visited the Real-Gymnasium and although we could not go into my former classroom at least my family could see the building, which still had its original front courtyard doors of heavy wood. But I was deeply disturbed by a plaque on the wall stating that during the ghetto period my gymnasium had been the headquarters of the *Judenrat*, one of the Jewish councils set up by the German occupiers throughout Eastern Europe to carry out the Nazi decrees. The *Judenrat* in Vilna, run by the autocratic Jacob Gens, was more powerful than most, and its own police force assembled Jews for slave labor and even mass execution. That my beloved *alma mater*, a center of Yiddish culture, had been used as a hub for the annihilation of Vilna Jewry was a perversion of the worst kind.

Then we got in our van and headed toward Belarus, a country that had been independent of the Soviet Union for the past decade. As soon as we got on the road we stuck out like a sore thumb. It was not just that we were seven Americans traveling in a poor, underdeveloped area, but also that our van happened to be a big, brand-new Mercedes, like nothing the locals had ever seen. It was in sharp contrast with the other modes of transportation we saw out the window: small, run-down cars that seemed made of tin, and even horse-drawn carts.

At the Belarusian border we had to wait for many hours. We'd been told to expect a long delay so Cheryl packed lunches for us. Many others in line got out of their cars too and were also having

In front of the sign, in Belarusian, indicating the village of Selub.
From right, Mark, Irwin, Elaine, Nathan, Aaron, Cheryl, and me

such roadside "picnics." When at long last our turn came, the border police scrutinized our passports, visas, and the documents for our amazing vehicle. It seemed like they'd never let us through. But after we slipped them a $10 bill and some packs of American cigarettes, they opened the gate in an instant.

We drove to Novogrudok but, even before we explored it, we went about ten miles north to the village of Selub. Cheryl's painstaking research had revealed that one of Norman's ancestors named Yitzchak, likely his great-grandfather, had moved with his family from there to Novogrudok in 1816. Because he had been from Selub, the family took the name Shelubski. Norman had distant relatives there long after his forebears had left and perhaps they influenced him; Selub was a Zionist stronghold.

As we drove through the countryside outside Novogrudok toward the Naliboki Puscha, I explained to my family how the dense forests so near the road allowed the partisan fighters to remain undetected as they prepared to ambush a German convoy. We went into the woods—even our fancy van got stuck in the mud a few times—and with the help of our guide found a full-scale model of a *ziemlanka,* the partisans' half-underground wooden bunkers, with branches on top. By a remarkable coincidence, we ran into a BBC film crew shooting a movie on the Bielski partisans. I was able to tell them how we lived in the *ziemlankas.* It was strange seeing actors and actresses dressed as peasants and partisans exactly where the real missions had taken place sixty years earlier.

After a few wrong turns we finally found the site of my camp in the Naliboki Puscha. I took Nathan by the hand to the base of a tall tree. In earshot of everyone I told him, "This is where we had a camp, this is where we cooked, this is where we had an oven." I wanted my family to get a close-up picture of the day-to-day struggle of fighting back.

We also went to the granite monument in the countryside commemorating the slaughter of fifty-one hundred Jews in December 1941, almost certainly including Norman's mother and brother. They had been taken from the Novogrudok courthouse about two miles south to pits that had already been dug in preparation for the mass executions. That's where we were standing now, in a grassy, demarcated area. It was cold comfort, but at least the inscription on the memorial's plaque, in Hebrew and Belarusian, designated the victims as Jews and the perpetrators as "the Nazis and their collaborators." The monument had been erected in 1997, and such wording would have been unacceptable when the region was under Soviet control. Holocaust memorials put up by the USSR usually referred to the perpetrators as "fascists," and even refrained from mentioning the word "Jews," although it was only against us that genocide had been carried out. Rather, we went unnamed, lumped together with all the "victims of Hitlerism."

As we walked, we found ourselves treading upon a rectangular mound, about 30 by 150 feet. An eerie feeling came upon each of us that we shared with one another later. We realized that we'd likely been tramping on holy ground atop the blood of the martyrs. Overcome by the ghostly sensation, we all quickly left the mound. For the rest of the trip, whenever we saw one of those monuments to the victims of the Shoah, we made a point of not stepping on any knoll on the grounds.

The next day in Novogrudok we were led by the well-informed and highly dedicated Tamara Vershitskaya, who spoke impeccable English. She was curator of the local museum, and is today its director. Tamara had devoted a corner of the museum to the Jewish community of the town, once large and vibrant, which dated from the fifteenth century. This exhibit was sorely needed; under the Soviets there had been so little education about the Jews that, growing up, Tamara herself did not know there had ever been any in Novogrudok. Yet the Jews had comprised around two-thirds of the town's population by 1900 and produced eminent rabbis and scholars.

Now there were only thirty Jews left, only three of them native Novogrudokers. Even more pitiful, among the thirty Jews were not the ten adult men needed for a *minyan*, or quorum, for services, so there could be no community-wide Jewish ceremonies. Tamara hoped to establish an entire wing of the museum devoted to the town's Jewish past and we all pitched in to give her a few hundred dollars toward that cause. It was money we knew would go a very long way in Belarus.

I was recently pleased to learn that an entire Museum of Jewish Resistance opened in Novogrudok in 2007, based on her initiative and with the help of private donors such as the Novogrudoker Jack Kagan, a historian and former partisan living in London. It includes a reproduction of the famous tunnel—Tamara had shown us the entrance to the actual one—through which about two hundred fifty Jewish prisoners, skilled craftsmen including Kagan and a good number of Zhetlers, escaped to the woods in September 1943. Many were killed along the way but about one hundred seventy made it to freedom and fought with the partisans.

After several attempts, we finally found Norman's former home on the 3rd of May Street (named for the date of the Polish constitution of 1791, an unsuccessful attempt to forestall annexation by the Russians). Mark and I had not been able to locate it in 1979 but, with Tamara's help, we now succeeded. The house was made of split logs on a rock foundation. Just as in the winter of 1944, when Norman and I stayed there with my ailing father, Sara and Morris, and Zus Bielski's in-laws, the large dwelling was still divided into three units. Its prewar charm was gone and a corrugated tin roof further added to its drab appearance.

The current residents were at first suspicious, but let us come in and look around. This time we found far less of the unease and distrust than Mark and I had experienced twenty years earlier.

As I walked through the rooms, conflicting emotions welled up inside me. It was where my husband, surrounded by a loving family, had grown into manhood, but also the spot from which his father, saying he was Nuchem Shelubski, was seized and sent to his death. It was the first place Norman and I had lived after the liberation and where we had our first taste of freedom, yet it was also the house in which my dear father, suffering terribly

On the streets of
my hometown with
Avrum Kaplan, the
last native-born Jew
to remain in Zhetel

from numerous diseases, died in the care of my sister. Could sorrow and joy be more entangled in a single place?

I had another connection with Novogrudok, my two years as a *desetiletka* student there from 1939 to 1941. We met with a Polish woman who had been a student in the same school around that time. She showed me the yearbook and I recognized many of my schoolmates. Then she brought out something that really took me back to those years, the attractive cloth badge, in the form of a heraldic insignia, that we proudly wore on our uniforms denoting the school just by its number, 919.

Before we left Novogrudok, we made contact with Jews, tiny as the community was. We met with an older Jewish couple and spoke to them at length in Yiddish. She was a Zhetler and although we didn't remember each other, we knew a few people in common. I found out from her that there were now only five

Jews left in my hometown, only one of them a native. His name was Avrum Kaplan and she had his phone number.

We arranged to meet on a street in Zhetel and I rushed ahead of my family to embrace him. Then Avrum led us into his small but well-kept house and introduced us to his non-Jewish wife. We talked for a long time, while I asked most of the questions. Three years my junior, Avrum had known my younger brother, Maeshe, better than me, but I was excited to see prewar photos of many of my relatives and friends, as well as my brother's, sister's and even my mother's closest companions.

The last Zhetel Jew to remain told us his story. Our lively conversation was in Yiddish and after every few sentences I'd turn to my family and translate. After a while, it became too much of a distraction. Avrum and I had so much to say to one another that I couldn't bear to interrupt our discussion. So Irwin served as the interpreter, and he not only rendered our words into English, but also mimicked my animated gestures. If I opened my eyes wide and spread out my arms in surprise at what I'd just heard, he'd do the same. We all laughed, a bit of levity we needed in Zhetel.

At sixteen Avrum had first been confined to the ghetto. Then he fled to the forest and survived in a family camp protected by the partisans. After liberation, he served in the Red Army for six years. When his military service was over, he was able to return to the same house his family had built in 1937 and he lived there ever since. Yet even in a place of such isolation, he still had connections to the wider Jewish world. His brother, a businessman in New York, regularly sent him the weekly Yiddish edition of the *Forward*, containing news and high-level opinion pieces on politics and culture.

His brother also sent him money. Without it he and his wife wouldn't have been able to get by. Avrum also collected reparations from Germany and received a small pension from his former job, but his living conditions confirmed the poverty we'd already seen for several days in Belarus. Even in 2001, his house lacked indoor plumbing and modern heating and he could barely afford food for himself and his wife. The value of the country's currency was unbelievably low. Irwin couldn't even change a $50 bill at a bank; they didn't have that much available in Belarusian rubles. The deprivation aside, I simply couldn't understand why Avrum had remained in Zhetel at all. To me, it was like living in a cemetery.

He led us through the town and, even more than when I'd visited in 1979, I was distressed by how much had been lost. Before the war there had been four synagogues in Zhetel; now only one was left standing and it was used as a fire station. I'd known that my house, my father's store, and the Sholem Aleichem School were gone without a trace, and now I learned that Aunt Nechamke's house was no longer standing either.

But I was completely overcome by grief when Avrum took us to the stone monuments on the grounds of the two *sh'chitehs* or slaughters, in 1942, the first taking the lives of around twelve hundred Jews, the second killing almost three thousand. In the first, my grandmother had literally been torn from our arms and later murdered. In the second, my aunt, uncle, and two of my cousins were executed. For me, standing at those spots was the most wrenching part of our trip. I wept openly and, just as she promised, Elaine was a great comfort to me. We held each other tightly as we walked the perimeter of those killing fields.

Before we left Zhetel I took my family to the pond where I'd fallen in when I was skating on its thin ice. They'd all heard the story several times about how other Jews had tried to save me: first the boy who himself fell in, and then the couple who pulled

The site of the second mass murder in Zhetel, August 6–8, 1942.
The plaque, in Russian, reads: "Here are buried 2,800 Zhetler Jews
brutally murdered by the German fascists—1942"

us both out. Seeing the actual pond again brought back my affection for that small, nurturing community now long gone. To have my loved ones with me in Zhetel, especially Aaron and Nathan, linked the three generations of our family more than ever. Mark's videotapes of our tour ensure that future generations of Shelubs will have the opportunity to learn where they came from.

Returning to Vilna for our departing flight we visited one last site of mass murder. At the wooded suburb of Ponary a hundred thousand people, mostly Jews, were killed by the Nazi *Einsatzgruppen* and their Lithuanian accomplices. Our only consolation in this place of unspeakable horror was the tall memorial, with newly inscribed plaques in Hebrew and Yiddish. Post-Soviet Lithuania had taken steps to mark the Holocaust, I could see, but as I would learn later, it still had a very long way to go.

IN THE SUMMER of 2011, Mark and I returned to Eastern Europe a fourth time as participants in a study tour conducted by Lehrhaus Judaica and the Jewish Community Center San Francisco. We began in Saint Petersburg, Russia, and went south through the Baltic capitals of Tallinn, Estonia; Riga, Latvia; and of course Vilna, Lithuania. In Estonia, I learned that many Jews had fled or been deported during the Soviet occupation but virtually all of those who remained, about fifteen hundred, were murdered by the Nazis in 1941.

Estonia had relatively few Jews before the war, but Latvia was once a major center of Jewish life and learning with a community of about one hundred thousand, almost half living in Riga. Ninety-five per cent of Latvian Jews were killed by the *Einsatzgruppen*. Some Estonian Jews returned home after the liberation but, needless to say, Jewish life in both countries is now dismal compared to what it had been before the war.

In Vilna, our group went to the large Choral Synagogue, built in 1903, and the only one still in use. That city once had over a hundred *shuls*. I was summoned to come up to speak in front of the ark and I told my fellow travelers my story of fighting back from the forests.

Mark and I stayed on for a three-day private tour. Our guide was Regina Kopilevich, part Jewish, part Lithuanian, who not only showed us important sites, but also brought us together with a wide range of people, including friends from my youth like Fania Brantsovsky. She had attended the Real-Gymnasium a year ahead of me, had been confined in the Vilna Ghetto, but fled to the forests in 1943 and joined a Soviet partisan group. For many years she was the librarian of the Vilnius Yiddish Institute—she continues to work there part-time—and is well known for her longtime advocacy of Holocaust education and commemoration in Lithuania. We first reunited during my summer Yiddish course in Vilna seven years earlier, and now, over dinner, I had more time to discuss the fate of my classmates and teachers. I found out that some education had gone on in the Vilna ghetto, and that the incarcerated Jews even set up Yiddish and Hebrew choirs. I also learned that many of the former Real-Gymnasium students gave some of their precious food coupons to their teachers. Tragically, this was not enough for our beloved Yiddish instructor and music teacher, Yakov Gershteyn. He died of hunger.

I didn't know it at the time—perhaps Fania did not want to upset me when we met—but she was going through quite an ordeal. In 2008, the police came to her house and informed her that she was under investigation for war crimes! Another Jewish woman who had fought back with the Soviet partisans, the biologist and Holocaust historian Dr. Rachel Margolis, was served notice to appear as a witness in the case of an alleged Jewish massacre of civilians; she also has a home in Israel and has not returned to Lithuania since. A year earlier the authorities had opened an investigation into the wartime activities of the world-famous partisan Yitzhak Arad, a former Israeli Brigadier General, and for more than two decades the chairman of Yad Vashem. Although their cases were eventually closed, rightwing media defamed all three as murderers of unarmed civilians.

Singling out these highly respected former partisans may seem utterly absurd to us but it serves the "double genocide" theory by which many Lithuanians equate their oppression under the USSR with the Final Solution. In maligning Brantsovsky, Margolis, and Arad they are trying to undermine the idea that Jews were the primary victims of the war; they want to shift the emphasis to Jews victimizing others.

Regina also put us in touch with the Brooklyn-born Yiddish scholar Dovid Katz who has long battled the Lithuanian government on precisely this issue. He had built up the Yiddish program at Oxford, taught at Vilnius University for twelve years, and now divides his time between Vilna and Great Britain. After a lunch in a Lithuanian restaurant, he invited us to his small, fifth-floor walk-up apartment, cluttered with piles of books.

The bearded, portly, and outgoing Dovid had us in stitches as he imitated the accents of French and American Jews learning Yiddish. But he's a serious researcher and videotaped an interview with me speaking in Yiddish, one of three thousand he's conducted. Before we left, he made sure we knew the extent to which East European governments, and Lithuania in particular, have "obfuscated" the Holocaust without actually denying it.

Regina took us to the Vilna Gaon Jewish State Museum where we saw a sketch of Alexander Bogen and were told they had other of his works in storage. At another part of the museum, the Green House, we saw an exhibit on the Holocaust and were gratified to see importance given there to the crimes of the local collaborators of the Nazis. The Green House is a kind of an oasis of Holocaust truth telling in Lithuania, run by the courageous Rachel Kostanian. She is still at her post today and we can only hope that she will be allowed to remain.

Then we went to the Chemistry Department of the Stefan Batory University (now Vilnius University) where Norman had been a student during the academic year 1938–39. Inside the main lecture hall, we saw the seats on the left side where Jews were required to sit and wondered if Norman had sat there, or stood in the back of the hall with those Jewish students who protested the discrimination. We also visited the vast Jewish cemetery in

Vilna and paid homage at the graves of my best friend's brother, Shmulke Kaplinski, and his wife, Chiena, who had both died in 1999.

Nothing prepared me for my third postwar visit to the Real-Gymnasium, now used as a building for art preservation. This time we were led into the central courtyard, where as a teenager I had relaxed with my classmates, and saw an imposing Holocaust memorial. Largely funded by American donors, it is an abstract stainless steel sculpture, *Flame of Hope*, created by the internationally recognized artist Leonardo Nierman. It was erected to commemorate the Jews who had been assembled there, when it served as the *Judenrat* headquarters, before they were taken to the killing pits at Ponary. If my high school could no longer be a center of Yiddish culture, I thought, let the building at least mark the terrible travesty it became under the Nazi rule. The sculpture, atop a large granite slab engraved with commemorative words, had just been completed before our arrival. Workmen were still laying paving stones around it as we took our photographs. It was scheduled to be dedicated later that week, almost seventy years after the Shoah.

But I was far from satisfied. It would have been fitting if here, of all places, the inscription had been in Yiddish and not just in Lithuanian, Russian, and English. There was no mention of the Real-Gymnasium having occupied the site before the war, and no indication that Lithuanian accomplices had participated in the mass murders. To make matters worse, I later learned that setting the sculpture inside the courtyard, instead of outside at the building's gates, has made it inaccessible to most visitors, given that the entrance is usually closed. Even those who make prior arrangements to enter the courtyard find the sculpture placed at an angle near a far corner so that only the nondescript title is clearly visible. To read the inscription, woefully insufficient though it is, one needs to walk behind *Flame of Hope* and stand in the narrow space between it and the building's walls. Several commentators have dubbed it the "hidden Holocaust memorial." It is the only one in Vilna.

As I think back on our trip, I can really appreciate how volatile, how unpredictable, the Lithuanian way of marking the Shoah has been, even after the collapse of communism. One set of government officials might allow for a proper memorial or museum exhibit, another might try to expunge from history the local collaborators, and yet another might equate the Soviet crimes with Hitler's annihilation of the Jews. Insult can be added to injury at any time. How, I wondered, could any Jew bear to live here?

On this trip we did not go into Belarus to Zhetel and Novogrudok for I already knew they were barren of Jewish life. Instead, still upset by our visit, Mark and I made last minute arrangements to fly to Israel, the perfect antidote to all the ruin we'd just witnessed in the Baltics.

Mark, Fred, and I in Vilna, 2011. (Courtesy Dorothy Shipps)

AS I TRY to make sense of my unlikely life I can see that for all of the hardship I've gone through, and loss I've had to bear, I've been blessed with the trait of perseverance. Elaine jokingly calls me Golda Meir for all that I've done in the face of adversity. It's almost a mantra for me when I say that I just put one foot in front of the other and go on. I don't know any other way. As the opening of the partisan hymn that I proudly sing goes, "Never say this is the last road."

And in my later years, I've continued to persevere—in telling my story. I'm still fighting back, now against ignorance and misconceptions. Of course, I harbor anger and grief, but I refuse to let it paralyze me. I want people to know that European Jewry was decimated, but also that some of us fought back. In the past decade I've spoken to at least twenty groups, mostly young people, because I feel teenagers are especially open to my message. They will be around long after the last survivors like me are gone and it will be left to them to keep alive the memory of the Holocaust.

My career as a public speaker was launched in 2003 by an earnest young man named Mitch Braff. With a background in commercial filmmaking, he had founded the locally based Jewish Partisan Educational Foundation three years earlier. He learned of my partisan past and, accompanied by his small film crew, interviewed me for several hours. We took an immediate liking to one another and when institutions called him requesting a former partisan as a speaker, I was at the top of his list along with Sonia Orbuch, a woman who had fought back in the province of Volynia, south of Belorussia, and who now lives in Marin. After a while, Mitch began receiving calls asking for Sonia or me specifically. He has been my "booking agent," so to speak, and picks me up and drives me to the events.

In addition to synagogues and Jewish Community Centers, I've spoken at Catholic high schools, non-sectarian private high schools, and the Jewish Community High School. I've tried not to lecture my audiences in the sense of talking *at* them, so much as sharing my experiences *with* them in a personal way. I encourage dialogue and, after my presentations, I take questions—and take my time in trying to answer them fully. High school girls seem especially affected by my message and often, after the question-and-answer session is over and I'm leaving the auditorium, one or two come up to talk with me. I hold their hands, look them in the eyes, and speak from my heart. To me each and every event is a special opportunity and I feel sorry when it's time to get back in the car and go home.

I've educated young people in Poland and Israel as well. I participated in the program known as *Shalhevet* (Hebrew for torch

In 2013 I received an award from San Francisco State University for my "inspirational" work as a Holocaust educator. Congratulating me is Dr. Anita Friedman, Executive Director of the Jewish Family and Children's Services

Mitch Braff and I speaking before a group of high school students

or flame) run by the Holocaust Center of Northern California (now the JFCS Holocaust Center) and the Bureau of Jewish Education (now Jewish LearningWorks). It matches a survivor with about thirty Bay Area high school juniors and seniors for a trip to Poland, including the death camps, and then a tour of Israel. In 2008, accompanied by Mark who served as the group's medical advisor, I was that survivor. In pre-tour meetings and on the trip itself I got close to many of the kids and one girl later wrote, "Every time I heard Mira's amazing story, I couldn't forget that she was about our age when it happened." When they got home and evaluated the tour, the students made very kind comments about my participation, but I was most heartened to learn that 88 percent of the kids on the trip "strongly agreed" that they now see themselves as a "witness" who will carry the lessons of the Holocaust forward.

I also had a rapport with a group of Polish students we met in Lodz. The plan was for the American and Polish teens to have lunch in one dining hall, while the adults ate in a separate room. Well, that arrangement didn't suit me. I left Mark and the rest of the staff and went off to be with the kids. Sure enough, I had a lively conversation with the Polish young people in their language.

I've participated too in large commemorative and educational events conducted by the JFCS Holocaust Center. The Day of Learning is a program involving six hundred students and teachers, and for seven years I've closed it with the partisan hymn. I've sung it many times at the community-wide Yom Hashoah event after the reading of the many names of local Jews' family members and friends who perished in the Holocaust.

The scale of our people's loss can barely be comprehended. My mother and my grandmother were killed in the Shoah, but still I'm far more fortunate than most. I came out of the fire alive, and so did my father, brother, and sister. This actually makes me one of the "lucky" ones because nine out of ten Polish Jews were slain, three million men, women, and children from that country alone.

Yet despite the enormity of the Holocaust, I believe we must make peace with the Germans and the other nations that collaborated with them. Reconciliation, not revenge is the goal I now seek. I cannot forgive someone of my generation because I don't know his or her responsibility for crimes committed during the war. But their children and grandchildren were not culpable, and I've been impressed with the compassion shown by the younger people.

I first became aware of this when I visited Mark on his kibbutz in 1981 and encountered many West German youths there as volunteers. They loved Israel, I could see, and loved being in the Jewish state. I felt similar feelings of good will from the dozens of Polish high school students I met in Lodz on the Shalhevet trip. Their friendliness, inquisitiveness, and empathy gave me hope for the future. Even in the Baltics and Belarus, I met some brave, honest educators and hope the day will come when youth there too will understand the heritage and suffering of the Jews, the people who used to live among them.

And hope, which is at the root of my resolve, is another trait that has enabled me to make it through, even in the most awful times.

I understand those who see the future more darkly. I know that genocide has taken place since the Holocaust, even in Europe, and that savage wars are raging in Africa and the Middle East even now. But still I have hope.

I recently reread a letter I sent in March 1947 from the Badgastein DP camp, less than two years after the war's end, and before the ashes of destruction had cooled. Even then I expressed hope, for the world and for my family. I wrote in English to Norman's Uncle Max in San Francisco of my yearning that we'd soon be together.

I made clear that, "We must hope, because a man without hope is nothing." Perhaps when I penned that line the partisan hymn was on my mind. It was written in the Vilna Ghetto by the twenty-one-year-old Hirsh Glick, who had been inspired by the Warsaw Ghetto Uprising several days before. The song that always stirs me opens with a message of promise and persistence.

> *Never say this is the last road for you,*
> *Though leaden skies may cover over days of blue*
> *As the hour that we longed for is so near,*
> *Our steps will beat out like drums: we are here!*

Who Can Be Courageous?

Irwin (Yitzchak) Shelub

Courage is force of will energized by the heart.
Yet the courageous person is aware of danger and also
mindful of risk.
In facing adversity one may see darkness and be suffused
with foreboding pessimism.
Another will see light and be fortified by unwavering optimism.
Regardless, courage can fuel both to act.

THE STORY OF MIRA AND NUCHEM is about a dreamer who finds light in the midst of calamity and a pragmatist who recognizes the darkness of impending disaster. They had differences as day and night, right and left, woman and man. But they complimented each other as husband and wife. These were two ambitious young students caught in the torrent of surging events that destroyed their world when the world engaged in cataclysmic war. Their story is one of courage that compelled them to endure, fight, and overcome when all was lost, or so it seemed.

As the ghetto was being liquidated Mira stood with her sister Sara behind a false wall in the family's chicken coop hiding place. That night she heard the beseeching calls of her distraught father searching for his lost daughters. For fear of entrapment by the Nazis, she would remain silent and endure her father's anguish. In a nearby town, Nuchem overheard an official demanding that his father, Yitzchak, present his son for arrest. Yitzchak insisted that he was Nuchem Shelubski. Throughout his life Nuchem would bear the burden of his loving father's ultimate act. Yitzchak would be murdered in place of his son.

Mira and Nuchem met in the woods as partisans, fell in love, and became an inseparable couple. They vowed to be one another's "life companion." Nuchem would rise to the rank of *Kommandier Roti*, company commander of platoons, in the valiant Ordzhonikidze brigade. One day he led his fellow partisans through the swampy terrain of a densely wooded forest, escaping Nazi troops that had them surrounded. They were dirty, hungry, thirsty, and exhausted. Suddenly, he turned to Mira and said, "No more, here I end it!" As he raised his pistol to his head Mira staunchly declared, "But you promised me an *Itzikel* (a little Yitzchak)." Nuchem responded to Mira. He re-holstered his pistol to fight on. He would lead the group to safety. They survived.

In America, the strong partisan leader achieved so much happiness. But finally he lost his lifelong struggle with childhood acquired heart disease. At the age of fifty-seven, Nuchem, now called Norman, would not survive cardiac surgery. Mira was crushed. She responded by obtaining a B.A. in History in her seventh decade and a Master's degree in her eighth. She would teach others, from young school children to adult groups of all persuasions. They all listened to a story of courage, the story of Mira and Nuchem.

In those desperate times of war, a young couple shunned hopelessness to discover themselves. With incomparable devotion to each other they tirelessly built a new way of life. They created a new world in a new land. In their own way they would again be Jewish, but not as in their youth in the villages of Poland. America was a place where no demonic force bent on their destruction would stigmatize their identity by a decree to wear a yellow star, deprecate their being by rounding them up, and attempt to annihilate their very existence through genocidal mass murder. America was the place where they would recall their past, revitalize their heritage, and proudly reclaim their Jewish legacy. In this "golden land," as Norman would so often repeat, they fulfilled the promise to resurrect the family and life that was decimated in the land they left behind. It is an impossible story that improbably happened.

After all that they had experienced in life, perhaps most remarkable was their perpetual vigor, their kindness, and their capacity to be happy. What radiated forth was personal warmth that intimately embraced family, endearingly engaged friends, and charmingly greeted acquaintances. They encountered frustration, disappointment, and tragedy even in San Francisco. Yet a relentless drive rooted in an indomitable spirit brought them through hardship to arrive at special moments of joy. They lived with quiet courage that shined. Now, in these pages, it glows.

The triumph of our Mom and Pop is their blessing to us, their children. Their blessing is our treasure. Their story is our story. In this book, page by page, those momentous events in the life and times of Mira Raznov and Nuchem Shelubski are a story for you. Whether dreamer or pragmatist, when facing events that cause us to feel an inescapable sense of despair, we can ignite the courage within.

They did.

Would I Have Been a Partisan?

Mark Shelub

I NEVER REALLY UNDERSTOOD THEIR STORY. If you had asked me a few years ago how they survived, I might have answered that my parents were partisans in a forest. What happened to them during those years was a mystery to me, and I couldn't have given you much detail. I would answer you differently now.

About three years ago, with my mother, I attended a partisan reunion in New York. The second day, a young "third generation" woman addressed us. If faced with the same situation, she told us, surely she would have been a partisan. While family and friends were *kvelling*, I was disappointed and upset. Why? What could possibly be upsetting about a wonderful, talented descendant of partisan survivors affirming her heritage? And yet, I wondered how she could say what she would have done in such unimaginable circumstances.

What *was* the right thing to do? Suppose the Nazis warned anyone leaving the ghetto that his or her remaining family members would be executed. Suppose elderly parents, perhaps disabled, were dependent on others for food and survival. Would one still flee to the forest? Why didn't my uncle Simcha leave his mother in the line of those marked for death, and try to escape with my father if he could? Was his the wrong decision or an act of ultimate courage? Proclaiming one would be a partisan makes light of the terrible reality of the times. Can anyone really say what he or she would have done?

Would I have been a partisan? I don't know. I do not know how I would have behaved in those conditions. I pray to God I would have known the right course of action, and had the courage to see it through.

"They went like sheep to the slaughter." I always despised those words. Primo Levi writes even of the *Sonderkommandos*, Jews who were forced to help in the operation of the death camps, that, "no one is authorized to judge them, not even those who lived through the experiences of the camp and even less those who did not live through it. I would invite anyone who dares pass judgment to... imagine, if he can, that he lived for months or years in a ghetto, tormented by chronic hunger, fatigue, promiscuity and humiliation; that he has seen die around him, one by one, his beloved; that he is cut off from the world, unable to receive or transmit news; that, finally, he is loaded onto a train, eighty or a hundred persons to a boxcar, that he travels into the unknown, blindly, for sleepless days and nights; and that he is at last flung inside the walls of an indecipherable inferno..." God forbid my parents' story may ever be used to judge what others could or should have done.

This book results in part from the many days Fred Rosenbaum and his wife, Dorothy Shipps, interviewed my mother. I had the good fortune of attending almost all of those lengthy sessions. As we progressed, it became clear that they both cared deeply about my parents' story. They exhaustively explored and brought to life my parents' experiences—even the small details—but always within the context of European history, and with attention to the standards of historical accuracy. I am very grateful to Fred and Dorothy for their wonderful work and dedication. But as we progressed, it became clear to me this story was not only about my parents and history.

This is also a story of miracles. There were many situations of "being in the right place at the right time." My parents survived when 95 percent of Jews in their region did not. It was exceedingly rare that all the children of one family lived, but my mother, her brother, and sister all survived. As a believing and questioning Jew, I see my parents' survival amidst unspeakable tragedy as miraculous, and I see God's hand in their story.

After the last few years of reliving their story, I can now tell you more of what happened to my parents during the war and how they reacted. But I also know that on a deeper level I cannot tell you how or why they survived. Yes, there was incredible human bravery and self-sacrifice, but there were miracles too— and I thank God for them. I thank God my parents survived and gave me the gift of life.

This is the story of "Never The Last Road." I thank God my parents had roads to travel, and the courage and heroism to travel them even in impossible circumstances. May we draw inspiration for our own lives from the lives of my parents. There were millions who had no roads at all. I will never judge them. I will never forget them.

The European Chronology of the
Raznov and Shelubski Families

· *Italic typeface refers to national, regional, or local political events.*

· Serif type refers to events in the lives of Mira and the Raznov family.

· Sans-serif type indicates events relating to Nuchem Shelubski and his family.

UNDER CZARIST RUSSIA (UNTIL 1917)

Early 1890s Yitzchak Shelubski and his future wife, Elke, are born to traditional families in Novogrudok.

Mid-1890s Chaim Michoel Raznov is born in the village of Alexandrovich near Zhetel, and Chana Rashke Rabinovich is born in Zhetel, both to traditional families.

1903–05 The first Bundist circles are formed in Zhetel.

c. 1907 Chaim Michoel's father dies and the family moves from the village to Zhetel.

August 1, 1914 World War I begins.

1914–1915 The retreating Russian Army loots Zhetel.

September 1915–Fall 1918 The German occupation of Zhetel and environs brings famine, crime, and disease.

November 11, 1918 World War I ends and Germany is defeated; the Polish Republic is proclaimed a week earlier.

IN THE POLISH REPUBLIC (1918–1939)

1919–1921 Poland surprisingly defeats the Soviet Union in a border war and the new country includes Zhetel, Novogrudok, and Vilna.

1920 The Bund is reconstituted in Zhetel

May 10, 1920 Nuchem is born in Novogrudok to Yitzchak and Elke Shelubski.

1921 *The Yiddishe Folkshule chartered by the Warsaw-based TSYSHO begins operations throughout Poland and will later oversee the Sholem Aleichem School in Zhetel*

September 15, 1922 Simcha, Nuchem's younger brother, is born in Novogrudok.

January 13, 1922 Mira Raznov is born in Zhetel, the first child in a family including her parents, Chaim Michoel and Chana Rashke, and Chana's mother, Henye.

April 10, 1925 Sara Raznov, Mira's younger sister, is born in Zhetel.

May 31, 1926 War hero Marshal Josef Pilsudski takes power and will rule Poland for almost a decade bringing some stability.

January 7, 1927 Maeshe Raznov, Mira's younger brother, is born in Zhetel.

September 1927 Mira enters the kindergarten of the Sholem Aleichem Yiddishe Folkshule in its new building.

Fall 1927 The Zionist Hebrew language school Tarbut opens in Zhetel.

Late 1920s Josef Stalin emerges as the unchallenged leader of the Soviet Union.

January 30, 1933 Adolf Hitler takes power in Germany.

June 1933 The first of a series of devastating fires destroys two hundred homes in Zhetel, including that of the Raznov family.

June 1934 Mira graduates from the Sholem Aleichem Yiddishe Folkshule.

September 1934–June 1935 Mira attends the Polish elementary school in Zhetel and receives a certificate of graduation.

Winter 1934–35 Skating on thin ice, Mira falls into a lake, a boy trying to rescue her falls in too, but both are saved by Jews living near the shore, and revived with vodka.

May 12, 1935 Marshal Pilsudski dies. He was a protector of the Jewish community and a period of increased anti-Semitism begins. The country will be ruled by a junta of rightwing military officers until the end of the Polish republic in the fall of 1939.

May 1935 Visiting her aunt and uncle in Vilna, Mira witnesses the funeral procession for Pilsudski's heart.

September 1935 Mira begins the famed Yiddish language Real-Gymnasium in Vilna on a scholarship and lives with her aunt Mareh, a dentist, and her uncle, her mother's brother Yisroel Ber Rabinovich.

February 1936 In another disastrous fire in Zhetel, the Sholem Aleichem Yiddishe Folkshule is destroyed.

November 9–10, 1938 Kristallnacht: Across Germany, Storm Troopers and civilians burn many hundreds of synagogues, kill almost a hundred Jews on the streets, and plunder Jewish property.

September 1938–June 1939 In her last year at the Real-Gymnasium in Vilna, Mira lives in an apartment with her girlfriend from Zhetel, Feigel Kaplinski.

June 1939 Nuchem Shelubski graduates from the Polish gymnasium in Baranovich.

August 22, 1939 The Ribbentrop-Molotov Nazi-Soviet Non-Aggression Pact is signed with a secret provision dividing Poland between the two countries.

September 1, 1939 *World War II begins as German troops invade Poland.*

UNDER SOVIET OCCUPATION (SEPTEMBER 1939–JUNE 1941)

September 17, 1939 *Soviet troops invade Poland from the east and the USSR soon annexes the eastern third of Poland. Zhetel and Novogrudok become part of the Byelorussian Soviet Socialist Republic.*

Fall 1939 *The Bund and other Jewish institutions are crushed by the Soviets.*

Fall 1939 Nuchem begins the Stefan Batory University in Vilna.

Fall 1939 *Lithuania is briefly under Soviet control, but becomes independent again and is neutral. In return for stationing troops there, the Soviets award Vilna to Lithuania. A year later the USSR will annex Lithuania.*

Fall 1939 *Hundreds of thousands of Jewish refugees from Nazi-occupied western and central Poland flee into Soviet-occupied eastern Poland.*

September 1939–June 1941 Mira does not return to Vilna, but rather enrolls in the Polish gymnasium in Novogrudok, where she lives in a dormitory. But the school is transformed into a ten-year Soviet secondary school with Russian as the language of instruction.

February 1940–June 1941 *About eight hundred eighty thousand people are deported from the Byelorussian Soviet Socialist Republic to Siberia, about 30 percent, or a quarter million of them, Jews,* including some friends of the Raznov family. *Many deportees are refugees from Nazi-occupied western Poland.*

UNDER NAZI OCCUPATION (JUNE 1941–JULY 1944)

June 22, 1941 *Nazi Germany launches Operation Barbarossa, a full-scale invasion of the Soviet Union.*

June 30, 1941 *German forces arrive in Zhetel.*

July 14, 1941 *Jews in Zhetel are required to wear the yellow star.*

July 23, 1941 *One hundred twenty leading Zhetel Jews (including one woman) are arrested by SS, almost all murdered in the forest.* Chaim Michoel's name is on the list, but he is bedridden with bronchitis and when Mira tells the Polish collaborators he is ill, they move on and his life is saved.

July 26, 1941 Three weeks after the Nazi occupation of Novogrudok, fifty-two prominent Jews are assembled in the market square and executed. Nuchem's father, Yitzchak, impersonating his son, is killed in that massacre, and Nuchem is spared, but will bear the burden of "survivor guilt" for the rest of his life.

Late July–early August 1941 *Zhetel Jews are required to turn over valuables—fur, jewelry, etc.—to the Germans.*

August 1941 *The Judenrat in Zhetel is formed. Alter Dvoretzky soon becomes Judenrat head.*

Late July 1941 Nuchem is among the first group to escape Novogrudok for the forest.

December 5–7, 1941 *Fifty-one hundred Novogrudok Jews are massacred in the first sh'chiteh, or slaughter, and the Novogrudok ghetto is soon formed.* Nuchem, who had returned to Novogrudok on a recruiting mission, is rounded up along with his brother and mother. In the Novogrudok courthouse Nuchem is spared because a family friend pulls him out of the line of those awaiting execution into the line of those selected to work for the Germans. But his brother remains with their mother on the line of the doomed and they both perish.

December 7, 1941 *The Japanese bomb Pearl Harbor and the United States enters World War II.*

February 22, 1942 *The Jews of Zhetel are confined to a ghetto.*

April 20, 1942 *Alter Dvoretzky and six other underground leaders escape Zhetel for the forest.*

April 30, 1942 *A selection is carried out in Zhetel and women, children, infirm and elderly are taken from the ghetto to a forest and shot.* Bubbe Henye is killed in that action.

May 11, 1942 *Alter Dvoretzky is killed by non-Jewish partisans in the forest.*

Spring 1942 *Tuvia, Zus, and Asael Bielski form the nucleus of their partisan fighting group, moving frequently in the forests of White Russia.*

August 6–7, 1942 After hiding in the chicken coup near their home in the Zhetel ghetto, Mira and Sara flee to the labor camp of Dvorets.

August 7, 1942 *The second slaughter in Novogrudok; most of those killed are refugees from the surrounding countryside who had been forcibly evacuated to Novogrudok earlier in the year.*

August 6–8, 1942 *In the second slaughter in Zhetel, the ghetto is liquidated. About two hundred Jewish craftsmen, including Aaron Gertsovsky, are transferred to the ghetto in Novogrudok.*

August 20, 1942 Nuchem Shelubski and Aaron Gertsovsky enter the Novogrudok ghetto and recruit a group of thirteen, with whom they flee to the forest.

August 30, 1942 Nuchem, Aaron and the other escapees from Novogrudok meet and join Hershel Kaplinski's group of twenty-five, largely Zhetlers, in the forest.

Early or mid-fall 1942 Mira and Sara are rescued by two partisans and taken from Dvorets to the Kaplinski camp in the Lipiczanska forest.

Mid-fall, 1942 Mira, Nuchem, and Sara serve in the fighters' unit; Mira's father, mother, and younger brother are in the family camp.

Mid-fall, 1942 Mira and Nuchem, known as Nonye, meet while on guard duty and soon fall in love.

November 21, 1942 Dr. Yechezkel Atlas, another partisan commander, is killed in battle.

November 1942 The Atlas, Kaplinski and other small units come under the supervision of the the Orlansky Otriad.

December 1942 The Germans attack the partisans in the Lipiczanska forest; Mira and Sara flee their base and experience a terrible ordeal in the winter forest.

December 1942 Hershel Kaplinski is killed in that battle.

Winter 1942–43 Maeshe, in the family camp, develops severe frostbite, although his mother cares for him and he is cured without medication.

Fall 1942–Summer 1943 As platoon leader, Nuchem participates in ambushes against the Germans in the Lipiczanska forest.

May 1943 The German army raids the family camp of partisans in the Lipiczanska Forest and Mira's mother, Chana Rashke, is killed.

May–June 1943 In response to anti-Semitism in the Orlanski brigade, about twenty-five fighters, including Nuchem and Mira, undertake a harsh journey through swampland, meet Tuvia Bielski in the Naliboki Forest, and register with the Soviets as partisans.

August 1, 1943 The "Big Hunt" begins, a German raid on the partisans in the Naliboki Forest.

Late August 1943 The Bielski group splits into a fighting unit with Zus Bielski as head of reconnaissance, and a family camp led by his older brother, Tuvia. The fighters' camp, named Ordzhonikidze, moves about fifty miles to the Bielskis' home area of Stankevich.

August 1943–July 1944 Nuchem is *Kommandier Roti*, or company commander, the head of fifty fighters carrying out missions against the Germans throughout the Naliboki forest.

June 6, 1944 *D-Day—Allied troops land in Normandy and begin the drive toward Berlin.*

Mid-July 1944 The Soviets liberate western Belorussia and Mira and her family and Nuchem are free. Nuchem and Mira vow to remain together for life, as do other couples in the partisan camp.

FROM LIBERATION TO IMMIGRATION (1944–1949)

Late July 1944 Mira and Nuchem return to his former house in Novogrudok, now dilapidated and split into three units, where Maeshe and Sara are caring for the ailing Chaim Michoel.

August 1944–May 1945 Mira and Nonye work as bureaucrats in Soviet-occupied Baranovich.

February 1945 *At the Yalta Conference of the "Big Three," Roosevelt and Churchill allow Stalin to retain the eastern third of Poland annexed by the Soviet Union in 1939.*

May 8, 1945 *VE-Day: The end of the war in Europe.*

September 2, 1945 *Japan formally surrenders ending World War II.*

Mid-1945–mid-1946 *Acts of violence, including a massacre in Kielce, are committed against surviving Jews throughout Poland.*

Mid-1945–mid-1947 Mira and Nuchem reside in the DP camp of Badgastein, Austria. Mira works as a translator for the American UNRRA social worker Mrs. Adams and also transcribes the accounts of former partisans. Nuchem is a Zionist activist.

Late 1945 The news of Chaim Michoel's death reaches Mira and Nuchem in Badgastein. Maeshe and then Sara soon arrive in the DP camp and all three children mourn their father.

Spring 1946 Maeshe and Sara leave Badgastein to study at the Technische Universitaet in Munich where they will remain for four years.

November 29, 1947 The UN adopts a partition plan dividing Palestine into Jewish and Arab states but the plan is not accepted by the Palestinians or Arab countries and not implemented.

Mid-1947–January 1949 After Badgastein is closed, Mira and Nuchem are transferred to the DP camp of Parsch near Salzburg where Mira works for the Sochnut, or Jewish Agency for Palestine, and Nuchem continues his Zionist activities.

April 6, 1948 Yitzchak Shelubski (later Irwin Shelub) is born to Mira and Nuchem in the Parsch DP camp.

May 14, 1948 In Tel Aviv, David Ben-Gurion declares the independence of the State of Israel and the armies of four neighboring Arab lands immediately attack the new country. During the War of Independence, ending in March 1949, six thousand Israelis, about 1 percent of the Jewish population, are killed.

June 25, 1948 President Truman signs the first DP Act admitting two hundred thousand Jewish refugees into the United States.

Fall 1948 Norman's uncle in San Francisco, furniture store owner Max Shaff, agrees to sponsor the Shelubski family's immigration to America.

January 1949 Mira, Nuchem and Yitzchak travel through Germany and sail from Bremerhaven to New York.

The Shelub–Raznov Ancestry
A reader's guide to those mentioned in the narrative

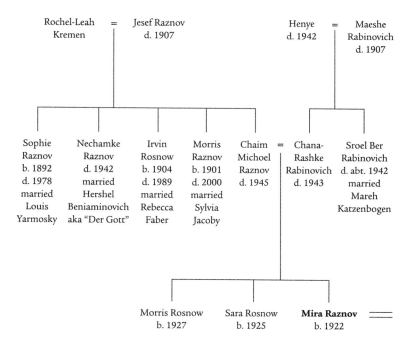

Rochel-Leah = Jesef Raznov   Henye = Maeshe
Kremen   d. 1907   d. 1942   Rabinovich
                                            d. 1907

Sophie   Nechamke   Irvin   Morris   Chaim = Chana-   Sroel Ber
Raznov   Raznov   Rosnow   Raznov   Michoel   Rashke   Rabinovich
b. 1892   d. 1942   b. 1904   b. 1901 Raznov   Rabinovich d. abt. 1942
d. 1978   married   d. 1989   d. 2000 d. 1945   d. 1943   married
married   Hershel   married   married   Mareh
Louis   Beniaminovich Rebecca   Sylvia   Katzenbogen
Yarmosky aka "Der Gott" Faber   Jacoby

Morris Rosnow   Sara Rosnow   Mira Raznov   =
b. 1927   b. 1925   b. 1922

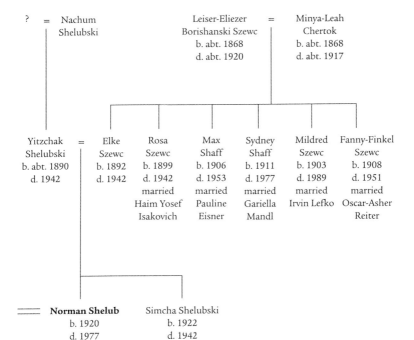

? = Nachum
    Shelubski

Leiser-Eliezer = Minya-Leah
Borishanski Szewc   Chertok
b. abt. 1868   b. abt. 1868
d. abt. 1920   d. abt. 1917

Yitzchak =	Elke	Rosa	Max	Sydney	Mildred	Fanny-Finkel
Shelubski	Szewc	Szewc	Shaff	Shaff	Szewc	Szewc
b. abt. 1890	b. 1892	b. 1899	b. 1906	b. 1911	b. 1903	b. 1908
d. 1942	d. 1942	d. 1942	d. 1953	d. 1977	d. 1989	d. 1951
		married	married	married	married	married
		Haim Yosef	Pauline	Gariella	Irvin Lefko	Oscar-Asher
		Isakovich	Eisner	Mandl		Reiter

Norman Shelub   Simcha Shelubski
b. 1920   b. 1922
d. 1977   d. 1942

Afterword and Acknowledgments

Fred Rosenbaum

WHEN MIRA AND HER FAMILY invited me to collaborate on her memoir I had recently co-authored the books of two others who had fought back from the forest. So I was familiar with interwar Poland, the partisan experience, the DP camps, and the survivors' struggle in America. I could see that hers was a stirring and uncommon story even within a field studded with sagas of resourcefulness and courage. Mira's life history seemed to call for examination and I was eager to be her partner in that endeavor.

She was born into a vibrant sector of Polish Jewry that has too often been overlooked. Although a child of the shtetl, her family was neither religious nor Zionist. She was imbued instead with deep devotion to the Yiddish language and its literature. Her schooling at the renowned Yiddish-language Real-Gymnasium in the heart of Vilna, the "Jerusalem of the North," put her in touch with the major Jewish intellectual currents of her day. During the Nazi occupation, the escape of her entire family from the ghetto was little short of miraculous. While most Jews in the resistance served in Soviet brigades, she joined all-Jewish or largely Jewish battalions. Never a forest wife who settled for any male protector, she would meet, fall in love with, and marry a man to whom she was exceedingly well suited; theirs would be a passionate love story ending only with his untimely death. In postwar America, Mira— remarkably ambitious, energetic, and focused—completed her education and succeeded in business and counseling. Seven decades after her liberation, she still practices her profession and gives presentations on the partisans.

Beyond her exceptional biography, I was intrigued by a revealing resource Mira brought to this project: the stories of eight other partisans that she transcribed in the Badgastein DP camp in 1945. I felt that these accounts, written less than a year after the liberation, would add much to the historical record.

Mira ardently recounted her experiences to my wife, Dorothy Shipps, and me during eight daylong interviews held in her San Francisco home over the course of three years beginning in 2011. The audiotapes of those discussions are the core source of this book.

Her three children added a great deal of information and insight about their parents and enriched the volume in the process. Dr. Mark Shelub actively participated in almost every one of our interviews with his mother and videotaped them as well. Dr. Irwin Shelub shared with me his perceptive observations about Mira and Norman's character traits, and improved the manuscript with many helpful suggestions. Elaine Shelub vividly recalled precious stories about growing up in this tight-knit American Jewish family.

Dorothy and I conducted interviews with others who have known Mira at different points in her long life: Fania Brantsovsky, who still resides in Vilna, attended the Real-Gymnasium a year ahead of Mira in the late 1930s. Chiena Ratner of Brooklyn was Mira's classmate at the gymnasium in Novogrudok from 1939 to 1941 and later her comrade in the Ordzhonikidze detachment in the Naliboki Forest. Stella Raukhman of the Jewish Family and Children's Services in San Francisco has long supervised Mira's counseling of émigrés from the former Soviet Union. My colleague at Lehrhaus Judaica, Rabbi Peretz Wolf-Prusan, co-led with Mira the Shalhevet tour to Poland and Israel for high school juniors and seniors. And Mitch Braff, the founder and director of the Jewish Partisan Education Foundation, launched and propelled Mira's public speaking career.

We also conducted a productive interview with Mira's sister, Sara Rosnow. Although it was not possible to interview their brother, Morris Rosnow, I learned a considerable amount from his videotaped testimony recorded in 1998 by the USC Shoah Foundation, which in the same year also filmed the valuable testimony of Sara and, in 1996, that of Mira. I thank the staff members at the Bobst Library of New York University for their efficiency and friendliness in accessing these interviews for me. Dr. Mark Shelub made available to me the videotape of the informative interview of his Aunt Sara that he conducted in 2008. Other important videotapes for my purposes were Mark's eight hour-long cassettes of the Shelub family trip to Vilna, Novogrudok, and Zhetel in 2001, a vital record of Mira's return, accompanied by her children and grandchildren, to the key places of her youth. His videotape of Mira's eightieth birthday party was of further help in understanding the special quality of her interaction with family and friends.

Two audiotapes provided by the Shelub family were also highly significant. One was that of Aaron Gertsovsky of Novogrudok, who infiltrated the ghetto with Norman to search for recruits, and later fought with alongside him in Hershel Kaplinski's partisan detachment. The second was a brief audiotape of Norman himself, recorded in the early 1970s, which described in detail a major mission he led in the Lipiczanska Forest. Beyond providing essential facts, simply hearing his voice made a deep impression on me.

THERE WERE MANY publications that helped me place Mira's life in historical context. For my research on her youth in Zhetel I benefited from that shtetl's Yizkor book (in Hebrew with an extensive English summary), *A Memorial to the Jewish Community in Zetel* (Zetel Association in Israel, 1957). Several of its photographs are reprinted in the early chapters of this volume. Similarly, *Novogrudok: The History of a Shtetl*, compiled by Jack Kagan (Valentine Mitchell, 2006), put into perspective her two years as a gymnasium student there, as well as Norman's upbringing and family life, ending with the mass murders of 1941–42. On the Polish shtetl in general, I was aided by *A Jewish Boyhood in Poland* by Norman Salsitz (Syracuse University, 1999), *Konin* by Theo Richmond (Pantheon, 1995), and *Shtetl* by Eva Hoffman (Vintage, 1999).

The stimulating milieu of Vilna in which Mira found herself in the late 1930s is well described in Lucy Dawidowicz's *From that Place and Time: A Memoir, 1938–1947* (Rutgers University Press, 2008). On the Jewish community of interwar Poland as a whole, I found Celia S. Heller's *On the Edge of Destruction* (Shocken, 1980) indispensable. For the Holocaust in Mira's region I drew upon Shalom Cholowsky's *Jews of Bielorussia During World War II* (Harwood, 1998), a work that includes much material on the resistance.

Regarding the partisans, I utilized my own earlier works: *Taking*

Risks co-authored with Joseph Pell (RDR Books, 2004) and *Here, There Are No Sarahs* co-authored with Sonia Shainwald Orbuch (RDR Books and the Judah L. Magnes Museum, 2009). Among the many other partisan memoirs, four were especially helpful: Nahum Kohn and Howard Roiter's *A Voice from the Forest* (Holocaust Library, 1980), Harold Werner's *Fighting Back* (Columbia, 1992), Shalom Yoran's *The Defiant* (St. Martin's Press, 1996), and Mira's friend Sulia Rubin's *Against the Tide* (Posner, 1980). Two informative histories in the field are Kenneth Slepyan's *Stalin's Guerillas* (University Press of Kansas, 2006) and Allan Levine's *Fugitives in the Forest* (Lyons Press, 2009). On the Bielski partisans in particular, I relied primarily upon Nechama Tec's path-breaking *Defiance* (Oxford, 1993) and Peter Duffy's popular *Bielski Brothers* (HarperCollins, 2004).

For Mira and Norman's two years in the Lipiczanska and Naliboki forests, there is no substitute for *Surviving the Holocaust with the Russian Jewish Partisans* (Valentine Mitchell, 1998) by Jack Kagan and Dov Cohen. Part memoir, part history, that work includes a detailed description of several of Norman's missions in the Ordzhonikidze detachment. I thank Irwin for bringing it to my attention and sending me a copy.

A memoir that helped me understand the atmosphere of grief and hope at the Badgastein DP camp is *Alicia* by Alicia Appleman (Bantam, 1988). On the new lives that Holocaust survivors made in America, William B. Helmreich's *Against All Odds* (Simon and Schuster, 1992), was highly illuminating.

One original document was both meaningful and moving. As I was completing the manuscript, Irwin found and sent me a revealing letter Mira had written from Badgastein in 1947 to Norman's uncle in San Francisco; she and I include a quotation from it on the final page of the foregoing narrative.

The Shelub family and I are honored to feature two sketches by Mira's cousin, the late Israeli artist Alexander Bogen, who was himself the commander of a partisan unit in the forests near Vilna. We deeply appreciate the permission granted by his son, Michael Bogen, and grandson, Amir Bogen, to reprint these exceptional works of art.

This volume owes a great deal to Professor Dovid Katz, formerly of Oxford University and one of the world's leading Yiddishists. In 2011, I spoke with him in his Vilna home about Lithuania's obfuscation of the Holocaust, and for the next three years he gave generously of his time in answering questions that came up in the course of my writing.

I greatly appreciate the corrections, suggestions, and encouragement of those who read the book in draft: Steven Zipperstein, Daniel E. Koshland Professor in Jewish Culture and History at Stanford University; my friend Judy Janec, former Director of Library and Archives at the JFCS Tauber Holocaust Library; Paul Orbuch, Founding President of the Jewish Partisans Educational Foundation; and my sister, Bobbi Leigh Zito. Katie Cook proofread the volume and I am grateful for her conscientious work.

The Jewish Family and Children's Services Holocaust Center is Lehrhaus Judaica's partner in this publication, and the Shelub family and I want to thank Morgan Blum, Director of Education, and JFCS Executive Director Dr. Anita Friedman, for their unwavering support.

I especially want to thank my wife, Dr. Dorothy Shipps, who took part in every interview with Mira and her children, and painstakingly edited the numerous versions of this manuscript, after all, a woman's story. Her many talents and good judgment enhanced the volume immeasurably.

Above all, I thank Mira for the rare opportunity to research and record her extraordinary life, and for her exuberance and affection as we worked together. Her intellect and intelligence, her sharp memory and gifts as a storyteller, made her an ideal co-author. She was steadfast in her commitment to this project, as with everything else she has undertaken.

Appendix: The Partisan Testimonies

IN THE FALL OF 1945, I was living with my husband, Nuchem Shelubski, in the Badgastein DP camp in the Austrian Alps. I worked
full-time as a translator for a devoted American UNRRA social
worker, Mrs. Adams. In my few leisure hours I interviewed others in the camp, all former Jewish partisans or those who spoke
of Jewish partisans killed in action. Told so close in time to the
events they describe, their stories form a record of the thoughts
and passions of Jewish partisans at war's end.

Still fresh in their minds was their struggle to prove, in the
words of one fighter, "that a Jew is not a coward." My interview-
ees speak of exploits against great odds, and the supreme sacri-
fice made by many of their comrades. Most of them focus on the
sights, sounds, and tactics of warfare in the forest, often including the minute details of battles won and lost. They proudly
list the number of German soldiers killed, the enemy weapons
captured, and the Soviet medals awarded. The last story offers a

woman's view of the aftereffects of intense combat and that one has entered my heart most deeply.

I transcribed the stories in Yiddish and, two-thirds of a century later, Lehrhaus Judaica engaged the Jewish educator, author, and translator Ken Blady to render eight of them into English for this volume. My co-author, Fred Rosenbaum, has added annotations in square brackets [ ] to clarify the narratives and place them in context. A facsimile of the original Yiddish document I wrote, along with the first draft of the English translation, is on file at the Tauber Holocaust Library and Education Program of the Jewish Family and Children's Services in San Francisco.

I am thankful for the opportunity I've had to tell my own story. Here, I share the experiences of eight of my former comrades-in-arms.

—MS

1. "Speaker," born in Pshemishl, Poland
As told by Gracer Rubin

It was the beginning of the year 1944. We were not able to implement the command from the Kiev headquarters to prevent the Germans from crossing the [long] Bug River near Kovel.

The battalion found itself in a very critical situation. To our rear was the Bug and facing us was the German front line. [After several months we had no choice but] to try to link up with the Red Army and it was decided that we would tear through the Shatzker forest.

On May 18, 1944, the Germans deployed four infantry regiments and two motorized divisions from the front with the intention of wiping us out. Our frame of mind was one of desperation, but while not discounting the overwhelming strength of the enemy, we doggedly took up the battle, which was fierce.

With only a few grenades we fought against German Tiger Tanks [heavily armored and capable of massive firepower]. The battle took ten days and we ran out of ammunition. That's when we decided to break through at any price in the direction of Brisk. However, the path was daunting: eighteen kilometers in deep mud. It was decided that all of the severely wounded, about sixty men, had to be left in the forest. We also left behind with them a commander, Zvade Vicekuv, and a Jewish doctor with the nom de guerre "Speaker."

The doctor was given an order that in the case of an enemy assault, he would have to poison all the wounded [because if they fell into German hands they would likely be tortured and could reveal valuable information about the partisans and the peasants allied with them].

But we would return, we told the doctor, and if the Germans had not attacked the group, we would gather our wounded comrades and care for them in whatever manner he deemed necessary.

A small number of us managed to cut though the enemy fire and, when the raid was over, ten other partisans and I received an order to go back to the Shatzker forest to find out what had happened to our wounded comrades. When we arrived, we beheld a most horrific sight: all the wounded were lying poisoned, and the medical doctor "Speaker" was lying there next to them with a revolver in his stiff hand. He had followed the command from headquarters and, not willing to part with his wounded friends in the battle, he chose to end his life with them.

2. Erich Stein, born in Hamburg, Germany, 1915

As told by Zorach Kremen, from the shtetl of Bilitza near Lida.
[Kremen was Norman's close friend in the DP camp.]

Before Hitler came to power Stein had studied at the maritime school in Hamburg, and then left for Italy where he completed his education. He went to work as the First Officer of an English cruise liner that sailed the Mediterranean and Black Seas.

In 1939, Stein was on a visit to Poland just when the war broke out. He [fled to Soviet-occupied Poland and] settled in Slonim in western White Russia. [In the fall of 1941,] after the Germans occupied Slonim, Stein was forced to work in a *Beutelager* [German for a camp or warehouse for storing booty] sorting captured Soviet ammunition, bombs, and cartridges.

When we founded [Slonim's] underground Anti-Fascist Committee, [whose members smuggled some of these weapons, under their clothing or in baskets, to the partisans] we had not been acquainted with Stein. We were suspicious of him but we didn't know why. [Perhaps it was because he was a German Jew.]

But after the second massacre in Slonim, which was perpetrated against the Jews on June 28 [and 29], 1942 [killing eight thousand], we drew him into our clandestine work. It turns out that during the entire period that Stein was in the storehouse he engaged in sabotage against the Germans as much as he could. Among other things, he managed to hide two thousand bullets for automatic weapons and two thousand tracer bullets [each with a pyrotechnic charge enabling a marksman to follow its trajectory and correct his aim]. This ammunition was more valuable than jewels in those days, both to the Germans and to us. He turned it over to the Jewish partisans together with a cache of weapons.

Before he went into the forest himself, Stein asked our permission to blow up the storehouse, which would also cause severe damage to the [nearby] Slonimer train station, supply depots, and two railway bridges. Yet the Germans had herded the remaining Jews into the courtyard of the storehouse and if Stein had blown it up, his action certainly would have wiped them out. The decision was a very painful one for the Jewish leadership. Comrade [Niania] Tsirinsky, as the duly appointed representative of the Slonimer Anti-Fascist Committee, didn't want to accept the responsibility for this plan, and there was no support for it in the forest.

But Stein was restless. One time he showed up in camp very pleased that he'd been able to construct a 45-millimeter canon, operable in one week. Stein was an expert marksman. With his left hand and only one shot he could hit a telephone wire on the mark. He took part in all of the battles of our group and proved himself a superb artillery commander.

An intrepid partisan, Stein was with me during a mission, which took place near Baranovich, in December 1942, when we blew up a small train on a bridge. Stein took it upon himself to blow up the train with a grenade, not having any other explosives. We had received thirty artillery pieces from our peasant allies. He fashioned a launcher from parts of two of the artillery pieces, blew up the German train and then, using the same method, he blew up two others.

On one occasion, after blowing up a train with German military personnel inside, we had an encounter which forced us to withdraw and we came up against a squadron of Germans and Ukrainians. We fled and scattered. Stein was shot to death.

The leadership of the group awarded Stein the Order of Hero

of the Soviet Union, and Partisan of the Patriotic War. Because of the prevailing anti-Semitism, the commander decided to pass up bestowing upon him the Order of Lenin. [In actuality, Stein was nominated for the Order of Hero of the Soviet Union, the highest honor the Soviet Union could bestow, but it was not awarded to him.]

3. Yoselevich, born in the shtetl of Bilitza near Lida, Poland, 1926

During the early period of the German occupation I was in the Zhetel ghetto [about thirty-five kilometers] from Lida. On July 11, 1942, five men and I fled with the goal of joining the partisans. For about five weeks our group was lost in the forest until we encountered the first Jewish partisans and together we took off for the Lipiczanska forest where a Jewish group was being organized under the leadership of Hershel Kaplinski.

On June 5, 1943 [a month after Kaplinski's death], our group of twelve was attacked by sixty Ukrainians who had escaped from a nearby prison. Lacking weapons, we scattered in different directions. In the onslaught, two men were killed and one woman was wounded.

Joining the Red Army [after our group was liberated by the Soviets], I was soon mobilized. On September 26, 1944, I went off to the front, which at that time was situated on the west bank of the Vistula. There, I was a liaison between the front line and the Fifth Artillery Division.

On February 8, 1945, during the German artillery counterassault, the telephone wires were damaged and communication was cut off.

The commander called me over and said, "The enemy fire is very heavy. We won't be able to accomplish anything until we reestablish communication with the front line. I believe that you, as a disciplined combatant, will be able carry out this important assignment." Disregarding the artillery fire and the noise from the explosives, tripping with every step, and crawling on all fours, I prepared myself for the task. Grabbing hold of the telephone cable with my left hand, and with the automatic rifle in my right hand, I managed to get back to my cohort and re-establish contact.

Thus, the command was carried out. But after going some two hundred meters from that place, I was wounded by a grenade splinter and I fell unconscious in the field. I was lying there like that for a couple of hours until a medic came and took me away. I was taken to a field hospital where I was operated on by a Jewish doctor, Captain Friedman. After a long stay in several hospitals, I was deemed unfit for active duty on June 18, 1945 [after VE Day], and as an invalid was discharged from the Red Army on December 9, 1945.

4. Yossel Sapozhnik, born in Berezne near Rovno, Poland Partisan of the Medvedev group in the Dimaner forest, twenty-five kilometers from Rovno.

In October 1943, a command came down to attack a long German convoy on the highway leading to Berezne, where a German command post was situated. On Shabbes our company of ninety with the commander in the lead, went out towards the road where the vehicles were to pass through. I was the only Jew in this company. Altogether, we had in our possession some explosives, a canon, some automatic rifles and handguns. The plan was to place mines on the highway and then to hide so that the Germans would not be able to see us. We camouflaged ourselves by the side of the road, and on the other side was a large field. When the Germans scattered, we thought, we could mow them down in that open space.

It was a cold night and our limbs were freezing. The air felt like a knife cutting into our organs, but we weren't able to light a fire because at any moment German thugs could come and snuff us out. And so we lay in wait there for a day and a night.

We finally came to the distressing realization that shooting would be virtually impossible because our fingers were frozen and we wouldn't be able to fire a rifle.

Suddenly, there was a great noise made by approaching vehicles. In a second everyone revived and we all stared in the same direction. We were ready to follow through with the ambush, which we had waited so long to carry out.

Our side remained still. The order was not to start shooting until the German drivers arrived at a predetermined spot. We were divided into groups and each had a specific objective, but we were supposed to open fire in unison. The fifth vehicle passed my position where I was lying right next to the commander. The vehicles, going at normal speed, finally arrived at the spot that we had picked. We opened fire, and out of a truck jumped five big *Schweinhunde* [German soldiers, literally pig-dogs] who came racing over to our crew. Three were shot down by the canon, and two by my automatic rifle. And then the commander ordered everyone to get up. We made a dash forward to get closer to the vehicles so that we could lob the grenades.

The first grenade that I threw at a German truck exploded and a couple of soldiers, including an officer, fell dead. The same was the case with the rest of the vehicles and their passengers. Everything was disrupted and the murderers were dead, [some of them] ripped to pieces with our bayonets until they died. We placed the enemy dead together and under their corpses planted explosives so if any Germans later came to take them away, they too would be blown up. The vehicles were so badly damaged that we had no use for them. We retreated and later that night, we arrived back at camp.

[To repeat:] I was the only Jew in the group. I received a special award for the first grenade which came from my hand, and which demolished a vehicle and all the Germans inside it.

5. [Zelig] Milikovsky, born in Slonim near Baranovich, Russia, 1914

As told by Zorach Kremen from Bilitza near Lida

After the second slaughter in Slonim, on June 28 [and 29], 1942, Comrade Milikovsky's carpentry workshop, illegally situated outside the ghetto [on *Barg* or Mountain Street] would be the only hiding place for we partisans. With some other comrades he had built it in a hidden bunker, which in the course of time would also serve as a storehouse for our weapons. As an expert marksman and saboteur, Milikovsky would personally handle the weapons, hide them, and distribute them in the forest when it was time to use them.

In August 1943, the Germans discovered and surrounded the bunker where Comrade Milikovsky and two others were hiding at the time. But he remained calm, and together with his comrades managed to outwit the murderers by stealthily escaping through an underground trapdoor and fleeing into the forest. Comrade

Milikovsky reached the 51st Jewish Partisans Group [in the Baranovich area]. There, he took part in all of their missions and distinguished himself as a sharpshooter and fearless partisan. [The 51st, with one hundred seventy-one fighters, lost seventy-two combatants, or 42 percent, a significantly higher death toll than most other partisan groups.]

[He continued to fight as a partisan until] his liberation by the Red Army, which he then joined. He fought on the White Russian front, where he took part in protecting the Bug and Vistula rivers. At the Vistula, he was killed in a battle with the barbarians.

The top brass decorated him posthumously for his bravery with the Order of the Red Star and the Partisan of the Patriotic War 1st Class.

6. Eliezer Lantzevitsky, born in Volkovysk, Poland, 1923

During the German occupation [which began in June 1941] I was in Volkovysk in the Bialystok district of the Byelorussian Soviet Socialist Republic. On September 1, 1942, when the decree was sent out to establish a ghetto in Volkovysk, my brother, and two friends and I decided to flee to the forest and join a partisan unit. Outside the city a German patrol detected us, and, because we ignored their command that we "stand still," they opened fire. My brother was shot dead, but the rest of us managed to get away. After eight days of wandering in the forest, we encountered [Soviet] partisans from the [battle-hardened] Bulak group who brought us over to their camp and accepted us.

In that group, I was accused of being a spy and told that I would be shot. Only after a long and intensive interrogation, during which I maintained that I am a Jew, and that I had come to the partisans to wreak vengeance on the Germans for the blood of our deceased, did they stop accusing me.

But the commander [Pavel Bulak, a known anti-Semite] still had some doubts: he couldn't believe that a Jew could be a good combatant, and what's more, be vengeful. He believed that a Jew would escape into the forest only to save his own skin. I replied that this was a slander and that I'd show him what Jews were capable of, and how they could take revenge.

From the day I received a rifle, I took part in all of the battles, always in the front lines, and I proved that a Jew is not a coward. In December 1942, I took part in destroying a security guard post in Halinka, between Slonim and Dereczyn, where we killed thirty policemen.

At that point, I was appointed the explosives specialist and in a short time my comrades and I wiped out three platoons of Germans on the Baranovich-Bialystok [railway] line.

For a couple of months before liberation, I was transferred to the specialist group NKGB [the Soviet Secret Police] where the commander took my opinions seriously, and I served as a demolitions man and blew up German trains along the Lida-Grodno line. In one of the last convoys, thirteen tank carriers were destroyed and more than three hundred Germans were killed and wounded. [I returned to my partisan unit and] just before the liberation, after crossing over the Baranovich-Lida line, we stumbled into a large group of AK [the anti-Semitic Polish Home Army] and fought a battle, which lasted about half an hour. But then we had to retreat, leaving behind our weapons and one injured person. The commander gave the order to retrieve the weapons and the wounded partisan. When he didn't call on me, I volunteered and took off with the other partisans to fulfill the command with honor.

I also took part in a battle with a German garrison allied with White Russian police in a village between Slonim and Dereczyn. We decided to surround it and assault at dawn, attacking from all directions. The battle stretched out for a couple of hours. The result was that we killed ninety-three Germans, captured twenty-four, and brought back two 82.2 mm light canons, several 51 mm explosive launchers, and two ammunition magazines. We were united with the Red Army on July 9, 1944 in the Lipiczanska forest. For my exploits, I was awarded the Order of the Red Star and the Partisan of the Patriotic War medal.

7. How My Friend Feivel Shreiber Was Killed
As told by a partisan from Berezne near Rovno

Our partisan unit [comprised of members of the group led by Colonel Dmitry Nikolaevich Medvedev, which earlier had rescued one hundred sixty Jews from various ghettos] was situated in the forest near the Polish village, Rudnia Bobrovska. On March 28, 1943, a command came from Moscow for our combat team to carry out an important mission in the [nearby] city of Rovno. The objective was to destroy the headquarters of the Reichskommissariat [German regional administration], in particular the quarters of the Reichskommissar [provincial governor, Erich] Koch. On the day we received the order, a group of seventy, led by the commander of our division, marched into the Dimaner forest in the direction of Rovno. In the group were four young women—two radio technicians and two medics. The trek was very difficult; more than once we had clashes with potato-heads [bands of pro-fascist peasants in the forest], and also Germans. Because the enemy was strong and we were a small number of partisans, we were forced to put a call out on Moscow Radio for a group of one hundred twenty men to help us. Among those who came to our rescue were two Jews, one of them being the nineteen-year-old Feivel Shreiber. Due to his courage and boldness he was the commander.

To battle the enemy posed such danger that our mission had to be postponed. But we deemed November 7, 1943 an auspicious moment to murder Reichskommissar Koch and German General Max Ilgen. That turned out to be the day when the Red Army liberated Kiev and was also the anniversary [as determined by the Gregorian or New Style calendar] of the October Revolution [in 1917]. [Koch survived the partisan attack but Ilgen was abducted in the raid and sent to Moscow for interrogation and execution.]

We had a great celebration. But in order to take revenge for the [kidnapping and imminent] death of the general, the Germans sent a couple of divisions against us to try to wipe us out. On the 8th of November, our spy network informed us that we were surrounded by the German thugs. Soon afterwards, there was a heavy bombardment. [Bombs dropped by Messerschmitt fighter planes] exploded in the woods everywhere around us. The forest was wrapped in a coat of fire and smoke and we found ourselves in a catastrophic and hopeless situation. Some individuals were ambushed; we saw dead and injured on our side. German intelligence got closer and closer. Because of the woeful shortage of bullets we knew we'd be at a great disadvantage in open combat, but our desperate circumstances gave us no choice. We went over our assault strategy with Feivel Shreiber. A ferocious battle out in the open field ensued.

The two Jewish lads rushed ahead with automatics in their hands and, by throwing themselves at the enemy, gave the rest of us a model of courage. But the adversary was not silent. A round of explosives smashed into the Jewish partisan commander, Feivel Shreiber.

The partisans' bravery [led to victory]. When it was over, the Germans left behind four hundred fifty of their dead and wounded, among them officers; three crates of small arms; fourteen machine-guns; many automatic rifles; and forty-five wagonloads of ammunition. The fallen hero received the medal of Partisan of the Patriotic War, 1st Class.

8. The Death of the Blind Partisan Koleh, born in Warsaw
As told by his nurse

In White Russia, deep in the mud of the Lipiczanska Forest, there lies a long narrow island. This is where fate cast me as a partisan, working in the hospital of the Lenin Brigade located there in May 1943.

The old gray swamps are coming to life. The still waters are covered with light green cobwebs, their little heads surfacing, small green leaves sending ahead barely blooming yellow flowers. How beautiful they look. Whose crown will reach highest to the sun? Now their branches are starting to sprout light-green flowers that seem astonished and curious as they look down from their heights to the earth. What will the new spring bring to the world today? The air is filled with birdsongs heralding new life. Now there's a beautiful harmony in the Lipiczanska Forest every day.

Life in the hospital was flowing calmly, undisturbed. Every once in a while a new sick or wounded patient was wheeled in. On one occasion three were brought in at once. An accident with a bayonet had set off an explosion underneath them and left one deaf, a second one blind, and a third with burns covering his whole body.

Koleh was the name of the most tragic one. It was my fate to sit by his side for a couple of nights and days. Here, next to this bed of suffering, of terrible human tragedy, I got a taste of what extreme torment is like. His first question to me was: "Nurse, is it possible that I will be able to see the blue in the sky again, the light of the sun, the green of the trees?"

"I remember that the world is so beautiful... In the battlefield, in the greatest battles, I bravely resisted death—today I blew up eight trains but after the ninth I myself was made a casualty..."

"*Ach*, my beloved mother—where are you? Will I ever see you again?... If you knew from so far away that your only son is suffering so much... Mother dear. *Yiddishe mameh.*"

"Nurse, what time is it?"

"Six o'clock, Koleh."

"Is it already early in the morning?"

"Yes."

"Nurse, why is it so dim for me? What does the doctor say? Will the night always surround me?"

"No, Koleh, a couple of days will go by and you'll be able to see," I replied with an unsure voice at this heartbreaking question as large, bitter tears came rolling down my face—the invalid wasn't able to see them. Opposite me was a corpse that was breathing, a corpse of a bright yesterday and a sinister today. Only yesterday he was painting promising plans for the future, which he had seen in rose colors...

Today a tragic incident disrupted everything, covered everything with a black mantle that would accompany him to the grave. Two eyes dripping with pus, like pits over a burned face, projected human helplessness.

My head is bowed. I am even more shriveled in the gaze of the

Almighty God who reigns supreme. How fortunate is the person who doesn't lose a God-given gift—the eyes. But as long as the eyes see, a person doesn't value this gift. It is like his property. I, too, never gave any thought to this. Now I came to understand the Yiddish expression *oyg in kup* ["an eye in the head," meaning something of incalculable value]. I feel how tiny and of little worth I am as a human being. A small accident and everything is lost... And from this blind partisan's tragedy I realized that only after a loss like this does one value one's own good fortune.

A faint voice from the other side of the room—"Nurse"—it disrupted my calm contemplation. I went over to the heavily wounded man from Warsaw. I made the bed where his injured leg lay but my eyes saw only two holes with pus, and scars on a wounded face...

Ach, I would give anything if only his eyes could see. He is after all my brother, [for] he is a partisan...

The doctor enters...

"Nurse, how are the sick ones doing today? How is Koleh doing?"

"Doctor, is everything irreparable? Is there perhaps a glimmer of hope that he'll still be able to see?"

"I'll take another look."

The doctor in his white coat went over, placed his hands on the burnt face and started to pull open the eyelids. I was standing on the other side of the bed and watched, my heart racing. Peeking out were two blood-covered eyes. I was waiting to hear a good word from the doctor: a life or death verdict was awaiting this young partisan.

A deadly silence. Then the doctor said: "Koleh, can you see this light?"

"No, doctor, I don't see anything."

Then, hard as a hammer, sharp as a hatchet, fell the doctor's "No."

"He won't be able to see. There is no hope. He will remain blind."

The day after tomorrow. Koleh is growing weaker. Last night was a very difficult one for him. He was shaking uncontrollably and calling out to his mother... In the morning, the rising sun, beaming down on the partisan woods, came to say good morning to the warriors and found Koleh in a greatly deteriorated state. He was even more agitated this morning than usual. After lunch he started to calm down a bit and in a barely audible voice called me over.

"Nurse, write down my address! Bashkiryeh..."

"Koleh, what do I need this for. It's not necessary."

"Please, nurse, write it down." He demanded this a couple of times and then asked me to read to him what I had written.

"But, Koleh, this is not important. You will recuperate soon and you'll write to your mother yourself. Your address is not important to us."

"Nurse, please read to me what you have written down. I beg you... I'm afraid something is going to happen to me tonight. *Ach,* beloved mother of mine."

I made a great effort to try to calm him, but I did not succeed. He lapsed into a coma and from time to time he would come out of it and start to babble words that were incomprehensible to me.

And that night, this brave partisan went out like an extinguished candle, ending a life that was no longer shining.